Henry James

Henry James OM (15 April 1843 – 28 February 1916) was an American-British author regarded as a key transitional figure between literary realism and literary modernism, and is considered by many to be among the greatest novelists in the English language. He was the son of Henry James Sr. and the brother of renowned philosopher and psychologist William James and diarist Alice James.

He is best known for a number of novels dealing with the social and marital interplay between émigré Americans, English people, and continental Europeans. Examples of such novels include The Portrait of a Lady, The Ambassadors, and The Wings of the Dove. His later works were increasingly experimental. In describing the internal states of mind and social dynamics of his characters, James often made use of a style in which ambiguous or contradictory motives and impressions were overlaid or juxtaposed in the discussion of a character's psyche.(Source: Wikipedia)

Literary works:

Watch and Ward (1871)
Roderick Hudson (1875)
The American (1877)
The Europeans (1878)
Confidence (1879)
Washington Square (1880)
The Portrait of a Lady (1881)
The Bostonians (1886)
The Princess Casamassima (1886)
The Reverberator (1888)
The Tragic Muse (1890)
The Other House (1896)
The Spoils of Poynton (1897)
What Maisie Knew (1897)
The Awkward Age (1899)
The Sacred Fount (1901)

THE SELECTED WORKS
OF
HENRY JAMES
VOL 14 (OF 36)

THE OUTCRY
PICTURE AND TEXT

PAPER SKY CLASSICS

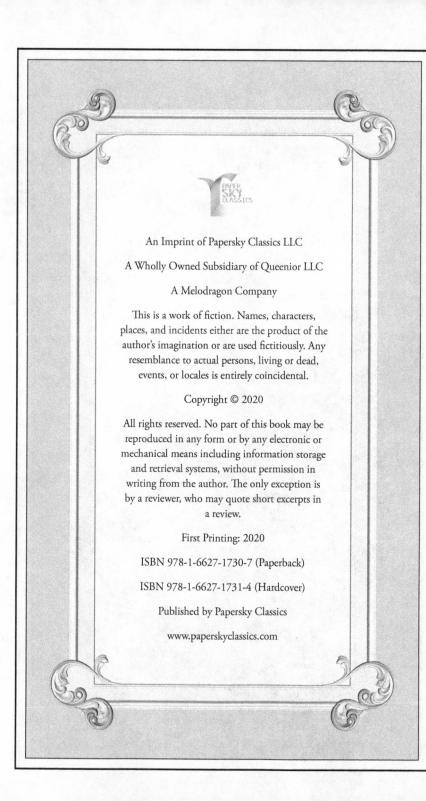

An Imprint of Papersky Classics LLC

A Wholly Owned Subsidiary of Queenior LLC

A Melodragon Company

Copyright © 2020

First Printing: 2020

ISBN 978-1-6627-1730-7 (Paperback)

ISBN 978-1-6627-1731-4 (Hardcover)

Published by Papersky Classics

www.paperskyclassics.com

Contents

THE
SELECTED
WORKS
OF
HENRY JAMES
VOL. 14 (OF 36)

THE OUTCRY

BOOK FIRST

I

No, my lord," Banks had replied, "no stranger has yet arrived. But I'll see if any one has come in—or who has." As he spoke, however, he observed Lady Sandgate's approach to the hall by the entrance giving upon the great terrace, and addressed her on her passing the threshold. "Lord John, my lady." With which, his duty majestically performed, he retired to the quarter—that of the main access to the spacious centre of the house—from which he had ushered the visitor.

This personage, facing Lady Sandgate as she paused there a moment framed by the large doorway to the outer expanses, the small pinkish paper of a folded telegram in her hand, had partly before him, as an immediate effect, the high wide interior, still breathing the quiet air and the fair pannelled security of the couple of hushed and stored centuries, in which certain of the reputed treasures of Dedborough Place beautifully disposed themselves; and then, through ample apertures and beyond the stately stone outworks of the great seated and supported house—uplifting terrace, balanced, balustraded steps and containing basins where splash and spray were at rest—all the rich composed extension of garden and lawn and park. An ancient, an assured elegance seemed to reign; pictures and preserved "pieces," cabinets and tapestries, spoke, each for itself, of fine selection and high distinction; while the originals of the old portraits, in more or less deserved salience, hung over the happy scene as the sworn members of a great guild might have sat, on the beautiful April day, at one of their annual feasts.

Such was the setting confirmed by generous time, but the handsome woman of considerably more than forty whose entrance had all but coincided with that of Lord John either belonged, for the eye, to no such complacent company or enjoyed a relation to it in which the odd twists and turns of history must have been more frequent than any dull avenue or easy sequence. Lady Sandgate was shiningly modern, and perhaps at no point more so than by the effect of her express repudiation of a mundane future certain to be more and more offensive to women of real quality and of formed taste. Clearly, at any rate, in her hands, the clue to the antique confidence had lost itself, and repose, however founded, had given way to curiosity—that is to speculation—however disguised. She might have consented, or even attained, to being but gracefully stupid, but she would presumably have confessed, if put on her trial for restlessness or for intelligence, that she *was*, after all, almost clever enough to be vulgar. Unmistakably, moreover, she had still, with her fine stature, her disciplined figure, her cherished complexion, her bright important hair, her kind bold eyes and her large constant smile, the degree of beauty that might pretend to put every other question by.

Lord John addressed her as with a significant manner that he might have had—that of a lack of need, or even of interest, for any explanation about herself: it would have been clear that he was apt to discriminate with sharpness among possible claims on his attention. "I luckily find *you* at least, Lady Sandgate—they tell me Theign's off somewhere."

She replied as with the general habit, on her side, of bland reassurance; it mostly had easier consequences—for herself—than the perhaps more showy creation of alarm. "Only off in the park—open to-day for a school-feast from Dedborough, as you may have made out from the avenue; giving good advice, at the top of his lungs, to four hundred and fifty children."

It was such a scene, and such an aspect of the personage so accounted for, as Lord John could easily take in, and his recognition familiarly smiled. "Oh he's so great on such occasions that I'm sorry to be missing it."

"I've *had* to miss it," Lady Sandgate sighed—"that is to miss the peroration. I've just left them, but he had even then been going on for twenty minutes, and I dare say that if you care to take a look you'll find him, poor dear victim of duty, still *at* it."

"I'll warrant—for, as I often tell him, he makes the idea of one's duty an awful thing to his friends by the extravagance with which he always overdoes it." And the image itself appeared in some degree to prompt this particular edified friend to look at his watch and consider. "I should like to come in for the grand *finale*, but I rattled over in a great measure to meet a party, as he calls himself—and calls, if you please, even me!—who's motoring down by appointment and whom I think I should be here to receive; as well as a little, I confess, in the hope of a glimpse of Lady Grace: if you can perhaps imagine *that!*"

"I can imagine it perfectly," said Lady Sandgate, whom evidently no perceptions of that general order ever cost a strain. "It quite sticks out of you, and every one moreover has for some time past been waiting to see. But you haven't then," she added, "come from town?"

"No, I'm for three days at Chanter with my mother; whom, as she kindly lent me her car, I should have rather liked to bring."

Lady Sandgate left the unsaid, in this connection, languish no longer than was decent. "But whom you doubtless had to leave, by her preference, just settling down to bridge."

"Oh, to sit down would imply that my mother at some moment of the day gets up——!"

"Which the Duchess never does?"—Lady Sand-gate only asked to be allowed to show how she saw it. "She fights to the last, invincible; gathering in the spoils and only routing her friends?" She abounded genially in her privileged vision. "Ah yes—we know something of that!"

Lord John, who was a young man of a rambling but not of an idle eye, fixed her an instant with a surprise that was yet not steeped in compassion. "You too then?"

She wouldn't, however, too meanly narrow it down. "Well, in this house generally; where I'm so often made welcome, you see, and where——"

"Where," he broke in at once, "your jolly good footing quite sticks out of *you*, perhaps you'll let me say!"

15

She clearly didn't mind his seeing her ask herself how she should deal with so much rather juvenile intelligence; and indeed she could only decide to deal quite simply. "You can't say more than I feel—and am proud to feel!—at being of comfort when they're worried."

This but fed the light flame of his easy perception—which lighted for him, if she would, all the facts equally. "And they're worried now, you imply, because my terrible mother is capable of heavy gains and of making a great noise if she isn't paid? I ought to mind speaking of that truth," he went on as with a practised glance in the direction of delicacy; "but I think I should like you to know that I myself am not a bit ignorant of why it has made such an impression here."

Lady Sandgate forestalled his knowledge. "Because poor Kitty Imber—who should either never touch a card or else learn to suffer in silence, as I've had to, goodness knows!—has thrown herself, with her impossible big debt, upon her father? whom she thinks herself entitled to 'look to' even more as a lovely young widow with a good jointure than she formerly did as the mere most beautiful daughter at home."

She had put the picture a shade interrogatively, but this was as nothing to the note of free inquiry in Lord John's reply. "You mean that our lovely young widows—to say nothing of lovely young wives—ought by this time to have made out, in predicaments, how to turn round?"

His temporary hostess, even with his eyes on her, appeared to decide after a moment not wholly to disown his thought. But she smiled for it. "Well, in that set——!"

"My mother's set?" However, if she could smile he could laugh. "I'm much obliged!"

"Oh," she qualified, "I don't criticise her Grace; but the ways and traditions and tone of this house——"

"Make it"—he took her sense straight from her—"the house in England where one feels most the false note of a dishevelled and bankrupt elder daughter breaking in with a list of her gaming debts—to say nothing of others!—and wishing to have at least those wiped out in the interest of her reputation? Exactly so," he went on before she could meet it with a diplomatic ambiguity; "and just that, I assure you, is a large part of the reason I like to come here—since I personally don't come with any such associations."

"Not the association of bankruptcy—no; as you represent the payee!"

The young man appeared to regard this imputation for a moment almost as a liberty taken. "How do you know so well, Lady Sandgate, what I represent?"

She bethought herself—but briefly and bravely. "Well, don't you represent, by your own admission, certain fond aspirations? Don't you represent the belief—very natural, I grant—that more than *one* perverse and extravagant flower will be unlikely on such a fine healthy old stem; and, consistently with that, the hope of arranging with our admirable host here that he shall lend a helpful hand to your commending yourself to dear Grace?"

Lord John might, in the light of these words, have felt any latent infirmity in such a pretension exposed; but as he stood there facing his chances he would have struck a spectator as resting firmly enough on some felt residuum of advantage: whether this were cleverness or luck, the strength of his backing or that of his sincerity. Even with the young woman to whom our friends' reference thus broadened still a vague quantity for us, you would have taken his sincerity as quite possible—and this despite an odd element in him that you might have described as a certain delicacy of brutality. This younger son of a noble matron recognised even by himself as terrible enjoyed in no immediate or aggressive manner any imputable private heritage or privilege of arrogance. He would on the contrary have irradiated fineness if his lustre hadn't been a little prematurely dimmed. Active yet insubstantial, he was slight and short and a trifle too punctually, though not yet quite lamentably, bald. Delicacy was in the arch of his eyebrow, the finish of his facial line, the economy of "treatment" by which his negative nose had been enabled to look important and his meagre mouth to smile its spareness away.

He had pleasant but hard little eyes—they glittered, handsomely, without promise—and a neatness, a coolness and an ease, a clear instinct for making point take, on his behalf, the place of weight and immunity that of capacity, which represented somehow the art of living at a high pitch and yet at a low cost. There was that in his satisfied air which still suggested sharp wants—and this was withal the ambiguity; for the temper of these appetites or views was certainly, you would have concluded, not such as always to sacrifice to form. If he really, for instance, wanted Lady Grace, the passion or the sense of his interest in it would scarce have been considerately irritable.

"May I ask what you mean," he inquired of Lady Sandgate, "by the question of my 'arranging'?"

"I mean that you're the very clever son of a very clever mother."

"Oh, I'm less clever than you think," he replied—"if you really think it of me at all; and mamma's a good sight cleverer!"

"Than I think?" Lady Sandgate echoed. "Why, she's the person in all our world I would gladly most resemble—for her general ability to put what she wants through." But she at once added: "That is *if*—!" pausing on it with a smile.

"If what then?"

"Well, if I could be absolutely certain to have all in her kinds of cleverness without exception—and to have them," said Lady Sandgate, "to the very end."

He definitely, he almost contemptuously declined to follow her. "The very end of what?"

She took her choice as amid all the wonderful directions there might be, and then seemed both to risk and to reserve something. "Say of her so wonderfully successful *general* career."

It doubtless, however, warranted him in appearing to cut insinuations short. "When you're as clever as she you'll be as good." To which he subjoined: "You don't begin to have the opportunity of knowing how good she is." This pronouncement, to whatever comparative obscurity it might appear to relegate her, his interlocutress had to take—he was so prompt with a more explicit challenge. "What is it exactly that you suppose yourself to know?"

Lady Sandgate had after a moment, in her supreme good humour, decided to take everything. "I always proceed on the assumption that I know everything, because that makes people tell me."

"It wouldn't make we," he quite rang out, "if I didn't want to! But as it happens," he allowed, "there's a question it would be convenient to me to put to you. You must be, with your charming unconventional relation with him, extremely in Theign's confidence."

She waited a little as for more. "Is that your question—*whether* I am?"

"No, but if you are you'll the better answer it"

She had no objection then to answering it beautifully. "We're the best friends in the world; he has been really my providence, as a lone woman with almost nobody and nothing of her own, and I feel my footing here, as so frequent and yet so discreet a visitor, simply perfect But I'm happy to say that—for my pleasure when I'm really curious—this doesn't close to me the sweet resource of occasionally guessing things."

"Then I hope you've ground for believing that if I go the right way about it he's likely to listen to me."

Lady Sandgate measured her ground—which scarce seemed extensive. "The person he most listens to just now—and in fact at any time, as you must have seen for yourself—is that arch-tormentor, or at least beautiful wheedler, his elder daughter."

"Lady Imber's *here?*" Lord John alertly asked.

"She arrived last night and—as we've other visitors—seems to have set up a side-show in the garden."

"Then she'll 'draw' of course immensely, as she always does. But her sister won't be in that case with her," the young man supposed.

19

"Because Grace feels herself naturally an independent show? So she well may," said Lady Sandgate, "but I must tell you that when I last noticed them there Kitty was in the very act of leading her away."

Lord John figured it a moment. "Lady Imber"—he ironically enlarged the figure—"*can* lead people away."

"Oh, dear Grace," his companion returned, "happens fortunately to be firm!"

This seemed to strike him for a moment as equivocal. "Not against *me*, however—you don't mean? You don't think she has a beastly prejudice——?"

"Surely you can judge about it; as knowing best what may—or what mayn't—have happened between you."

"Well, I try to judge"—and such candour as was possible to Lord John seemed to sit for a moment on his brow. "But I'm in fear of seeing her too much as I want to see her."

There was an appeal in it that Lady Sandgate might have been moved to meet "Are you absolutely in earnest about her?"

"Of course I am—why shouldn't I be? But," he said with impatience, "I want help."

"Very well then, that's what Lady Imber's giving you." And as it appeared to take him time to read into these words their full sense, she produced others, and so far did help him—though the effort was in a degree that of her exhibiting with some complacency her own unassisted control of stray signs and shy lights. "By telling her, by bringing it home to her, that if she'll make up her mind to accept you the Duchess will do the handsome thing. Handsome, I mean, by Kitty."

Lord John, appropriating for his convenience the truth in this, yet regarded it as open to a becoming, an improving touch from himself. "Well, and by *me*." To which he added with more of a challenge in it: "But you really know what my mother will do?"

"By my system," Lady Sandgate smiled, "you see I've guessed. What your mother will do is what brought you over!"

"Well, it's that," he allowed—"and something else."

"Something else?" she derisively echoed. "I should think 'that,' for an ardent lover, would have been enough."

"Ah, but it's all one Job! I mean it's one idea," he hastened to explain—"if you think Lady Imber's really acting on her."

"Mightn't you go and see?"

"I would in a moment if I hadn't to look out for another matter too." And he renewed his attention to his watch. "I mean getting straight at my American, the party I just mentioned————"

But she had already taken him up. "You too have an American and a 'party,' and yours also motors down————?"

"Mr. Breckenridge Bender." Lord John named him with a shade of elation.

She gaped at the fuller light "You *know* my Breckenridge?—who I hoped was coming for me!"

Lord John as freely, but more gaily, wondered. "Had he told you so?"

She held out, opened, the telegram she had kept folded in her hand since her entrance. "He has sent me that—which, delivered to me ten minutes ago out there, has brought me in to receive him."

The young man read out this missive. "'Failing to find you in Bruton Street, start in pursuit and hope to overtake you about four.'" It did involve an ambiguity. "Why, he has been engaged these three days to coincide with myself, and not to fail of him has been part of my business."

Lady Sandgate, in her demonstrative way, appealed to the general rich scene. "Then why does he say it's me he's pursuing?"

He seemed to recognise promptly enough in her the sense of a menaced monopoly. "My dear lady, he's pursuing expensive works of art."

"By which you imply that I'm one?" She might have been wound up by her disappointment to almost any irony.

"I imply—or rather I affirm—that every handsome woman is! But what he arranged with me about," Lord John explained, "was that he should see the Dedborough pictures in general and the great Sir Joshua in particular—of which he had heard so much and to which I've been thus glad to assist him."

This news, however, with its lively interest, but deepened the listener's mystification. "Then why—this whole week that I've been in the house—hasn't our good friend here mentioned to me his coming?"

"Because our good friend here has had no reason"—Lord John could treat it now as simple enough. "Good as he is in all ways, he's so best of all about showing the house and its contents that I haven't even thought necessary to write him that I'm introducing Breckenridge."

"I should have been happy to introduce him," Lady Sandgate just quavered—"if I had at all known he wanted it."

Her companion weighed the difference between them and appeared to pronounce it a trifle he didn't care a fig for. "I surrender you that privilege then—of presenting him to his host—if I've seemed to you to snatch it from you." To which Lord John added, as with liberality unrestricted, "But I've been taking him about to see what's worth while—as only last week to Lady Lappington's Longhi."

This revelation, though so casual in its form, fairly drew from Lady Sandgate, as she took it in, an interrogative wail. "Her Longhi?"

"Why, don't you know her great Venetian family group, the What-do-you-call-'ems?—seven full-length figures, each one a gem, for which he paid her her price before he left the house."

She could but make it more richly resound—almost stricken, lost in her wistful thought: "Seven full-length figures? Her price?"

"Eight thousand—slap down. Bender knows," said Lord John, "what he wants."

"And does he want only"—her wonder grew and grew—

"What-do-you-call-'ems'?"

"He most usually wants what he can't have." Lord John made scarce more of it than that. "But, awfully hard up as I fancy her, Lady Lappington went *at* him."

It determined in his friend a boldly critical attitude. "How horrible—at the rate things are leaving us!" But this was far from the end of her interest. "And is that the way he pays?"

"Before he leaves the house?" Lord John lived it amusedly over. "Well, *she* took care of that."

"How incredibly vulgar!" It all had, however, for Lady Sandgate, still other connections—which might have attenuated Lady Lappington's case, though she didn't glance at this. "He makes the most scandalous eyes—the ruffian!—at my great-grandmother." And then as richly to enlighten any blankness: "My tremendous Lawrence, don't you know?—in her wedding-dress, down to her knees; with such extraordinarily speaking eyes, such lovely arms and hands, such wonderful flesh-tints: universally considered the masterpiece of the artist."

Lord John seemed to look a moment not so much at the image evoked, in which he wasn't interested, as at certain possibilities lurking behind it. "And are you going to *sell* the masterpiece of the artist?"

She held her head high. "I've indignantly refused—for all his pressing me so hard."

"Yet that's what he nevertheless pursues you to-day to keep up?"

The question had a little the ring of those of which the occupant of a witness-box is mostly the subject, but Lady Sandgate was so far as this went an imperturbable witness. "I need hardly fear it perhaps if—in the light of what you tell me of your arrangement with him—his pursuit becomes, where I am concerned, a figure of speech."

"Oh," Lord John returned, "he kills two birds with one stone—he sees both Sir Joshua and you."

This version of the case had its effect, for the moment, on his fair associate. "Does he want to buy *their* pride and glory?"

The young man, however, struck on his own side, became at first but the bright reflector of her thought. "Is that wonder for sale?"

She closed her eyes as with the shudder of hearing such words. "Not, surely, by *any* monstrous chance! Fancy dear, proud Theign————!"

"I can't fancy him—no!" And Lord John appeared to renounce the effort. "But a cat may look at a king and a sharp funny Yankee at anything."

These things might be, Lady Sandgate's face and gesture apparently signified; but another question diverted her. "You're clearly a wonderful showman, but do you mind my asking you whether you're on such an occasion a—well, a closely interested one?"

"'Interested'?" he echoed; though it wasn't to gain time, he showed, for he would in that case have taken more. "To the extent, you mean, of my little percentage?" And then as in silence she but kept a slightly grim smile on him: "Why do you ask if—with your high delicacy about your great-grandmother—you've nothing to place?"

It took her a minute to say, while her fine eye only rolled; but when she spoke that organ boldly rested and the truth vividly appeared. "I ask because people like you, Lord John, strike me as dangerous to the—how shall I name it?—the common weal; and because of my general strong feeling that we don't want any more of our national treasures (for I regard my great-grandmother as national) to be scattered about the world."

"There's much in this country and age," he replied in an off-hand manner, "to be said about *that*," The present, however, was not the time to say it all; so he said something else instead, accompanying it with a smile that signified sufficiency. "To my friends, I need scarcely remark to you, I'm all the friend."

She had meanwhile seen the butler reappear by the door that opened to the terrace, and though the high, bleak, impersonal approach of this functionary was ever, and more and more at every step, a process to defy interpretation, long practice evidently now enabled her to suggest, as she turned again to her fellow-visitor a reading of it. "It's the friend then clearly who's wanted in the park."

She might, by the way Banks looked at her, have snatched from his hand a missive addressed to another; though while he addressed himself to her companion he allowed for her indecorum sufficiently to take it up where she had left it. "By her ladyship, my lord, who sends to hope you'll join them below the terrace."

"Ah, Grace hopes," said Lady Sandgate for the young man's encouragement. "There you are!"

Lord John took up the motor-cap he had lain down on coming in. "I rush to Lady Grace, but don't demoralise Bender!" And he went forth to the terrace and the gardens.

Banks looked about as for some further exercise of his high function. "Will you have tea, my lady?"

This appeared to strike her as premature. "Oh, thanks—when they all come in."

"They'll scarcely *all*, my lady"—he indicated respectfully that he knew what he was talking about. "There's tea in her ladyship's tent; but," he qualified, "it has also been ordered for the saloon."

"Ah then," she said cheerfully, "Mr. Bender will be glad—!" And she became, with this, aware of the approach of another visitor. Banks considered, up and down, the gentleman ushered in, at the left, by the footman who had received him at the main entrance to the house. "Here he must be, my lady." With which he retired to the spacious opposite quarter, where he vanished, while the footman, his own office performed, retreated as he had come, and Lady Sandgate, all hospitality, received the many-sided author of her specious telegram, of Lord John's irritating confidence and of Lady Lappington's massive cheque.

II

Having greeted him with an explicitly gracious welcome and both hands out, she had at once gone on: "You'll of course have tea?—in the saloon."

But his mechanism seemed of the type that has to expand and revolve before sounding. "Why; the very first thing?"

She only desired, as her laugh showed, to accommodate. "Ah, have it the last if you like!"

"You see your English teas—!" he pleaded as he looked about him, so immediately and frankly interested in the place and its contents that his friend could only have taken this for the very glance with which he must have swept Lady Lappington's inferior scene.

"They're too much for you?"

"Well, they're too many. I think I've had two or three on the road— at any rate my man did. I like to do business before—" But his sequence dropped as his eye caught some object across the wealth of space.

She divertedly picked it up. "Before tea, Mr. Bender?"

"Before everything, Lady Sandgate." He was immensely genial, but a queer, quaint, rough-edged distinctness somehow kept it safe—for himself.

"Then you've *come* to do business?" Her appeal and her emphasis melted as into a caress—which, however, spent itself on his large high person as he consented, with less of demonstration but more of attention, to look down upon her. She could therefore but reinforce it by an intenser note. "To tell me you *will* treat?"

Mr. Bender had six feet of stature and an air as of having received benefits at the hands of fortune. Substantial, powerful, easy, he shone as with a glorious cleanness, a supplied and equipped and appointed sanity and security; aids to action that might have figured a pair of very ample wings—wide pinions for the present conveniently folded, but that he would certainly on occasion agitate for great efforts and spread for great flights. These things would have made him quite an admirable, even a worshipful, image of full-blown life and character, had not the affirmation and the emphasis halted in one important particular. Fortune, felicity, nature, the perverse or interfering old fairy at his cradle-side—whatever the ministering power might have been—had simply overlooked and neglected his vast wholly-shaven face, which thus showed not so much for perfunctorily scamped as for not treated, as for neither formed nor fondled nor finished, at all. Nothing seemed to have been done for it but what the razor and the sponge, the tooth-brush and the looking-glass could officiously do; it had in short resisted any possibly finer attrition at the hands of fifty years of offered experience. It had developed on the lines, if lines they could be called, of the mere scoured and polished and initialled "mug" rather than to any effect of a composed physiognomy; though we must at the same time add that its wearer carried this featureless disk as with the warranted confidence that might have attended a warning headlight or a glaring motor-lamp. The object, however one named it, showed you at least where he was, and most often that he was straight upon you. It was fearlessly and resistingly across the path of his advance that Lady Sandgate had thrown herself, and indeed with such success that he soon connected her demonstration with a particular motive. "For your grandmother, Lady Sandgate?" he then returned.

"For my grandmother's *mother*, Mr. Bender—the most beautiful woman of her time and the greatest of all Lawrences, no matter whose; as you quite acknowledged, you know, in our talk in Bruton Street."

Mr. Bender bethought himself further—yet drawing it out; as if the familiar fact of his being "made up to" had never had such special softness and warmth of pressure. "Do you want very, *very* much——?"

She had already caught him up. "'Very, very much' for her? Well, Mr. Bender," she smilingly replied, "I think I should like her full value."

"I mean"—he kindly discriminated—"do you want so badly to work her off?"

"It would be an intense convenience to me—so much so that your telegram made me at once fondly hope you'd be arriving to conclude."

Such measure of response as he had good-naturedly given her was the mere frayed edge of a mastering detachment, the copious, impatient range elsewhere of his true attention. Somehow, however, he still seemed kind even while, turning his back upon her, he moved off to look at one of the several, the famous Dedborough pictures—stray specimens, by every presumption, lost a little in the whole bright bigness. "'Conclude'?" he echoed as he approached a significantly small canvas. "You ladies want to get there before the road's so much as laid or the country's safe! Do you know what this *here* is?" he at once went on.

"Oh, you can't have *that!*" she cried as with full authority—"and you must really understand that you can't have everything. You mustn't expect to ravage Dedborough."

He had his nose meanwhile close to the picture. "I guess it's a bogus Cuyp—but I know Lord Theign *has* things. He won't do business?"

"He's not in the least, and can never be, in my tight place," Lady Sandgate replied; "but he's as proud as he's kind, dear man, and as solid as he's proud; so that if you came down under a different impression—!" Well, she could only exhale the folly of his error with an unction that represented, whatever he might think of it, all her competence to answer for their host.

He scarce thought of it enough, on any side, however, to be diverted from prior dispositions. "I came on an understanding that I should find my friend Lord John, and that Lord Theign would, on his introduction, kindly let me look round. But being before lunch in Bruton Street I knocked at your door——"

"For another look," she quickly interposed, "at my Lawrence?"

"For another look at *you*, Lady Sandgate—your great-grandmother wasn't required. Informed you were here, and struck with the coincidence of my being myself presently due," he went on, "I despatched you my wire, on coming away, just to keep up your spirits."

"You *don't* keep them up, you depress them to anguish," she almost passionately protested, "when you don't tell me you'll treat!"

He paused in his preoccupation, his perambulation, conscious evidently of no reluctance that was worth a scene with so charming and so hungry a woman. "Well, if it's a question of your otherwise suffering torments, may I have another interview with the old lady?"

"Dear Mr. Bender, she's in the flower of her youth; she only yearns for interviews, and you may have," Lady Sandgate earnestly declared, "as many as you like."

"Oh, you must be there to protect me!"

"Then as soon as I return——!"

"Well,"—it clearly cost him little to say—"I'll come right round."

She joyously registered the vow. "Only meanwhile then, please, never a word!"

"Never a word, certainly. But where all this time," Mr. Bender asked, "is Lord John?"

Lady Sandgate, as he spoke, found her eyes meeting those of a young woman who, presenting herself from without, stood framed in the doorway to the terrace; a slight fair grave young woman, of middle, stature and simply dressed, whose brow showed clear even under the heavy shade of a large hat surmounted with big black bows and feathers. Her eyes had vaguely questioned those of her elder, who at once replied to the gentleman forming the subject of their inquiry: "Lady Grace must know." At this the young woman came forward, and Lady Sandgate introduced the visitor. "My dear Grace, this is Mr. Breckenridge Bender."

The younger daughter of the house might have arrived in preoccupation, but she had urbanity to spare. "Of whom Lord John has told me," she returned, "and whom I'm glad to see. Lord John," she explained to his waiting friend, "is detained a moment in the park, open to-day to a big Temperance school-feast, where our party is mostly gathered; so that if you care to go out—!" She gave him in fine his choice.

But this was clearly a thing that, in the conditions, Mr. Bender wasn't the man to take precipitately; though his big useful smile disguised his prudence. "Are there any pictures in the park?"

Lady Grace's facial response represented less humour perhaps, but more play. "We find our park itself rather a picture."

Mr. Bender's own levity at any rate persisted. "With a big Temperance school-feast?"

"Mr. Bender's a great judge of pictures," Lady Sandgate said as to forestall any impression of excessive freedom.

"Will there be more tea?" he pursued, almost presuming on this.

It showed Lady Grace for comparatively candid and literal. "Oh, there'll be plenty of tea."

This appeared to determine Mr. Bender. "Well, Lady Grace, I'm after pictures, but I take them 'neat.' May I go right round here?"

"Perhaps, love," Lady Sandgate at once said, "you'll let me show him."

"A moment, dear"—Lady Grace gently demurred. "Do go round," she conformably added to Mr. Bender; "take your ease and your time. Everything's open and visible, and, with our whole company dispersed, you'll have the place to yourself."

He rose, in his genial mass, to the opportunity. "I'll be in clover—sure!" But present to him was the richest corner of the pasture, which he could fluently enough name. "And I'll find 'The Beautiful Duchess of Waterbridge'?"

She indicated, off to the right, where a stately perspective opened, the quarter of the saloon to which we have seen Mr. Banks retire. "At the very end of *those* rooms."

He had wide eyes for the vista. "About thirty in a row, hey?" And he was already off. "I'll work right through!"

III

Left with her friend, Lady Grace had a prompt question. "Lord John warned me he was 'funny'—but you already know him?"

There might have been a sense of embarrassment in the way in which, as to gain time, Lady Sandgate pointed, instead of answering, to the small picture pronounced upon by Mr. Bender. "He thinks your little Cuyp a fraud."

"That one?" Lady Grace could but stare. "The wretch!" However, she made, without alarm, no more of it; she returned to her previous question. "You've met him before?"

"Just a little—in town. Being 'after pictures'" Lady Sandgate explained, "he has been after my great-grandmother."

"She," said Lady Grace with amusement, "must have found him funny! But he can clearly take care of himself, while Kitty takes care of Lord John, and while you, if you'll be so good, go back to support father—in the hour of his triumph: which he wants you so much to witness that he complains of your desertion and goes so far as to speak of you as sneaking away."

Lady Sandgate, with a slight flush, turned it over. "I delight in his triumph, and whatever I do is at least above board; but if it's a question of support, aren't you yourself failing him quite as much?"

This had, however, no effect on the girl's confidence. "Ah, my dear, I'm not at all the same thing, and as I'm the person in the world he least misses—" Well, such a fact spoke for itself.

"You've been free to return and wait for Lord John?"—that was the sense in which the elder woman appeared to prefer to understand it as speaking.

The tone of it, none the less, led her companion immediately, though very quietly, to correct her. "I've not come back to wait for Lord John."

"Then he hasn't told you—if you've talked—with what idea he has come?"

Lady Grace had for a further correction the same shade of detachment. "Kitty has told me—what it suits her to pretend to suppose."

"And Kitty's pretensions and suppositions always go with what happens—at the moment, among all her wonderful happenings—to suit her?"

Lady Grace let that question answer itself—she took the case up further on. "What I can't make out is why this *should* so suit her!"

"And what *I* can't!" said Lady Sandgate without gross honesty and turning away after having watched the girl a moment. She nevertheless presently faced her again to follow this speculation up. "Do you like him enough to risk the chance of Kitty's being for once right?"

Lady Grace gave it a thought—with which she moved away. "I don't know how much I like him!"

"Nor how little!" cried her friend, who evidently found amusement in the tone of it. "And you're not disposed to take the time to find out? He's at least better than the others."

"The 'others'?"—Lady Grace was blank for them.

"The others of his set."

"Oh, his set! That wouldn't be difficult—by what I imagine of some of them. But he means well enough," the girl added; "he's very charming and does me great honour."

It determined in her companion, about to leave her, another brief arrest. "Then may I tell your father?"

This in turn brought about in Lady Grace an immediate drop of the subject. "Tell my father, please, that I'm expecting Mr. Crimble; of whom I've spoken to him even if he doesn't remember, and who bicycles this afternoon ten miles over from where he's staying—with some people we don't know—to look at the pictures, about which he's awfully keen."

Lady Sandgate took it in. "Ah, like Mr. Bender?"

"No, not at all, I think, like Mr. Bender."

This appeared to move in the elder woman some deeper thought "May I ask then—if one's to meet him—who he is?"

"Oh, father knows—or ought to—that I sat next him, in London, a month ago, at dinner, and that he then told me he was working, tooth and nail, at what he called the wonderful modern science of Connoisseurship—which is upsetting, as perhaps you're not aware, all the old-fashioned canons of art-criticism, everything we've stupidly thought right and held dear; that he was to spend Easter in these parts, and that he should like greatly to be allowed some day to come over and make acquaintance with our things. I told him," Lady Grace wound up, "that nothing would be easier; a note from him arrived before dinner——"

Lady Sandgate jumped the rest "And it's for him you've come in."

"It's for him I've come in," the girl assented with serenity.

"Very good—though he sounds most detrimental! But will you first just tell me *this*—whether when you sent in ten minutes ago for Lord John to come out to you it was wholly of your own movement?" And she followed it up as her young friend appeared to hesitate. "Was it because you knew why he had arrived?"

The young friend hesitated still. "'Why '?"

"So particularly to speak to you."

"Since he was expected and mightn't know where I was," Lady Grace said after an instant, "I wanted naturally to be civil to him."

"And had he time there to tell you," Lady Sand-gate asked, "how very civil he wants to be to you?"

"No, only to tell me that his friend—who's off there—was coming; for Kitty at once appropriated him and was still in possession when I came away." Then, as deciding at last on perfect frankness, Lady Grace went on: "If you want to know, I sent for news of him because Kitty insisted on my doing so; saying, so very oddly and quite in her own way, that she herself didn't wish to 'appear in it.' She had done nothing but say to me for an hour, rather worryingly, what you've just said—that it's me he's what, like Mr. Bender, she calls 'after'; but as soon as he appeared she pounced on him, and I left him—I assure you quite resignedly—in her hands."

"She wants"—it was easy for Lady Sandgate to remark—"to talk of you to him."

"I don't know *what* she wants," the girl replied as with rather a tired patience; "Kitty wants so many things at once. She always wants money, in quantities, to begin with—and all to throw so horribly away; so that whenever I see her 'in' so very deep with any one I always imagine her appealing for some new tip as to how it's to be come by."

"Kitty's an abyss, I grant you, and with my disinterested devotion to your father—in requital of all his kindness to me since Lord Sandgate's death and since your mother's—I can never be too grateful to you, my dear, for your being so different a creature. But what is she going to gain financially," Lady Sand-gate pursued with a strong emphasis on her adverb, "by working up our friend's confidence in your listening to him—if you *are* to listen?"

"I haven't in the least engaged to listen," said Lady Grace—"it will depend on the music he makes!" But she added with light cynicism: "Perhaps she's to gain a commission!"

"On his fairly getting you?" And then as the girl assented by silence: "Is he in a position to pay her one?" Lady Sandgate asked.

"I dare say the Duchess is!"

"But do you see the Duchess *producing* money—with all that Kitty, as we're not ignorant, owes her? Hundreds and hundreds and hundreds!"—Lady Sandgate piled them up.

Her young friend's gesture checked it. "Ah, don't tell me how many—it's too sad and too ugly and too wrong!" To which, however, Lady Grace added:

"But perhaps that will be just her way!" And then as her companion seemed for the moment not quite to follow: "By letting Kitty off her debt."

"You mean that Kitty goes free if Lord John wins your promise?"

"Kitty goes free."

"She has her creditor's release?"

"For every shilling."

"And if he only fails?"

"Why then of course," said now quite lucid Lady Grace, "she throws herself more than ever on poor father."

"Poor father indeed!"—Lady Sandgate richly sighed it

It appeared even to create in the younger woman a sense of excess. "Yes—but he after all and in spite of everything adores her."

"To the point, you mean"—for Lady Sandgate could clearly but wonder—"of really sacrificing you?"

The weight of Lady Grace's charming deep eyes on her face made her pause while, at some length, she gave back this look and the interchange determined in the girl a grave appeal. "You think I *should* be sacrificed if I married him?"

Lady Sandgate replied, though with an equal emphasis, indirectly. "*Could* you marry him?"

Lady Grace waited a moment "Do you mean for Kitty?"

"For himself even—if they should convince you, among them, that he cares for you."

Lady Grace had another delay. "Well, he's his awful mother's son."

"Yes—but you wouldn't marry his mother."

"No—but I should only be the more uncomfortably and intimately conscious of her."

"Even when," Lady Sandgate optimistically put it, "she so markedly likes you?"

This determined in the girl a fine impatience. "She doesn't 'like' me, she only *wants* me—which is a very different thing; wants me for my father's so particularly beautiful position, and my mother's so supremely great people, and for everything we have been and have done, and still are and still have: except of course poor not-at-all-model Kitty."

To this luminous account of the matter Lady Sand-gate turned as to a genial sun-burst. "I see indeed—for the general immaculate connection."

The words had no note of irony, but Lady Grace, in her great seriousness, glanced with deprecation at the possibility. "Well, we *haven't* had false notes. We've scarcely even had bad moments."

"Yes, you've been beatific!"—Lady Sandgate enviously, quite ruefully, felt it. But any further treatment of the question was checked by the re-entrance of the footman—a demonstration explained by the concomitant appearance of a young man in eyeglasses and with the ends of his trousers clipped together as for cycling. "This must be your friend," she had only time to say to the daughter of the house; with which, alert and reminded of how she was awaited elsewhere, she retreated before her companion's visitor, who had come in with his guide from the vestibule. She passed away to the terrace and the gardens, Mr. Hugh Crimble's announced name ringing in her ears— to some effect that we are as yet not qualified to discern.

IV

Lady Grace had turned to meet Mr. Hugh Crimble, whose pleasure in at once finding her lighted his keen countenance and broke into easy words. "So awfully kind of you—in the midst of the great doings I noticed—to have found a beautiful minute for me."

"I left the great doings, which are almost over, to every one's relief, I think," the girl returned, "so that your precious time shouldn't be taken to hunt for me."

It was clearly for him, on this bright answer, as if her white hand were holding out the perfect flower of felicity. "You came in from your revels on purpose—with the same charity you showed me from that first moment?" They stood smiling at each other as in an exchange of sympathy already confessed—and even as if finding that their relation had grown during the lapse of contact; she recognising the effect of what they had originally felt as bravely as he might name it. What the fine, slightly long oval of her essentially quiet face—quiet in spite of certain vague depths of reference to forces of the strong high order, forces involved and implanted, yet also rather spent in the process—kept in range from under her redundant black hat was the strength of expression, the directness of communication, that her guest appeared to borrow from the unframed and unattached nippers unceasingly perched, by their mere ground-glass rims, as she remembered, on the bony bridge of his indescribably authoritative (since it was at the same time decidedly inquisitive) young nose. She must, however, also have embraced in this contemplation, she must more or less again have interpreted, his main physiognomic mark, the degree to which his clean jaw was underhung and his lower lip protruded; a lapse of regularity made evident by a suppression of beard and moustache as complete as that practised by Mr. Bender—though without the appearance consequent in the latter's case, that of the flagrantly vain appeal in the countenance for some other exhibition of a history, of a process of production, than this so superficial one. With the interested and interesting girl sufficiently under our attention while we thus try to evoke her, we may even make out some wonder in her as to why the so perceptibly protrusive lower lip of this acquaintance of an hour or two should positively have contributed to his being handsome instead of much more logically interfering with it. We might in fact in such a case even have followed her into another and no less refined a speculation—the question of whether the surest seat of his good looks mightn't after all be his high, fair, if somewhat narrow, forehead, crowned with short crisp brown hair and which, after a fashion of its own, predominated without overhanging. He spoke after they had stood just face to face almost long enough for awkwardness. "I haven't forgotten one item of your kindness to me on that rather bleak occasion."

"Bleak do you call it?" she laughed. "Why I found it, rather, tropical— 'lush.' My neighbour on the other side wanted to talk to me of the White City."

"Then you made it doubtless bleak for *him*, let us say. *I* couldn't let you alone, I remember, about *this*—it was like a shipwrecked signal to a sail on the horizon." "This" obviously meant for the young man exactly what surrounded him; he had begun, like Mr. Bender, to be conscious of a thick solicitation of the eye—and much more than he, doubtless, of a tug at the imagination; and he broke—characteristically, you would have been sure—into a great free gaiety of recognition.

"Oh, we've nothing particular in the hall," Lady Grace amiably objected.

"Nothing, I see, but Claudes and Cuyps! I'm an ogre," he said—"before a new and rare feast!"

She happily took up his figure. "Then won't you begin—as a first course—with tea after your ride? If the other, that is—for there has been an ogre before you—has left any."

"Some tea, with pleasure"—he looked all his longing; "though when you talk of a fellow-feaster I should have supposed that, on such a day as this especially, you'd find yourselves running a continuous *table d'hôte*."

"Ah, we can't work sports in our gallery and saloon—the banging or whacking and shoving amusements that are all most people care for; unless, perhaps," Lady Grace went on, "your own peculiar one, as I understand you, of playing football with the old benighted traditions and attributions you everywhere meet: in fact I think you said the old idiotic superstitions."

Hugh Crimble went more than half-way to meet this description of his fondest activity; he indeed even beckoned it on. "The names and stories and styles—the so often vain legend, not to be too invidious—of author or subject or school?" But he had a drop, no less, as from the sense of a cause sometimes lost. "Ah, that's a game at which we *all* can play!"

"Though scarcely," Lady Grace suggested, "at which we all can score."

The words appeared indeed to take meaning from his growing impression of the place and its charm—of the number of objects, treasures of art, that pressed for appreciation of their importance. "Certainly," he said, "no one can ever have scored much on sacred spots of *this* order—which express so the grand impunity of their pride, their claims, their assurance!"

"We've had great luck," she granted—"as I've just been reminded; but ever since those terrible things you told me in town—about the tremendous tricks of the whirligig of time and the aesthetic fools' paradise in which so many of us live—I've gone about with my heart in my mouth. Who knows that while I talk Mr. Bender mayn't be pulling us to pieces?"

Hugh Crimble had a shudder of remembrance. "Mr. Bender?"

"The rich American who's going round."

It gave him a sharper shock. "The wretch who bagged Lady Lappington's Longhi?"

Lady Grace showed surprise. "Is he a wretch?"

Her visitor but asked to be extravagant. "Rather—the scoundrel. He offered his infernal eight thousand down."

"Oh, I thought you meant he had played some trick!"

"I wish he had—he could then have been collared."

"Well," Lady Grace peacefully smiled, "it's no use his offering *us* eight thousand—or eighteen or even eighty!"

Hugh Crimble stared as at the odd superfluity of this reassurance, almost crude on exquisite lips and contradicting an imputation no one would have indecently made. "Gracious goodness, I hope not! The man surely doesn't *suppose* you'd traffic."

She might, while she still smiled at him, have been fairly enjoying the friendly horror she produced. "I don't quite know what he supposes. But people *have* trafficked; people do; people are trafficking all round."

"Ah," Hugh Crimble cried, "that's what deprives me of my rest and, as a lover of our vast and beneficent art-wealth, poisons my waking hours. That art-wealth is at the mercy of a leak there appears no means of stopping." She had tapped a spring in him, clearly, and the consequent flood might almost at any moment become copious. "Precious things are going out of our distracted country at a quicker rate than the very quickest—a century and more ago—of their ever coming in."

She was sharply struck, but was also unmistakably a person in whom stirred thought soon found connections and relations. "Well, I suppose our art-wealth came in—save for those awkward Elgin Marbles!—mainly by purchase too, didn't it? We ourselves largely took it away from somewhere, didn't we? We didn't *grow* it all."

"We grew some of the loveliest flowers—and on the whole to-day the most exposed." He had been pulled up but for an instant. "Great Gainsboroughs and Sir Joshuas and Romneys and Sargents, great Turners and Constables and old Cromes and Brabazons, form, you'll recognise, a vast garden in themselves. What have we ever for instance more successfully grown than your splendid 'Duchess of Waterbridge'?"

The girl showed herself ready at once to recognise under his eloquence anything he would. "Yes—it's our Sir Joshua, I believe, that Mr. Bender has proclaimed himself particularly 'after.'"

It brought a cloud to her friend's face. "Then he'll be capable of anything."

"Of anything, no doubt, but of making my father capable—! And you haven't at any rate," she said, "so much as seen the picture."

"I beg your pardon—I saw it at the Guildhall three years ago; and am almost afraid of getting again, with a fresh sense of its beauty, a livelier sense of its danger."

Lady Grace, however, was so far from fear that she could even afford pity. "Poor baffled Mr. Bender!"

"Oh, rich and confident Mr. Bender!" Crimble cried. "Once given his money, his confidence is a horrid engine in itself—there's the rub! I dare say"—the young man saw it all—"he has brought his poisonous cheque."

She gave it her less exasperated wonder. "One has heard of that, but only in the case of some particularly pushing dealer."

"And Mr. Bender, to do him justice, isn't a particularly pushing dealer?"

"No," Lady Grace judiciously returned; "I think he's not a dealer at all, but just what you a moment ago spoke of yourself as being."

He gave a glance at his possibly wild recent past. "A fond true lover?"

"As we *all* were in our lucky time—when we rum-aged Italy and Spain."

He appeared to recognise this complication—of Bender's voracious integrity; but only to push it away. "Well, I don't know whether the best lovers are, or ever were, the best buyers—but I feel to-day that they're the best keepers."

The breath of his emphasis blew, as her eyes showed, on the girl's dimmer fire. "It's as if it were suddenly in the air that you've brought us some light or some help—that you may do something really good for us."

"Do you mean 'mark down,' as they say at the shops, all your greatest claims?"

His chord of sensibility had trembled all gratefully into derision, and not to seem to swagger he had put his possible virtue at its lowest. This she beautifully showed that she beautifully saw. "I dare say that if you did even that we should have to take it from you."

"Then it may very well be," he laughed back, "the reason why I feel, under my delightful, wonderful impression, a bit anxious and nervous and afraid."

"That shows," she returned, "that you suspect us of horrors hiding from justice, and that your natural kindness yet shrinks from handing us over!"

Well, clearly, she might put it as she liked—it all came back to his being more charmed. "Heaven knows I've wanted a chance at you, but what should you say if, having then at last just taken you in in your so apparent perfection, I should feel it the better part of valour simply to mount my 'bike' again and spin away?"

"I should be sure that at the end of the avenue you'd turn right round and come back. You'd think again of Mr. Bender."

"Whom I don't, however, you see—if he's prowling off there—in the least want to meet." Crimble made the point with gaiety. "I don't know what I mightn't do to him—and yet it's not of my temptation to violence, after all, that I'm most afraid. It's of the brutal mistake of one's breaking—with one's priggish, precious modernity and one's possibly futile discriminations—into a *general* situation or composition, as we say, so serene and sound and right. What should one do here, out of respect for that felicity, but hold one's breath and walk on tip-toe? The very celebrations and consecrations, as you tell me, instinctively stay outside. I saw that all," the young man went on with more weight in his ardour, "I saw it, while we talked in London, as your natural setting and your native air—and now ten minutes on the spot have made it sink into my spirit. You're a case, all together, of enchanted harmony, of perfect equilibrium—there's nothing to be done or said."

His friend listened to this eloquence with her eyes lowered, then raising them to meet, with a vague insistence, his own; after which something she had seen there appeared to determine in her another motion. She indicated the small landscape that Mr. Bender had, by Lady Sandgate's report, rapidly studied and denounced. "For what do you take that little picture?"

Hugh Crimble went over and looked. "Why, don't you know? It's a jolly little Vandermeer of Delft."

"It's not a base imitation?"

He looked again, but appeared at a loss. "An imitation of Vandermeer?"

"Mr. Bender thinks of Cuyp."

It made the young man ring out: "Then Mr. Bender's doubly dangerous!"

"Singly is enough!" Lady Grace laughed. "But you see you *have* to speak."

"Oh, to *him*, rather, after that—if you'll just take me to him."

"Yes then," she said; but even while she spoke Lord John, who had returned, by the terrace, from his quarter of an hour passed with Lady Imber, was there practically between them; a fact that she had to notice for her other visitor, to whom she was hastily reduced to naming him.

His lordship eagerly made the most of this tribute of her attention, which had reached his ear; he treated it—her "Oh Lord John!"—as a direct greeting. "Ah Lady Grace! I came back particularly to find you."

She could but explain her predicament. "I was taking Mr. Crimble to see the pictures." And then more pointedly, as her manner had been virtually an introduction of that gentleman, an introduction which Lord John's mere noncommittal stare was as little as possible a response to: "Mr. Crimble's one of the quite new connoisseurs."

"Oh, I'm at the very lowest round of the ladder. But I aspire!" Hugh laughed.

"You'll mount!" said Lady Grace with friendly confidence.

He took it again with gay deprecation. "Ah, if by that time there's anything left here to mount *on!*"

"Let us hope there will be at least what Mr. Bender, poor man, won't have been able to carry off." To which Lady Grace added, as to strike a helpful spark from the personage who had just joined them, but who had the air of wishing to preserve his detachment: "It's to Lord John that we owe Mr. Bender's acquaintance."

Hugh looked at the gentleman to whom they were so indebted. "Then do you happen to know, sir, what your friend means to *do* with his spoil?"

The question got itself but dryly treated, as if it might be a commercially calculating or interested one. "Oh, not sell it again."

"Then ship it to New York?" the inquirer pursued, defining himself somehow as not snubbed and, from this point, not snubbable.

That appearance failed none the less to deprive Lord John of a betrayed relish for being able to displease Lady Grace's odd guest by large assent. "As fast as ever he can—and you can land things there *now*, can't you? in three or four days."

"I dare say. But can't he be induced to have a little mercy?" Hugh sturdily pursued.

Lord John pushed out his lips. "A 'little'? How much do you want?"

"Well, one wants to be able somehow to stay his hand."

"I doubt if you can any more stay Mr. Bender's hand than you can empty his purse."

"Ah, the Despoilers!" said Crimble with strong expression. "But it's *we*," he added, "who are base."

"'Base'?"—and Lord John's surprise was apparently genuine.

"To want only to 'do business,' I mean, with our treasures, with our glories."

Hugh's words exhaled such a sense of peril as to draw at once Lady Grace. "Ah, but if we're above that *here*, as you know———!"

He stood smilingly corrected and contrite. "Of course I know—but you must forgive me if I have it on the brain. And show me first of all, won't you? the Moretto of Brescia."

"You know then about the Moretto of Brescia?"

44

"Why, didn't you tell me yourself?" It went on between them for the moment quite as if there had been no Lord John.

"Probably, yes," she recalled; "so how I must have swaggered!" After which she turned to the other visitor with a kindness strained clear of urgency. "Will you also come?"

He confessed to a difficulty—which his whole face begged her also to take account of. "I hoped you'd be at leisure—for something I've so at heart!"

This had its effect; she took a rapid decision and turned persuasively to Crimble—for whom, in like manner, there must have been something in *her* face. "Let Mr. Bender himself then show you. And there are things in the library too."

"Oh yes, there are things in the library." Lord John, happy in his gained advantage and addressing Hugh from the strong ground of an initiation already complete, quite sped him on the way.

Hugh clearly made no attempt to veil the penetration with which he was moved to look from one of these counsellors to the other, though with a ready "Thank-you!" for Lady Grace he the next instant started in pursuit of Mr. Bender.

V

"Your friend seems remarkably hot!" Lord John remarked to his young hostess as soon as they had been left together.

"He has cycled twenty miles. And indeed," she smiled, "he does appear to care for what he cares for!"

Her companion then, during a moment's silence, might have been noting the emphasis of her assent. "Have you known him long?"

"No—not long."

"Nor seen him often?"

"Only once—till now."

"Oh!" said Lord John with another pause. But he soon proceeded. "Let us leave him then to cool! I haven't cycled twenty miles, but I've motored forty very much in the hope of *this*, Lady Grace—the chance of being able to assure you that I too care very much for what I care for." To which he added on an easier note, as to carry off a slight awkwardness while she only waited: "You certainly mustn't let yourself—between us all—be worked to death."

"Oh, such days as this—I" She made light enough of her burden.

"They don't come often to *me* at least, Lady Grace! I hadn't grasped in advance the scale of your fête," he went on; "but since I've the great luck to find you alone—!" He paused for breath, however, before the full sequence.

She helped him out as through common kindness, but it was a trifle colourless. "Alone or in company, Lord John, I'm always very glad to see you."

"Then that assurance helps me to wonder if you don't perhaps gently guess what it is I want to say." This time indeed she left him to his wonder, so that he had to support himself. "I've tried, all considerately—these three months—to let you see for yourself how I feel. I feel very strongly, Lady Grace; so that at last"—and his impatient sincerity took after another instant the jump—"well, I regularly worship you. You're my absolute ideal. I think of you the whole time."

She measured out consideration as if it had been a yard of pretty ribbon. "Are you sure you *know* me enough?"

"I think I know a perfect woman when I see one!" Nothing now at least could have been more prompt, and while a decent pity for such a mistake showed in her smile he followed it up. "Isn't what you rather mean that you haven't cared sufficiently to know *me*? If so, that can be little by little mended, Lady Grace." He was in fact altogether gallant about it. "I'm aware of the limits of what I have to show or to offer, but I defy you to find a limit to my possible devotion."

She deferred to that, but taking it in a lower key. "I believe you'd be very good to me."

"Well, isn't *that* something to start with?"—he fairly pounced on it. "I'll do any blest thing in life you like, I'll accept any condition you impose, if you'll only tell me you see your way."

"Shouldn't I have a little more first to see yours?" she asked. "When you say you'll do anything in life I like, isn't there anything you yourself want strongly enough to do?"

He cast a stare about on the suggestions of the scene. "Anything that will make money, you mean?"

"Make money or make reputation—or even just make the time pass."

"Oh, what I have to look to in the way of a career?" If that was her meaning he could show after an instant that he didn't fear it. "Well, your father, dear delightful man, has been so good as to give me to understand that he backs me for a decent deserving creature; and I've noticed, as you doubtless yourself have, that when Lord Theign backs a fellow——!"

He left the obvious moral for her to take up—which she did, but all interrogatively. "The fellow at once comes in for something awfully good?"

"I don't in the least mind your laughing at me," Lord John returned, "for when I put him the question of the lift he'd give me by speaking to you first he bade me simply remember the complete personal liberty in which he leaves you, and yet which doesn't come—take my word!" said the young man sagely—"from his being at all indifferent."

"No," she answered—"father isn't indifferent. But father's 'great'"

"Great indeed!"—her friend took it as with full comprehension. This appeared not to prevent, however, a second and more anxious thought. "Too great for *you?*"

"Well, he makes me feel—even as his daughter—my extreme comparative smallness."

47

It was easy, Lord John indicated, to see what she meant "He's a *grand seigneur*, and a serious one—that's what he is: the very type and model of it, down to the ground. So you can imagine," the young man said, "what he makes me feel—most of all when he's so awfully good-natured to me. His being as 'great' as you say and yet backing me—such as I am!—doesn't *that* strike you as a good note for me, the best you could possibly require? For he really *would* like what I propose to you."

She might have been noting, while she thought, that he had risen to ingenuity, to fineness, on the wings of his argument; under the effect of which her reply had the air of a concession. "Yes—he would like it."

"Then he *has* spoken to you?" her suitor eagerly asked.

"He hasn't needed—he has ways of letting one know."

"Yes, yes, he has ways; all his own—like everything else he has. He's wonderful."

She fully agreed. "He's wonderful."

The tone of it appeared somehow to shorten at once for Lord John the rest of his approach to a conclusion. "So you do see your way?"

"Ah—!" she said with a quick sad shrinkage.

"I mean," her visitor hastened to explain, "if he does put it to you as the very best idea he has for you. When he does that—as I believe him ready to do—will you really and fairly listen to him? I'm certain, honestly, that when you know me better—!" His confidence in short donned a bravery.

"I've been feeling this quarter of an hour," the girl returned, "that I do know you better."

"Then isn't that all I want?—unless indeed I ought perhaps to ask rather if it isn't all *you* do! At any rate," said Lord John, "I may see you again here?"

She waited a moment. "You must have patience with me."

"I *am* having it But *after* your father's appeal."

"Well," she said, "that must come first."

"Then you won't dodge it?"

She looked at him straight "I don't dodge, Lord John."

He admired the manner of it "You look awfully handsome as you say so—and you see what *that* does to me." As to attentuate a little the freedom of which he went on: "May I fondly hope that if Lady Imber too should wish to put in another word for me——?"

"Will I listen to her?"—it brought Lady Grace straight down. "No, Lord John, let me tell you at once that I'll do nothing of the sort Kitty's quite another affair, and I never listen to her a bit more than I can help."

Lord John appeared to feel, on this, that he mustn't too easily, in honour, abandon a person who had presented herself to him as an ally. "Ah, you strike me as a little hard on her. Your father himself—in his looser moments!—takes pleasure in what she says."

Our young woman's eyes, as they rested on him after this remark, had no mercy for its extreme feebleness. "If you mean that she's the most reckless rattle one knows, and that she never looks so beautiful as when she's at her worst, and that, always clever for where she makes out her interest, she has learnt to 'get round' him till he only sees through her eyes—if you mean *that* I understand you perfectly. But even if you think me horrid for reflecting so on my nearest and dearest, it's not on the side on which he has most confidence in his elder daughter that his youngest is moved to have most confidence in *him*."

Lord John stared as if she had shaken some odd bright fluttering object in his face; but then recovering himself: "He hasn't perhaps an absolutely boundless confidence—"

"In any one in the world but himself?"—she had taken him straight up. "He hasn't indeed, and that's what we must come to; so that even if he likes you as much as you doubtless very justly feel, it won't be because you are right about your being nice, but because *he* is!"

"You mean that if I were wrong about it he would still insist that he isn't?"

Lady Grace was indeed sure. "Absolutely—if he had begun so! He began so with Kitty—that is with allowing her everything."

Lord John appeared struck. "Yes—and he still allows her two thousand."

"I'm glad to hear it—she has never told me how much!" the girl undisguisedly smiled.

"Then perhaps I oughtn't!"—he glowed with the light of contrition.

"Well, you can't help it now," his companion remarked with amusement.

"You mean that he ought to allow *you* as much?" Lord John inquired. "I'm sure you're right, and that he will," he continued quite as in good faith; "but I want you to understand that I don't care in the least what it may be!"

The subject of his suit took the longest look at him she had taken yet. "You're very good to say so!"

If this was ironic the touch fell short, thanks to his perception that they had practically just ceased to be alone. They were in presence of a third figure, who had arrived from the terrace, but whose approach to them was not so immediate as to deprive Lord John of time for another question. "Will you let *him* tell you, at all events, how good he thinks me?—and then let me come back and have it from you again?"

Lady Grace's answer to this was to turn, as he drew nearer, to the person by whom they were now joined. "Lord John desires you should tell me, father, how good you think him."

"'Good,' my dear?—good for what?" said Lord Theign a trifle absurdly, but looking from one of them to the other.

"I feel I must ask *him* to tell you."

"Then I shall give him a chance—as I should particularly like you to go back and deal with those overwhelming children."

"Ah, they don't overwhelm *you*, father!"—the girl put it with some point.

"If you mean to say I overwhelmed *them*, I dare say I did," he replied—"from my view of that vast collective gape of six hundred painfully plain and perfectly expressionless faces. But that was only for the time: I pumped advice—oh *such* advice!—and they held the large bucket as still as my pet pointer, when I scratch him, holds his back. The bucket, under the stream—"

"Was bound to overflow?" Lady Grace suggested.

"Well, the strong recoil of the wave of intelligence has been not unnaturally followed by the formidable break. You must really," Lord Theign insisted, "go and deal with it."

His daughter's smile, for all this, was perceptibly cold. "You work people up, father, and then leave others to let them down."

"The two things," he promptly replied, "require different natures." To which he simply added, as with the habit of authority, though not of harshness, "Go!"

It was absolute and she yielded; only pausing an instant to look as with a certain gathered meaning from one of the men to the other. Faintly and resignedly sighing she passed away to the terrace and disappeared.

"The nature that *can* let you down—I rather like it, you know!" Lord John threw off. Which, for an airy elegance in them, were perhaps just slightly rash words—his companion gave him so sharp a look as the two were left together.

VI

Face to face with his visitor the master of Dedborough betrayed the impression his daughter appeared to have given him. "She didn't want to go?" And then before Lord John could reply: "What the deuce is the matter with her?"

Lord John took his time. "I think perhaps a little Mr. Crimble."

"And who the deuce is a little Mr. Crimble?"

"A young man who was just with her—and whom she appears to have invited."

"Where is he then?" Lord Theign demanded.

"Off there among the pictures—which he seems partly to have come for."

"Oh!"—it made his lordship easier. "Then he's all right—on such a day."

His companion could none the less just wonder. "Hadn't Lady Grace told you?"

"That he was coming? Not that I remember." But Lord Theign, perceptibly preoccupied, made nothing of this. "We've had other fish to fry, and you know the freedom I allow her."

His friend had a vivid gesture. "My dear man, I only ask to profit by it!" With which there might well have been in Lord John's face a light of comment on the pretension in such a quarter to allow freedom.

Yet it was a pretension that Lord Theign sustained—as to show himself far from all bourgeois narrowness. "She has her friends by the score—at this time of day." There was clearly a claim here also—to *know* the time of day. "But in the matter of friends where, by the way, is your own—of whom I've but just heard?"

"Oh, off there among the pictures too; so they'll have met and taken care of each other." Accounting for this inquirer would be clearly the least of Lord John's difficulties. "I mustn't appear to Bender to have failed him; but I must at once let you know, before I join him, that, seizing my opportunity, I have just very definitely, in fact very pressingly, spoken to Lady Grace. It hasn't been perhaps," he continued, "quite the pick of a chance; but that seemed never to come, and if I'm not too fondly mistaken, at any rate, she listened to me without abhorrence. Only I've led her to expect—for our case—that you'll be so good, without loss of time, as to say the clinching word to her yourself."

"Without loss, you mean, of—a—my daughter's time?" Lord Theign, confessedly and amiably interested, had accepted these intimations—yet with the very blandness that was not accessible to hustling and was never forgetful of its standing privilege of criticism. He had come in from his public duty, a few minutes before, somewhat flushed and blown; but that had presently dropped—to the effect, we should have guessed, of his appearing to Lord John at least as cool as the occasion required. His appearance, we ourselves certainly should have felt, was in all respects charming—with the great note of it the beautiful restless, almost suspicious, challenge to you, on the part of deep and mixed things in him, his pride and his shyness, his conscience, his taste and his temper, to deny that he was admirably simple. Obviously, at this rate, he had a passion for simplicity—simplicity, above all, of relation with you, and would show you, with the last subtlety of displeasure, his impatience of your attempting anything more with himself. With such an ideal of decent ease he would, confound you, "sink" a hundred other attributes—or the recognition at least and the formulation of them—that you might abjectly have taken for granted in him: just to show you that in a beastly vulgar age you had, and small wonder, a beastly vulgar imagination. He sank thus, surely, in defiance of insistent vulgarity, half his consciousness of his advantages, flattering himself that mere facility and amiability, a true effective, a positively ideal suppression of reference in any one to anything that might complicate, alone floated above. This would be quite his religion, you might infer—to cause his hands to ignore in whatever contact any opportunity, however convenient, for an unfair pull. Which habit it was that must have produced in him a sort of ripe and radiant fairness; if it be allowed us, that is, to figure in so shining an air a nobleman of fifty-three, of an undecided rather than a certified frame or outline, of a head thinly though neatly covered and not measureably massive, of an almost trivial freshness, of a face marked but by a fine inwrought line or two and lighted by a merely charming expression. You might somehow have traced back the whole character so presented to an ideal privately invoked—that of his establishing in the formal garden of his suffered greatness such easy seats and short perspectives, such winding paths and natural-looking waters, as would mercifully break up the scale. You would perhaps indeed have reflected at the same time that the thought of so much mercy was almost more than anything else the thought of a great option and a great margin—in fine of fifty alternatives. Which remarks of ours, however, leave his lordship with his last immediate question on his hands.

"Well, yes—*that*, of course, in all propriety," his companion has meanwhile replied to it. "But I was thinking a little, you understand, of the importance of our own time."

Divinably Lord Theign put himself out less, as we may say, for the comparatively matter-of-course haunters of his garden than for interlopers even but slightly accredited. He seemed thus not at all to strain to "understand" in this particular connection—it would be his familiarly amusing friend Lord John, clearly, who must do most of the work for him. "'Our own' in the sense of yours and mine?"

"Of yours and mine and Lady Imber's, yes—and a good bit, last not least, in that of my watching and waiting mother's." This struck no prompt spark of apprehension from his listener, so that Lord John went on: "The last thing she did this morning was to remind me, with her fine old frankness, that she would like to learn without more delay where, on the whole question, she *is*, don't you know? What she put to me"—the younger man felt his ground a little, but proceeded further—"what she put to me, with her rather grand way of looking *all* questions straight in the face, you see, was: Do we or don't we, decidedly, take up practically her very handsome offer—'very handsome' being, I mean, what *she* calls it; though it strikes even me too, you know, as rather decent."

Lord Theign at this point resigned himself to know. "Kitty has of course rubbed into me how decent she herself finds it. She hurls herself again on me—successfully!—for everything, and it suits her down to the ground. She pays her beastly debt—that is, I mean to say," and he took himself up, though it was scarce more than perfunctory, "discharges her obligations—by her sister's fair hand; not to mention a few other trifles for which I naturally provide."

Lord John, a little unexpectedly to himself on the defensive, was yet but briefly at a loss. "Of course we take into account, don't we? not only the fact of my mother's desire (intended, I assure you, to be most flattering) that Lady Grace shall enter our family with all honours, but her expressed readiness to facilitate the thing by an understanding over and above——"

"Over and above Kitty's release from her damnable payment?"—Lord Theign reached out to what his guest had left rather in the air. "Of course we take *everything* into account—or I shouldn't, my dear fellow, be discussing with you at all a business one or two of whose aspects so little appeal to me: especially as there's nothing, you easily conceive, that a daughter of mine can come in for by entering even your family, or any other (as a family) that she wouldn't be quite as sure of by just staying in her own. The Duchess's idea, at any rate, if I've followed you, is that if Grace does accept you she settles on you twelve thousand; with the condition—"

Lord John was already all there. "Definitely, yes, of your settling the equivalent on Lady Grace."

"And what do you call the equivalent of twelve thousand?"

"Why, tacked on to a value so great and so charming as Lady Grace herself, I dare say such a sum as nine or ten would serve."

"And where the mischief, if you please, at this highly inconvenient time, am I to pick up nine or ten thousand?"

Lord John declined, with a smiling, a fairly irritating eye for his friend's general resources, to consider that question seriously. "Surely you can have no difficulty whatever—!"

"Why not?—when you can see for yourself that I've had this year to let poor dear old Hill Street! Do you call it the moment for me to have *liked* to see myself all but cajoled into planking down even such a matter as the very much lower figure of Kitty's horrid incubus?"

"Ah, but the inducement and the *quid pro quo*," Lord John brightly indicated, "are here much greater! In the case you speak of you will only have removed the incubus—which, I grant you, she must and you must feel as horrid. In this other you pacify Lady Imber *and* marry Lady Grace: marry her to a man who has set his heart on her and of whom she has just expressed—to himself—a very kind and very high opinion."

"She has expressed a very high opinion of you?"—Lord Theign scarce glowed with credulity.

But the younger man held his ground. "She has told me she thoroughly likes me and that—though a fellow feels an ass repeating such things—she thinks me perfectly charming."

"A tremendous creature, eh, all round? Then," said Lord Theign, "what does she want more?"

"She very possibly wants nothing—but I'm to that beastly degree, you see," his visitor patiently explained, "in the cleft stick of my fearfully positive mother's wants. Those are her 'terms,' and I don't mind saying that they're most disagreeable to me—I quite hate 'em: there! Only I think it makes a jolly difference that I wouldn't touch 'em with a long pole if my personal feeling— in respect to Lady Grace—wasn't so immensely enlisted."

"I assure you I'd chuck 'em out of window, my boy, if I didn't believe you'd be really good to her," Lord Theign returned with the properest spirit.

It only encouraged his companion. "You *will* just tell her then, now and here, how good you honestly believe I shall be?"

This appeal required a moment—a longer look at him. "You truly hold that that friendly guarantee, backed by my parental weight, will do your job?"

"That's the conviction I entertain."

Lord Theign thought again. "Well, even if your conviction's just, that still doesn't tell me into which of my very empty pockets it will be of the least use for me to fumble."

"Oh," Lord John laughed, "when a man has such a tremendous assortment of breeches—!" He pulled up, however, as, in his motion, his eye caught the great vista of the open rooms. "If it's a question of pockets—and what's *in* 'em—here precisely is my man!" This personage had come back from his tour of observation and was now, on the threshold of the hall, exhibited to Lord Theign as well. Lord John's welcome was warm. "I've had awfully to fail you, Mr. Bender, but I was on the point of joining you. Let me, however, still better, introduce you to our host."

VII

Mr. Bender indeed, formidably advancing, scarce had use for this assistance. "Happy to meet you—especially in your beautiful home, Lord Theign." To which he added while the master of Dedborough stood good-humouredly passive to his approach: "I've been round, by your kind permission and the light of nature, and haven't required support; though if I had there's a gentleman there who seemed prepared to allow me any amount." Mr. Bender, out of his abundance, evoked as by a suggestive hand this contributory figure. "A young, spare, nervous gentleman with eye-glasses—I guess he's an author. A friend of yours too?" he asked of Lord John.

The answer was prompt and emphatic. "No, the gentleman is no friend at all of mine, Mr. Bender."

"A friend of my daughter's," Lord Theign easily explained. "I hope they're looking after him."

"Oh, they took care he had tea and bread and butter to any extent; and were so good as to move something," Mr. Bender conscientiously added, "so that he could get up on a chair and see straight into the Moretto."

This was a touch, however, that appeared to affect Lord John unfavourably. "Up on a chair? I say!"

Mr. Bender took another view. "Why, I got right up myself—a little more and I'd almost have begun to paw it! He got me quite interested"—the proprietor of the picture would perhaps care to know—"in that Moretto."

And it was on these lines that Mr. Bender continued to advance. "I take it that your biggest value, however, Lord Theign, is your splendid Sir Joshua. Our friend there has a great deal to say about that too—but it didn't lead to our moving any more furniture." On which he paused as to enjoy, with a show of his fine teeth, his host's reassurance. "It *has* yet, my impression of that picture, sir, led to something else. Are you prepared, Lord Theign, to entertain a proposition?"

Lord Theign met Mr. Bender's eyes while this inquirer left these few portentous words to speak for themselves. "To the effect that I part to you with 'The Beautiful Duchess of Waterbridge'? No, Mr. Bender, such a proposition would leave me intensely cold."

Lord John had meanwhile had a more headlong cry. "My dear Bender, I *envy* you!"

"I guess you don't envy me," his friend serenely replied, "as much as I envy Lord Theign." And then while Mr. Bender and the latter continued to face each other searchingly and firmly: "What I allude to is an overture of a strong and simple stamp—such as perhaps would shed a softer light on the difficulties raised by association and attachment. I've had some experience of first shocks, and I'd be glad to meet you as man to man."

Mr. Bender was, quite clearly, all genial and all sincere; he intended no irony and used, consciously, no great freedom. Lord Theign, not less evidently, saw this, and it permitted him amusement. "As rich man to poor man is how I'm to understand it? For me to meet *you*," he added, "I should have to be tempted—and I'm not even temptable. So there we are," he blandly smiled.

His blandness appeared even for a moment to set an example to Lord John. "'The Beautiful Duchess of Waterbridge,' Mr. Bender, is a golden apple of one of those great family trees of which respectable people don't lop off the branches whose venerable shade, in this garish and denuded age, they so much enjoy."

Mr. Bender looked at him as if he had cut some irrelevant caper. "Then if they don't sell their ancestors where in the world are all the ancestors bought?"

"Doesn't it for the moment sufficiently answer your question," Lord Theign asked, "that they're definitely not bought at Dedborough?"

"Why," said Mr. Bender with a wealthy patience, "you talk as if it were my interest to be *reasonable*—which shows how little you understand. I'd be ashamed—with the lovely ideas I have—if I didn't make you kick." And his sturdy smile for it all fairly proclaimed his faith. "Well, I guess I can wait!"

This again in turn visibly affected Lord John: marking the moment from which he, in spite of his cultivated levity, allowed an intenser and more sustained look to keep straying toward their host. "Mr. Bender's bound to *have* something!"

It was even as if after a minute Lord Theign had been reached by his friend's mute pressure. "'Something'?"

"Something, Mr. Bender?" Lord John insisted.

It made their visitor rather sharply fix him. "Why, have *you* an interest, Lord John?"

This personage, though undisturbed by the challenge, if such it was, referred it to Lord Theign. "Do you authorise me to speak—a little—as if I have an interest?"

Lord Theign gave the appeal—and the speaker—a certain attention, and then appeared rather sharply to turn away from them. "My dear fellow, you may amuse yourself at my expense as you like!"

"Oh, I don't mean at your expense," Lord John laughed—"I mean at Mr. Bender's!"

"Well, go ahead, Lord John," said that gentleman, always easy, but always too, as you would have felt, aware of everything—"go ahead, but don't sweetly hope to create me in any desire that doesn't already exist in the germ. The attempt has often been made, over here—has in fact been organised on a considerable scale; but I guess I've got some peculiarity, for it doesn't seem as if the thing could be done. If the germ is there, on the other hand," Mr. Bender conceded, "it develops independently of all encouragement."

Lord John communicated again as in a particular sense with Lord Theign. "He thinks I really mean to *offer* him something!"

Lord Theign, who seemed to wish to advertise a degree of detachment from the issue, or from any other such, strolled off, in his restlessness, toward the door that opened to the terrace, only stopping on his way to light a cigarette from a matchbox on a small table. It was but after doing so that he made the remark: "Ah, Mr. Bender may easily be too much for you!"

"That makes me the more sorry, sir," said his visitor, "not to have been enough for *you!*"

"I risk it, at any rate," Lord John went on—"I put you, Bender, the question of whether you wouldn't Move,' as you say, to acquire that Moretto."

Mr. Bender's large face had a commensurate gaze. "As I say? I haven't said anything of the sort!"

"But you do 'love' you know," Lord John slightly overgrimaced.

"I don't when I don't want to. I'm different from most people—I can love or not as I like. The trouble with that Moretto," Mr. Bender continued, "is that it ain't what I'm after."

His "after" had somehow, for the ear, the vividness of a sharp whack on the resisting surface of things, and was concerned doubtless in Lord John's speaking again across to their host. "The worst he can do for me, you see, is to refuse it."

Lord Theign, who practically had his back turned and was fairly dandling about in his impatience, tossed out to the terrace the cigarette he had but just lighted. Yet he faced round to reply: "It's the very first time in the history of this house (a long one, Mr. Bender) that a picture, or anything else in it, has been offered——!"

It was not imperceptible that even if he hadn't dropped Mr. Bender mightn't have been markedly impressed. "Then it must be the very first time such an offer has failed."

"Oh, it isn't that we in the least press it!" Lord Theign quite naturally laughed.

"Ah, I beg your pardon—I press it very hard!" And Lord John, as taking from his face and manner a cue for further humorous license, went so far as to emulate, though sympathetically enough, their companion's native form. "You don't mean to say you don't feel the interest of that Moretto?"

Mr. Bender, quietly confident, took his time to reply. "Well, if you had seen me up on that chair you'd have thought I did."

"Then you must have stepped down from the chair properly impressed."

"I stepped down quite impressed with that young man."

"Mr. Crimble?"—it came after an instant to Lord John. "With *his* opinion, really? Then I hope he's aware of the picture's value."

"You had better ask him," Mr. Bender observed.

"Oh, we don't depend here on the Mr. Crimbles!" Lord John returned.

Mr. Bender took a longer look at him. "Are you aware of the value yourself?"

His friend resorted again, as for the amusement of the thing, to their entertainer. "Am I aware of the value of the Moretto?"

Lord Theign, who had meanwhile lighted another cigarette, appeared, a bit extravagantly smoking, to wish to put an end to his effect of hovering aloof.

"That question needn't trouble us—when I see how much Mr. Bender himself knows about it."

"Well, Lord Theign, I only know what that young man puts it at." And then as the others waited, "Ten thousand," said Mr. Bender.

"Ten thousand?" The owner of the work showed no emotion.

"Well," said Lord John again in Mr. Bender's style, "what's the matter with ten thousand?"

The subject of his gay tribute considered. "There's nothing the matter with ten thousand."

"Then," Lord Theign asked, "is there anything the matter with the picture?"

"Yes, sir—I guess there is."

It gave an upward push to his lordship's eyebrows. "But what in the world——?"

"Well, that's just the question!"

The eyebrows continued to rise. "Does he pretend there's a question of whether it *is* a Moretto?"

"That's what he was up there trying to find out."

"But if the value's, according to himself, ten thousand——?"

"Why, of course," said Mr. Bender, "it's a fine work anyway."

"Then," Lord Theign brought good-naturedly out, "what's the matter with *you*, Mr. Bender?"

That gentleman was perfectly clear. "The matter with me, Lord Theign, is that I've no use for a ten thousand picture."

"'No use?'"—the expression had an oddity. "But what's it your idea to do with such things?"

"I mean," Mr. Bender explained, "that a picture of that rank is not what I'm after."

"The figure," said his noble host—speaking thus, under pressure, commercially—"is beyond what you see your way to?"

But Lord John had jumped at the truth. "The matter with Mr. Bender is that he sees his way much further."

"Further?" their companion echoed.

"The matter with Mr. Bender is that he wants to give millions."

Lord Theign sounded this abyss with a smile. "Well, there would be no difficulty about *that*, I think!"

"Ah," said his guest, "you know the basis, sir, on which I'm ready to pay."

"On the basis then of the Sir Joshua," Lord John inquired, "how far would you go?"

Mr. Bender indicated by a gesture that on a question reduced to a moiety by its conditional form he could give but semi-satisfaction. "Well, I'd go all the way."

"He wants, you see," Lord John elucidated, "an *ideally* expensive thing."

Lord Theign appeared to decide after a moment to enter into the pleasant spirit of this; which he did by addressing his younger friend. "Then why shouldn't I make even the Moretto as expensive as he desires?"

"Because you can't do violence to *that* master's natural modesty," Mr. Bender declared before Lord John had time to speak. And conscious at this moment of the reappearance of his fellow-explorer, he at once supplied a further light. "I guess this gentleman at any rate can tell you."

VIII

Hugh Crimble had come back from his voyage of discovery, and it was visible as he stood there flushed and quite radiant that he had caught in his approach Lord Theign's last inquiry and Mr. Bender's reply to it. You would have imputed to him on the spot the lively possession of a new idea, the sustaining sense of a message important enough to justify his irruption. He looked from one to the other of the three men, scattered a little by the sight of him, but attached eyes of recognition then to Lord Theign's, whom he remained an instant longer communicatively smiling at. After which, as you might have gathered, he all confidently plunged, taking up the talk where the others had left it. "I should say, Lord Theign, if you'll allow me, in regard to what you appear to have been discussing, that it depends a good deal on just that question—of what your Moretto, at any rate, may be presumed or proved to 'be.' Let me thank you," he cheerfully went on, "for your kind leave to go over your treasures."

The personage he so addressed was, as we know, nothing if not generally affable; yet if that was just then apparent it was through a shade of coolness for the slightly heated familiarity of so plain, or at least so free, a young man in eye-glasses, now for the first time definitely apprehended. "Oh, I've scarcely 'treasures'—but I've some things of interest."

Hugh, however, entering the opulent circle, as it were, clearly took account of no breath of a chill. "I think possible, my lord, that you've a great treasure—if you've really so high a rarity as a splendid Manto-vano."

"A 'Mantovano'?" You wouldn't have been sure that his lordship didn't pronounce the word for the first time in his life.

"There have been supposed to be only *seven* real examples about the world; so that if by an extraordinary chance you find yourself the possessor of a magnificent eighth——"

But Lord John had already broken in. "Why, there you *are*, Mr. Bender!"

"Oh, Mr. Bender, with whom I've made acquaintance," Hugh returned, "was there as it began to work in me—"

"That your Moretto, Lord Theign"—Mr. Bender took their informant up—"isn't, after all, a Moretto at all." And he continued amusedly to Hugh: "It began to work in you, sir, like very strong drink!"

"Do I understand you to suggest," Lord Theign asked of the startling young man, "that my precious picture isn't genuine?"

Well, Hugh knew exactly what he suggested. "As a picture, Lord Theign, as a great portrait, one of the most genuine things in Europe. But it strikes me as probable that from far back—for reasons!—there has been a wrong attribution; that the work has been, in other words, traditionally, obstinately miscalled. It has passed for a Moretto, and at first I quite took it for one; but I suddenly, as I looked and looked and saw and saw, began to doubt, and now I know *why* I doubted."

Lord Theign had during this speech kept his eyes on the ground; but he raised them to Mr. Crimble's almost palpitating presence for the remark: "I'm bound to say that I hope you've some very good grounds!"

"I've three or four, Lord Theign; they seem to me of the best—as yet. They made me wonder and wonder—and then light splendidly broke."

His lordship didn't stint his attention. "Reflected, you mean, from *other* Mantovanos—that I don't know?"

"I mean from those I know myself," said Hugh; "and I mean from fine analogies with one in particular."

"Analogies that in all these years, these centuries, have so remarkably not been noticed?"

"Well," Hugh competently explained, "they're a sort of thing the very sense of, the value and meaning of, are a highly modern—in fact a quite recent growth."

Lord John at this professed with cordiality that he at least quite understood. "Oh, we know a lot more about our pictures and things than ever our ancestors did!"

"Well, I guess it's enough for *me*," Mr. Bender contributed, "that your ancestors knew enough to get 'em!"

"Ah, that doesn't go so far," cried Hugh, "unless we ourselves know enough to keep 'em!"

The words appeared to quicken in a manner Lord Theign's view of the speaker. "Were *your* ancestors, Mr. Crimble, great collectors?"

Arrested, it might be, in his general assurance, Hugh wondered and smiled. "Mine—collectors? Oh, I'm afraid I haven't any—to speak of. Only it has seemed to me for a long time," he added, "that on that head we should all feel together."

Lord Theign looked for a moment as if these were rather large presumptions; then he put them in their place a little curtly. "It's one thing to keep our possessions for ourselves—it's another to keep them for other people."

"Well," Hugh good-humouredly returned, "I'm perhaps not so absolutely sure of myself, if you press me, as that I sha'n't be glad of a higher and wiser opinion—I mean than my own. It would be awfully interesting, if you'll allow me to say so, to have the judgment of one or two of the great men."

"You're not yourself, Mr. Crimble, one of the great men?" his host asked with tempered irony.

"Well, I guess he's going to be, anyhow," Mr. Bender cordially struck in; "and this remarkable exhibition of intelligence may just let him loose on the world, mayn't it?"

"Thank you, Mr. Bender!"—and Hugh obviously tried to look neither elated nor snubbed. "I've too much still to learn, but I'm learning every day, and I shall have learnt immensely this afternoon."

"Pretty well at my expense, however," Lord Theign laughed, "if you demolish a name we've held for generations so dear."

"You may have held the name dear, my lord," his young critic answered; "but my whole point is that, if I'm right, you've held the picture itself cheap."

"Because a Mantovano," said Lord John, "is so much greater a value?"

Hugh met his eyes a moment "Are you talking of values pecuniary?"

"What values are *not* pecuniary?"

Hugh might, during his hesitation, have been imagined to stand off a little from the question. "Well, some things have in a higher degree that one, and some have the associational or the factitious, and some the clear artistic."

"And some," Mr. Bender opined, "have them *all*—in the highest degree. But what you mean," he went on, "is that a Mantovano would come higher under the hammer than a Moretto?"

"Why, sir," the young man returned, "there aren't any, as I've just stated, to 'come.' I account—or I easily can—for every one of the very small number."

"Then do you consider that you account for this one?"

"I believe I shall if you'll give me time."

"Oh, time!" Mr. Bender impatiently sighed. "But we'll give you all we've got—only I guess it isn't much." And he appeared freely to invite their companions to join in this estimate. They listened to him, however, they watched him, for the moment, but in silence, and with the next he had gone on: "How much higher—if your idea is correct about it—would Lord Theign's picture come?"

Hugh turned to that nobleman. "Does Mr. Bender mean come to *him*, my lord?"

Lord Theign looked again hard at Hugh, and then harder than he had done yet at his other invader. "I don't know *what* Mr. Bender means!" With which he turned off.

"Well, I guess I mean that it would come higher to me than to any one! But how *much* higher?" the American continued to Hugh.

"How much higher to *you?*"

"Oh, I can size *that*. How much higher as a Mantovano?"

Unmistakably—for us at least—our young man was gaining time; he had the instinct of circumspection and delay. "To any one?"

67

"To any one."

"Than as a Moretto?" Hugh continued.

It even acted on Lord John's nerves. "That's what we're talking about—really!"

But Hugh still took his ease; as if, with his eyes first on Bender and then on Lord Theign, whose back was practically presented, he were covertly studying signs. "Well," he presently said, "in view of the very great interest combined with the very great rarity, more than—ah more than can be estimated off-hand."

It made Lord Theign turn round. "But a fine Moretto has a very great rarity and a very great interest."

"Yes—but not on the whole the same amount of either."

"No, not on the whole the same amount of either!"—Mr. Bender judiciously echoed it. "But how," he freely pursued, "are you going to find out?"

"Have I your permission, Lord Theign," Hugh brightly asked, "to attempt to find out?"

The question produced on his lordship's part a visible, a natural anxiety. "What would it be your idea then to *do* with my property?"

"Nothing at all here—it could all be done, I think, at Verona. What besets, what quite haunts me," Hugh explained, "is the vivid image of a Mantovano—one of the glories of the short list—in a private collection in that place. The conviction grows in me that the two portraits must be of the same original. In fact I'll bet my head," the young man quite ardently wound up, "that the wonderful subject of the Verona picture, a very great person clearly, is none other than the very great person of yours."

Lord Theign had listened with interest. "Mayn't he be that and yet from another hand?"

"It isn't another hand"—oh Hugh was quite positive. "It's the hand of the very same painter."

"How can you prove it's the same?"

"Only by the most intimate internal evidence, I admit—and evidence that of course has to be estimated."

"Then who," Lord Theign asked, "is to estimate it?"

"Well,"—Hugh was all ready—"will you let Pap-pendick, one of the first authorities in Europe, a good friend of mine, in fact more or less my master, and who is generally to be found at Brussels? I happen to know he knows your picture—he once spoke to me of it; and he'll go and look again at the Verona one, he'll go and judge our issue, if I apply to him, in the light of certain new tips that I shall be able to give him."

Lord Theign appeared to wonder. "If you 'apply' to him?"

"Like a shot, I believe, if I ask it of him—as a service."

"A service to *you?* He'll be very obliging," his lordship smiled.

"Well, I've obliged *him!*" Hugh readily retorted.

"The obligation will be to we"—Lord Theign spoke more formally.

"Well, the satisfaction," said Hugh, "will be to all of us. The things Pappendick has seen he intensely, ineffaceably keeps in mind, to every detail; so that he'll tell me—as no one else really can—if the Verona man is *your* man."

"But then," asked Mr. Bender, "we've got to believe anyway what he says?"

"The market," said Lord John with emphasis, "would have to believe it—that's the point."

"Oh," Hugh returned lightly, "the market will have nothing to do with it, I hope; but I think you'll feel when he has spoken that you really know where you are."

Mr. Bender couldn't doubt of that. "Oh, if he gives us a bigger thing we won't complain. Only, how long will it take him to get there? I want him to start right away."

"Well, as I'm sure he'll be deeply interested——"

"We *may*"—Mr. Bender took it straight up—"get news next week?"

Hugh addressed his reply to Lord Theign; it was already a little too much as if he and the American between them were snatching the case from that possessor's hands. "The day I hear from Pappendick you shall have a full report. And," he conscientiously added, "if I'm proved to have been unfortunately wrong——!"

His lordship easily pointed the moral. "You'll have caused me some inconvenience."

"Of course I shall," the young man unreservedly agreed—"like a wanton meddling ass!" His candour, his freedom had decidedly a note of their own. "But my conviction, after those moments with your picture, was too strong for me not to speak—and, since you allow it, I face the danger and risk the test."

"I allow it of course in the form of business." This produced in Hugh a certain blankness. "'Business'?" "If I consent to the inquiry I pay for the inquiry." Hugh demurred. "Even if I turn out mistaken?" "You make me in any event your proper charge." The young man thought again, and then as for vague accommodation: "Oh, my charge won't be high!"

"Ah," Mr. Bender protested, "it ought to be handsome if the thing's marked *up*!" After which he looked at his watch. "But I guess I've got to go, Lord Theign, though your lovely old Duchess—for it's to *her* I've lost my heart—does cry out for me again."

"You'll find her then still there," Lord John observed with emphasis, but with his eyes for the time on Lord Theign; "and if you want another look at her I'll presently come and take one too."

"I'll order your car to the garden-front," Lord Theign added to this; "you'll reach it from the saloon, but I'll see you again first."

Mr. Bender glared as with the round full force of his pair of motor lamps. "Well, if you're ready to talk about anything, I am. Good-bye, Mr. Crimble."

"Good-bye, Mr. Bender." But Hugh, addressing their host while his fellow-guest returned to the saloon, broke into the familiarity of confidence. "As if you *could* be ready to 'talk'!"

This produced on the part of the others present a mute exchange that could only have denoted surprise at all the irrepressible young outsider thus projected upon them took for granted. "I've an idea," said Lord John to his friend, "that you're quite ready to talk with *me*."

Hugh then, with his appetite so richly quickened, could but rejoice. "Lady Grace spoke to me of things in the library."

"You'll find it *that* way"—Lord Theign gave the indication.

"Thanks," said Hugh elatedly, and hastened away.

Lord John, when he had gone, found relief in a quick comment. "Very sharp, no doubt—but he wants taking down."

The master of Dedborough wouldn't have put it so crudely, but the young expert did bring certain things home. "The people my daughters, in the exercise of a wild freedom, do pick up——!"

"Well, don't you see that all you've got to do—on the question we're dealing with—is to claim your very own wild freedom? Surely I'm right in feeling you," Lord John further remarked, "to have jumped at once to my idea that Bender is heaven-sent—and at what they call the psychologic moment, don't they?—to point that moral. Why look anywhere else for a sum of money that—smaller or greater—you can find with perfect ease in that extraordinarily bulging pocket?"

Lord Theign, slowly pacing the hall again, threw up his hands. "Ah, with 'perfect ease' can scarcely be said!"

"Why not?—when he absolutely thrusts his dirty dollars down your throat."

"Oh, I'm not talking of ease to *him*," Lord Theign returned—"I'm talking of ease to myself. I shall have to make a sacrifice."

"Why not then—for so great a convenience—gallantly make it?"

"Ah, my dear chap, if you want me to sell my Sir Joshua——!"

But the horror in the words said enough, and Lord John felt its chill. "I don't make a point of that—God forbid! But there are other things to which the objection wouldn't apply."

"You see how it applies—in the case of the Moret-to—for *him*. A mere Moretto," said Lord Theign, "is too cheap—for a Yankee 'on the spend.'"

"Then the Mantovano wouldn't be."

"It remains to be proved that it *is* a Mantovano."

"Well," said Lord John, "go into it."

"Hanged if I won't!" his friend broke out after a moment. "It *would* suit me. I mean"—the explanation came after a brief intensity of thought—"the possible size of his cheque would."

"Oh," said Lord John gaily, "I guess there's no limit to the possible size of his cheque!"

"Yes, it would suit me, it would suit me!" the elder man, standing there, audibly mused. But his air changed and a lighter question came up to him as he saw his daughter reappear at the door from the terrace. "Well, the infant horde?" he immediately put to her.

Lady Grace came in, dutifully accounting for them. "They've marched off—in a huge procession."

"Thank goodness! And our friends?"

"All playing tennis," she said—"save those who are sitting it out." To which she added, as to explain her return: "Mr. Crimble has gone?"

Lord John took upon him to say. "He's in the library, to which you addressed him—making discoveries."

"Not then, I hope," she smiled, "to our disadvantage!"

"To your very great honour and glory." Lord John clearly valued the effect he might produce.

"Your Moretto of Brescia—do you know what it really and spendidly is?" And then as the girl, in her surprise, but wondered: "A Mantovano, neither more nor less. Ever so much more swagger."

"A Mantovano?" Lady Grace echoed. "Why, how tremendously jolly!"

Her father was struck. "Do you know the artist—of whom I had never heard?"

"Yes, something of the little that *is* known." And she rejoiced as her knowledge came to her. "He's a tremendous swell, because, great as he was, there are but seven proved examples——"

"With this of yours," Lord John broke in, "there are eight."

"Then why haven't I known about him?" Lord Theign put it as if so many other people were guilty for this.

His daughter was the first to plead for the vague body. "Why, I suppose in order that you should have exactly this pleasure, father."

"Oh, pleasures not desired are like acquaintances not sought—they rather bore one!" Lord Theign sighed. With which he moved away from her.

Her eyes followed him an instant—then she smiled at their guest. "Is he bored at having the higher prize—if you're sure it *is* the higher?"

"Mr. Crimble is sure—because if he isn't," Lord John added, "he's a wretch."

"Well," she returned, "as he's certainly not a wretch it must be true. And fancy," she exclaimed further, though as more particularly for herself, "our having suddenly incurred this immense debt to him!"

"Oh, I shall pay Mr. Crimble!" said her father, who had turned round.

The whole question appeared to have provoked in Lord John a rise of spirits and a flush of humour. "Don't you let him stick it on."

His host, however, bethinking himself, checked him. "Go *you* to Mr. Bender straight!"

Lord John saw the point. "Yes—till he leaves. But I shall find you here, shan't I?" he asked with all earnestness of Lady Grace.

She had an hesitation, but after a look at her father she assented. "I'll wait for you."

"Then *à tantôt!*" It made him show for happy as, waving his hand at her, he proceeded to seek Mr. Bender in presence of the object that most excited that gentleman's appetite—to say nothing of the effect involved on Lord John's own.

IX

Lord Theign, when he had gone, revolved—it might have been nervously—about the place a little, but soon broke ground. "He'll have told you, I understand, that I've promised to speak to you for him. But I understand also that he has found something to say for himself."

"Yes, we talked—a while since," the girl said. "At least *he* did."

"Then if you listened I hope you listened with a good grace."

"Oh, he speaks very well—and I've never disliked him."

74

It pulled her father up. "Is that *all*—when I think so much of him?"

She seemed to say that she had, to her own mind, been liberal and gone far; but she waited a little. "Do you think very, *very* much?"

"Surely I've made my good opinion clear to you!"

Again she had a pause. "Oh yes, I've seen you like him and believe in him—and I've found him pleasant and clever."

"He has never had," Lord Theign more or less ingeniously explained, "what I call a real show." But the character under discussion could after all be summed up without searching analysis. "I consider nevertheless that there's plenty in him."

It was a moderate claim, to which Lady Grace might assent. "He strikes me as naturally quick and—well, nice. But I agree with you than he hasn't had a chance."

"Then if you can see your way by sympathy and confidence to help him to one I dare say you'll find your reward."

For a third time she considered, as if a certain curtness in her companion's manner rather hindered, in such a question, than helped. Didn't he simplify too much, you would have felt her ask, and wasn't his visible wish for brevity of debate a sign of his uncomfortable and indeed rather irritated sense of his not making a figure in it? "Do you desire it very particularly?" was, however, all she at last brought out.

"I should like it exceedingly—if you act from conviction. Then of course only; but of one thing I'm myself convinced—of what he thinks of yourself and feels for you."

"Then would you mind my waiting a little?" she asked. "I mean to be absolutely sure of myself." After which, on his delaying to agree, she added frankly, as to help her case: "Upon my word, father, I should like to do what would please you."

But it determined in him a sharper impatience. "Ah, what would please *me!* Don't put it off on 'me'! Judge absolutely for yourself"—he slightly took himself up—"in the light of my having consented to do for him what I always *hate* to do: deviate from my normal practice of never intermeddling. If I've deviated now you can judge. But to do so all round, of course, take—in reason!—your time."

"May I ask then," she said, "for still a little more?"

He looked for this, verily, as if it was not in reason. "You know," he then returned, "what he'll feel that a sign of."

"Well, I'll tell him what I mean."

"Then I'll send him to you."

He glanced at his watch and was going, but after a "Thanks, father," she had stopped him. "There's one thing more." An embarrassment showed in her manner, but at the cost of some effect of earnest abruptness she surmounted it. "What does your American—Mr. Bender—want?"

Lord Theign plainly felt the challenge. "'My' American? He's none of mine!"

"Well then Lord John's."

"He's none of his either—more, I mean, than any one else's. He's every one's American, literally—to all appearance; and I've not to tell *you*, surely, with the freedom of your own visitors, how people stalk in and out here."

"No, father—certainly," she said. "You're splendidly generous."

His eyes seemed rather sharply to ask her then how he could improve on that; but he added as if it were enough: "What the man must by this time want more than anything else is his car."

"Not then anything of ours?" she still insisted.

"Of 'ours'?" he echoed with a frown. "Are you afraid he has an eye to something of *yours?*"

"Why, if we've a new treasure—which we certainly have if we possess a Mantovano—haven't we all, even I, an immense interest in it?" And before he could answer, "Is *that* exposed?" she asked.

Lord Theign, a little unready, cast about at his storied halls; any illusion to the "exposure" of the objects they so solidly sheltered was obviously unpleasant to him. But then it was as if he found at a stroke both his own reassurance and his daughter's. "How can there be a question of it when he only wants Sir Joshuas?"

"He wants ours?" the girl gasped.

"At absolutely any price."

"But you're not," she cried, "discussing it?"

He hesitated as between chiding and contenting her—then he handsomely chose. "My dear child, for what do you take me?" With which he impatiently started, through the long and stately perspective, for the saloon.

She sank into a chair when he had gone; she sat there some moments in a visible tension of thought, her hands clasped in her lap and her dropped eyes fixed and unperceiving; but she sprang up as Hugh Crimble, in search of her, again stood before her. He presented himself as with winged sandals.

"What luck to find you! I must take my spin back."

"You've seen everything as you wished?"

"Oh," he smiled, "I've seen wonders."

She showed her pleasure. "Yes, we've got some things."

"So Mr. Bender says!" he laughed. "You've got five or six—"

"Only five or six?" she cried in bright alarm.

"'Only'?" he continued to laugh. "Why, that's enormous, five or six things of the first importance! But I think I ought to mention to you," he added, "a most barefaced 'Rubens' there in the library."

"It isn't a Rubens?"

"No more than I'm a Ruskin."

"Then you'll brand us—expose us for it?"

"No, I'll let you off—I'll be quiet if you're good, if you go straight. I'll only hold it *in terrorem*. One can't be sure in these dreadful days—that's always to remember; so that if you're not good I'll come down on you with it. But to balance against that threat," he went on, "I've made the very grandest find. At least I believe I have!"

She was all there for this news. "Of the Manto-vano—hidden in the other thing?"

Hugh wondered—almost as if she had been before him. "You don't mean to say *you've* had the idea of that?"

"No, but my father has told me."

"And is your father," he eagerly asked, "really gratified?"

With her conscious eyes on him—her eyes could clearly be very conscious about her father—she considered a moment. "He always prefers old associations and appearances to new; but I'm sure he'll resign himself if you see your way to a certainty."

"Well, it will be a question of the weight of expert opinion that I shall invoke. But I'm not afraid," he resolutely said, "and I shall make the thing, from its splendid rarity, the crown and flower of your glory."

Her serious face shone at him with a charmed gratitude. "It's awfully beautiful then your having come to us so. It's awfully beautiful your having brought us this way, in a flash—as dropping out of a chariot of fire—more light and what you apparently feel with myself as more honour."

"Ah, the beauty's in your having yourself done it!" he returned. He gave way to the positive joy of it. "If I've brought the 'light' and the rest—that's to say the very useful information—who in the world was it brought *me?*"

She had a gesture of protest "You'd have come in some other way."

"I'm not so sure! I'm beastly shy—little as I may seem to show it: save in great causes, when I'm horridly bold and hideously offensive. Now at any rate I only know what *has* been." She turned off for it, moving away from him as with a sense of mingled things that made for unrest; and he had the next moment grown graver under the impression. "But does anything in it all," he asked, "trouble you?"

She faced about across the wider space, and there was a different note in what she brought out. "I don't know what forces me so to *tell* you things."

"'Tell' me?" he stared. "Why, you've told me nothing more monstrous than that I've been welcome!"

"Well, however that may be, what did you mean just now by the chance of our not 'going straight'? When you said you'd expose our bad—or is it our false?—Rubens in the event of a certain danger."

"Oh, in the event of your ever being bribed"—he laughed again as with relief. And then as her face seemed to challenge the word: "Why, to let anything—of your best!—ever leave Dedborough. By which I mean really of course leave the country." She turned again on this, and something in her air made him wonder. "I hope you don't feel there *is* such a danger? I understood from you half an hour ago that it was unthinkable."

"Well, it *was*, to me, half an hour ago," she said as she came nearer. "But if it has since come up?"

"'If' it has! But *has* it? In the form of that monster? What Mr. Bender wants is the great Duchess," he recalled.

"And my father won't sell *her*? No, he won't sell the great Duchess—there I feel safe. But he greatly needs a certain sum of money—or he thinks he does—and I've just had a talk with him."

"In which he has told you that?"

79

"He has told me nothing," Lady Grace said—"or else told me quite other things. But the more I think of them the more it comes to me that he feels urged or tempted—"

"To despoil and denude these walls?" Hugh broke in, looking about in his sharper apprehension.

"Yes, to satisfy, to save my sister. *Now* do you think our state so ideal?" she asked—but without elation for her hint of triumph.

He had no answer for this save "Ah, but you terribly interest me. May I ask what's the matter with your sister?"

Oh, she wanted to go on straight now! "The matter is—in the first place—that she's too dazzlingly, dreadfully beautiful."

"More beautiful than you?" his sincerity easily risked.

"Millions of times." Sad, almost sombre, she hadn't a shade of coquetry. "Kitty has debts—great heaped-up gaming debts."

"But to such amounts?"

"Incredible amounts it appears. And mountains of others too. She throws herself all on our father."

"And he *has* to pay them? There's no one else?" Hugh asked.

She waited as if he might answer himself, and then as he apparently didn't, "He's only afraid there *may* be some else—that's how she makes him do it," she said. And "Now do you think," she pursued, "that I don't tell you things?"

He turned them over in his young perception and pity, the things she told him. "Oh, oh, oh!" And then, in the great place, while as, just spent by the effort of her disclosure, she moved from him again, he took them all in. "That's the situation that, as you say, may force his hand."

"It absolutely, I feel, does force it." And the renewal of her appeal brought her round. "Isn't it too lovely?"

His frank disgust answered. "It's too damnable!"

"And it's you," she quite terribly smiled, "who—by the 'irony of fate'!—have given him help."

He smote his head in the light of it. "By the Mantovano?"

"By the possible Mantovano—as a substitute for the impossible Sir Joshua. You've made him aware of a value."

"Ah, but the value's to be fixed!"

"Then Mr. Bender will fix it!"

"Oh, but—as he himself would say—I'll fix Mr. Bender!" Hugh declared. "And he won't buy a pig in a poke."

This cleared the air while they looked at each other; yet she had already asked: "What in the world can you do, and how in the world can you do it?"

Well, he was too excited for decision. "I don't quite see now, but give me time." And he took out his watch as already to measure it. "Oughtn't I before I go to say a word to Lord Theign?"

"Is it your idea to become a lion in his path?"

"Well, say a cub—as that's what I'm afraid he'll call me! But I think I should speak to him."

She drew a conclusion momentarily dark. "He'll have to learn in that case that I've told you of my fear."

"And is there any good reason why he shouldn't?"

She kept her eyes on him and the darkness seemed to clear. "No!" she at last replied, and, having gone to touch an electric bell, was with him again. "But I think I'm rather sorry for you."

"Does that represent a reason why I should be so for you?"

For a little she said nothing; but after that: "None whatever!"

81

"Then is the sister of whom you speak Lady Imber?"

Lady Grace, at this, raised her hand in caution: the butler had arrived, with due gravity, in answer to her ring; to whom she made known her desire. "Please say to his lordship—in the saloon or wherever—that Mr. Crimble must go." When Banks had departed, however, accepting the responsibility of this mission, she answered her friend's question. "The sister of whom I speak is Lady Imber."

"She loses then so heavily at bridge?"

"She loses more than she wins."

Hugh gazed as with interest at these oddities of the great. "And yet she still plays?"

"What else, in her set, should she do?"

This he was quite unable to say; but he could after a moment's exhibition of the extent to which he was out of it put a question instead. "So *you're* not in her set?"

"I'm not in her set."

"Then decidedly," he said, "I don't want to save her. I only want—"

He was going on, but she broke in: "I know what you want!"

He kept his eyes on her till he had made sure—and this deep exchange between them had a beauty. "So you're now *with* me?"

"I'm now *with* you!"

"Then," said Hugh, "shake hands on it"

He offered her his hand, she took it, and their grasp became, as you would have seen in their fine young faces, a pledge in which they stood a minute locked. Lord Theign came upon them from the saloon in the midst of the process; on which they separated as with an air of its having consisted but of Hugh's leave-taking. With some such form of mere civility, at any rate, he appeared, by the manner in which he addressed himself to Hugh, to have supposed them occupied.

"I'm sorry my daughter can't keep you; but I must at least thank you for your interesting view of my picture."

Hugh indulged in a brief and mute, though very grave, acknowledgment of this expression; presently speaking, however, as on a resolve taken with a sense of possibly awkward consequences: "May I—before you're sure of your indebtedness—put you rather a straight question, Lord Theign?" It sounded doubtless, and of a sudden, a little portentous—as was in fact testified to by his lordship's quick stiff stare, full of wonder at so free a note. But Hugh had the courage of his undertaking. "If I contribute in ny modest degree to establishing the true authorship of the work you speak of, may I have from you an assurance that my success isn't to serve as a basis for any peril—or possibility—of its leaving the country?"

Lord Theign was visibly astonished, but had also, independently of this, turned a shade pale. "You ask of me an 'assurance'?"

Hugh had now, with his firmness and his strained smile, quite the look of having counted the cost of his step. "I'm afraid I *must*, you see."

It pressed at once in his host the spring of a very grand manner. "And pray by what right here do you do anything of the sort?"

"By the right of a person from whom you, on your side, are accepting a service."

Hugh had clearly determined in his opponent a rise of what is called spirit. "A service that you half an hour ago thrust on me, sir—and with which you may take it from me that I'm already quite prepared to dispense."

"I'm sorry to appear indiscreet," our young man returned; "I'm sorry to have upset you in any way. But I can't overcome my anxiety—"

Lord Theign took the words from his lips. "And you therefore invite me—at the end of half an hour in this house!—to account to you for my personal intentions and my private affairs and make over my freedom to your hands?"

Hugh stood there with his eyes on the black and white pavement that stretched about him—the great loz-enged marble floor that might have figured that ground of his own vision which he had made up his mind to "stand." "I can only see the matter as I see it, and I should be ashamed not to have seized any chance to appeal to you." Whatever difficulty he had had shyly to face didn't exist for him now. "I entreat you to think again, to think *well*, before you deprive us of such a source of just envy."

"And you regard your entreaty as helped," Lord Theign asked, "by the beautiful threat you are so good as to attach to it?" Then as his monitor, arrested, exchanged a searching look with Lady Grace, who, showing in her face all the pain of the business, stood off at the distance to which a woman instinctively retreats when a scene turns to violence as precipitately as this one appeared to strike her as having turned: "I ask you that not less than I should like to know whom you speak of as 'deprived' of property that happens—for reasons that I don't suppose you also quarrel with!—to be mine."

"Well, I know nothing about threats, Lord Theign," Hugh said, "but I speak of *all* of us—of all the people of England; who would deeply deplore such an act of alienation, and whom, for the interest they bear you, I beseech you mercifully to consider."

"The interest they bear me?"—the master of Dedborough fairly bristled with wonder. "Pray how the devil do they show it?"

"I think they show it in all sorts of ways"—and Hugh's critical smile, at almost any moment hovering, played over the question in a manner seeming to convey that he meant many things.

"Understand then, please," said Lord Theign with every inch of his authority, "that they'll show it best by minding their own business while I very particularly mind mine."

"You simply do, in other words," Hugh explicitly concluded, "what happens to be convenient to you."

"In very distinct preference to what happens to be convenient to *you!* So that I need no longer detain you," Lord Theign added with the last dryness and as if to wind up their brief and thankless connection.

The young man took his dismissal, being able to do no less, while, unsatisfied and unhappy, he looked about mechanically for the cycling-cap he had laid down somewhere in the hall on his arrival. "I apologise, my lord, if I seem to you to have ill repaid your hospitality. But," he went on with his uncommended cheer, "my interest in your picture remains."

Lady Grace, who had stopped and strayed and stopped again as a mere watchful witness, drew nearer hereupon, breaking her silence for the first time. "And please let me say, father, that mine also grows and grows."

It was obvious that this parent, surprised and disconcerted by her tone, judged her contribution superfluous. "I'm happy to hear it, Grace—but yours is another affair."

"I think on the contrary that it's quite the same one," she returned—"since it's on my hint to him that Mr. Crimble has said to you what he has." The resolution she had gathered while she awaited her chance sat in her charming eyes, which met, as she spoke, the straighter paternal glare. "I let him know that I supposed you to think of profiting by the importance of Mr. Bender's visit."

"Then you might have spared, my dear, your—I suppose and hope well-meant—interpretation of my mind." Lord Theign showed himself at this point master of the beautiful art of righting himself as without having been in the wrong. "Mr. Bender's visit will terminate—as soon as he has released Lord John—without my having profited in the smallest particular."

Hugh meanwhile evidently but wanted to speak for his friend. "It was Lady Grace's anxious inference, she will doubtless let me say for her, that my idea about the Moretto would add to your power—well," he pushed on not without awkwardness, "of 'realising' advantageously on such a prospective rise."

Lord Theign glanced at him as for positively the last time, but spoke to Lady Grace. "Understand then, please, that, as I detach myself from any association with this gentleman's ideas—whether about the Moretto or about anything else—his further application of them ceases from this moment to concern us."

The girl's rejoinder was to address herself directly to Hugh, across their companion. "Will you make your inquiry for *me* then?"

The light again kindled in him. "With all the pleasure in life!" He had found his cap and, taking them together, bowed to the two, for departure, with high emphasis of form. Then he marched off in the direction from which he had entered.

Lord Theign scarce waited for his disappearance to turn in wrath to Lady Grace. "I denounce the indecency, wretched child, of your public defiance of me!"

They were separated by a wide interval now, and though at her distance she met his reproof so unshrinkingly as perhaps to justify the terms into which it had broken, she became aware of a reason for his not following it up. She pronounced in quick warning "Lord John!"—for their friend, released from among the pictures, was rejoining them, was already there.

He spoke straight to his host on coming into sight. "Bender's at last off, but"—he indicated the direction of the garden front—"you may still find him, out yonder, prolonging the agony with Lady Sand-gate."

Lord Theign remained a moment, and the heat of his resentment remained. He looked with a divided discretion, the pain of his indecision, from his daughter's suitor and his approved candidate to that contumacious young woman and back again; then choosing his course in silence he had a gesture of almost desperate indifference and passed quickly out by the door to the terrace.

It had left Lord John gaping. "What on earth's the matter with your father?"

"What on earth indeed?" Lady Grace unaidingly asked. "Is he discussing with that awful man?"

"Old Bender? Do you think him so awful?" Lord John showed surprise—which might indeed have passed for harmless amusement; but he shook everything off in view of a nearer interest. He quite waved old Bender away. "My dear girl, what do *we* care—?"

"I care immensely, I assure you," she interrupted, "and I ask of you, please, to tell me!"

Her perversity, coming straight and which he had so little expected, threw him back so that he looked at her with sombre eyes. "Ah, it's not for such a matter I'm here, Lady Grace—I'm here with that fond question of my own." And then as she turned away, leaving him with a vehement motion of protest: "I've come for your kind answer—the answer your father instructed me to count on."

"I've no kind answer to give you!"—she raised forbidding hands. "I entreat you to leave me alone."

There was so high a spirit and so strong a force in it that he stared as if stricken by violence. "In God's name then what has happened—when you almost gave me your word?"

"What has happened is that I've found it impossible to listen to you." And she moved as if fleeing she scarce knew whither before him.

He had already hastened around another way, however, as to meet her in her quick circuit of the hall. "That's all you've got to say to me after what has passed between us?"

He had stopped her thus, but she had also stopped him, and her passionate denial set him a limit. "I've got to say—sorry as I am—that if you *must* have an answer it's this: that never, Lord John, never, can there be anything more between us." And her gesture cleared her path, permitting her to achieve her flight. "Never, no, never," she repeated as she went—"never, never, never!" She got off by the door at which she had been aiming to some retreat of her own, while aghast and defeated, left to make the best of it, he sank after a moment into a chair and remained quite pitiably staring before him, appealing to the great blank splendour.

BOOK SECOND

I

LADY SANDGATE, on a morning late in May, entered her drawing-room by the door that opened at the right of that charming retreat as a person coming in faced Bruton Street; and she met there at this moment Mr. Gotch, her butler, who had just appeared in the much wider doorway forming opposite the Bruton Street windows an apartment not less ample, lighted from the back of the house and having its independent connection with the upper floors and the lower. She showed surprise at not immediately finding the visitor to whom she had been called.

"But Mr. Crimble———?"

"Here he is, my lady." And he made way for that gentleman, who emerged from the back room; Gotch observing the propriety of a prompt withdrawal.

"I went in for a minute, with your servant's permission," Hugh explained, "to see your famous Lawrence—which is splendid; he was so good as to arrange the light." The young man's dress was of a form less relaxed than on the occasion of his visit to Dedborough; yet the soft felt hat that he rather restlessly crumpled as he talked marked the limit of his sacrifice to vain appearances.

Lady Sandgate was at once interested in the punctuality of his reported act. "Gotch thinks as much of my grandmother as I do—and even seems to have ended by taking her for his very own."

"One sees, unmistakably, from her beauty, that you at any rate are of her line," Hugh allowed himself, not without confidence, the amusement of replying; "and I must make sure of another look at her when I've a good deal more time."

His hostess heard him as with a lapse of hope. "You hadn't then come *for* the poor dear?" And then as he obviously hadn't, but for something quite else: "I thought, from so prompt an interest, that she might be coveted—!" It dropped with a yearning sigh.

"You imagined me sent by some prowling collector?" Hugh asked. "Ah, I shall never do their work—unless to betray them: *that* I shouldn't in the least mind!—and I'm here, frankly, at this early hour, to ask your consent to my seeing Lady Grace a moment on a particular business, if she can kindly give me time."

"You've known then of her being with me?"

"I've known of her coming to you straight on leaving Dedborough," he explained; "of her wishing not to go to her sister's, and of Lord Theign's having proceeded, as they say, or being on the point of proceeding, to some foreign part."

"And you've learnt it from having seen her—these three or four weeks?"

"I've met her—but just barely—two or three times: at a 'private view' at the opera, in the lobby, and that sort of thing. But she hasn't told you?"

Lady Sandgate neither affirmed nor denied; she only turned on him her thick lustre. "I wanted to see how much *you'd* tell." She waited even as for more, but this not coming she helped herself. "Once again at dinner?"

"Yes, but alas not near her!"

"Once then at a private view?—when, with the squash they usually are, you might have been very near her indeed!"

The young man, his hilarity quickened, took but a moment for the truth. "Yes—it *was* a squash!"

"And once," his hostess pursued, "in the lobby of the opera?"

"After 'Tristan'—yes; but with some awful grand people I didn't know."

She recognised; she estimated the grandeur. "Oh, the Pennimans are nobody! But now," she asked, "you've come, you say, on 'business'?"

"Very important, please—which accounts for the hour I've ventured and the appearance I present."

"I don't ask you too much to 'account,'" Lady Sandgate kindly said; "but I can't not wonder if she hasn't told you what things have happened."

He cast about. "She has had no chance to tell me anything—beyond the fact of her being here."

"Without the reason?"

"'The reason'?" he echoed.

She gave it up, going straighter. "She's with me then as an old firm friend. Under my care and protection."

"I see"—he took it, with more penetration than enthusiasm, as a hint in respect to himself. "She puts you on your guard."

Lady Sandgate expressed it more graciously. "She puts me on my honour—or at least her father does."

"As to her seeing *me*"

"As to *my* seeing at least—what may happen to her."

"Because—you say—things *have* happened?"

His companion fairly sounded him. "You've only talked—when you've met—of 'art'?"

"Well," he smiled, "'art is long'!"

"Then I hope it may see you through! But you should know first that Lord Theign is presently due—"

"*Here*, back already from abroad?"—he was all alert.

"He has not yet gone—he comes up this morning to start."

"And stops here on his way?"

"To take the *train de luxe* this afternoon to his annual Salsomaggiore. But with so little time to spare," she went on reassuringly, "that, to simplify—

91

as he wired me an hour ago from Dedborough—he has given rendezvous here to Mr. Bender, who is particularly to wait for him."

"And who may therefore arrive at any moment?"

She looked at her bracelet watch. "Scarcely before noon. So you'll just have your chance—"

"Thank the powers then!"—Hugh grasped at it. "I shall have it best if you'll be so good as to tell me first—well," he faltered, "what it is that, to my great disquiet, you've further alluded to; what it is that has occurred."

Lady Sandgate took her time, but her good-nature and other sentiments pronounced. "Haven't you at least guessed that she has fallen under her father's extreme reprobation?"

"Yes, so much as that—that she must have greatly annoyed him—I have been supposing. But isn't it by her having asked me to act for her? I mean about the Mantovano—which I *have* done."

Lady Sandgate wondered. "You've 'acted'?"

"It's what I've come to tell her at last—and I'm all impatience."

"I see, I see"—she had caught a clue. "He hated that—yes; but you haven't really made out," she put to him, "the *other* effect of your hour at Dedborough?" She recognised, however, while she spoke, that his divination had failed, and she didn't trouble him to confess it. "Directly you had gone she 'turned down' Lord John. Declined, I mean, the offer of his hand in marriage."

Hugh was clearly as much mystified as anything else. "He proposed there—?"

"He had spoken, that day, *before*—before your talk with Lord Theign, who had every confidence in her accepting him. But you came, Mr. Crimble, you went; and when her suitor reappeared, just after you *had* gone, for his answer—"

"She wouldn't have him?" Hugh asked with a precipitation of interest.

But Lady Sandgate could humour almost any curiosity. "She wouldn't look at him."

He bethought himself. "But had she said she would?"

"So her father indignantly considers."

"That's the *ground* of his indignation?"

"He had his reasons for counting on her, and it has determined a painful crisis."

Hugh Crimble turned this over—feeling apparently for something he didn't find. "I'm sorry to hear such things, but where's the connection with me?"

"Ah, you know best yourself, and if you don't see any——!" In that case, Lady Sandgate's motion implied, she washed her hands of it.

Hugh had for a moment the air of a young man treated to the sweet chance to guess a conundrum—which he gave up. "I really don't see any, Lady Sandgate. But," he a little inconsistently said, "I'm greatly obliged to you for telling me."

"Don't mention it!—though I think it *is* good of me," she smiled, "on so short an acquaintance." To which she added more gravely: "I leave you the situation—but I'm willing to let you know that I'm all on Grace's side."

"So am I, *rather!*—please let me frankly say."

He clearly refreshed, he even almost charmed her. "It's the very least you can say!—though I'm not sure whether you say it as the simplest or as the very subtlest of men. But in case you don't know as I do how little the particular candidate I've named——"

"Had a right or a claim to succeed with her?" he broke in—all quick intelligence here at least. "No, I don't perhaps know as well as you do—but I think I know as well as I just yet require."

"There you are then! And if you did prevent," his hostess maturely pursued, "what wouldn't have been—well, good or nice, I'm quite on your side too."

Our young man seemed to feel the shade of ambiguity, but he reached at a meaning. "You're with me in my plea for our defending at any cost of effort or ingenuity—"

"The precious picture Lord Theign exposes?"—she took his presumed sense faster than he had taken hers. But she hung fire a moment with her reply to it. "Well, will you keep the secret of everything I've said or say?"

"To the death, to the stake, Lady Sandgate!"

"Then," she momentously returned, "I only want, too, to make Bender impossible. If you ask me," she pursued, "how I arrange that with my deep loyalty to Lord Theign——"

"I don't ask you anything of the sort," he interrupted—"I wouldn't ask you for the world; and my own bright plan for achieving the *coup* you mention——"

"You'll have time, at the most," she said, consulting afresh her bracelet watch, "to explain to Lady Grace." She reached an electric bell, which she touched—facing then her visitor again with an abrupt and slightly embarrassed change of tone. "You do think *my* great portrait splendid?"

He had strayed far from it and all too languidly came back. "Your Lawrence there? As I said, magnificent."

But the butler had come in, interrupting, straight from the lobby; of whom she made her request. "Let her ladyship know—Mr. Crimble."

Gotch looked hard at Hugh and the crumpled hat—almost as if having an option. But he resigned himself to repeating, with a distinctness that scarce fell short of the invidious, "Mr. Crimble," and departed on his errand.

Lady Sandgate's fair flush of diplomacy had meanwhile not faded. "Couldn't you, with your immense cleverness and power, get the Government to do something?"

"About your picture?" Hugh betrayed on this head a graceless detachment. "You too then want to sell?"

Oh she righted herself. "Never to a private party!"

"Mr. Bender's not after it?" he asked—though scarce lighting his reluctant interest with a forced smile.

"Most intensely after it. But never," cried the proprietress, "to a bloated alien!"

"Then I applaud your patriotism. Only why not," he asked, "carrying that magnanimity a little further, set us all an example as splendid as the object itself?"

"Give it you for nothing?" She threw up shocked hands. "Because I'm an aged female pauper and can't make *every* sacrifice."

Hugh pretended—none too convincingly—to think. "Will you let them have it very cheap?"

"Yes—for less than such a bribe as Bender's."

"Ah," he said expressively, "that might be, and still——!"

"Well," she had a flare of fond confidence. "I'll find out what he'll offer—if you'll on your side do what you can—and then ask them a third less." And she followed it up—as if suddenly conceiving him a prig. "See here, Mr. Crimble, I've been—and this very first time I—charming to you."

"You have indeed," he returned; "but you throw back on it a lurid light if it has all been for *that!*"

"It has been—well, to keep things as I want them; and if I've given you precious information mightn't you on your side—"

"Estimate its value in cash?"—Hugh sharply took her up. "Ah, Lady Sandgate, I *am* in your debt, but if you really bargain for your precious information I'd rather we assume that I haven't enjoyed it."

She made him, however, in reply, a sign for silence; she had heard Lady Grace enter the other room from the back landing, and, reaching the nearer

95

door, she disposed of the question with high gay bravery. "I won't bargain with the Treasury!"—she had passed out by the time Lady Grace arrived.

II

As Hugh recognised in this friend's entrance and face the light of welcome he went, full of his subject, straight to their main affair. "I haven't been able to wait, I've wanted so much to tell you—I mean how I've just come back from Brussels, where I saw Pappen-dick, who was free and ready, by the happiest chance, to start for Verona, which he must have reached some time yesterday."

The girl's responsive interest fairly broke into rapture. "Ah, the dear sweet thing!"

"Yes, he's a brick—but the question now hangs in the balance. Allowing him time to have got into relation with the picture, I've begun to expect his wire, which will probably come to my club; but my fidget, while I wait, has driven me"—he threw out and dropped his arms in expression of his soft surrender—"well, just to do *this*: to come to you here, in my fever, at an unnatural hour and uninvited, and at least let you know I've 'acted.'"

"Oh, but I simply rejoice," Lady Grace declared, "to be acting *with* you."

"Then if you are, if you are," the young man cried, "why everything's beautiful and right!"

"It's all I care for and think of now," she went on in her bright devotion, "and I've only wondered and hoped!"

Well, Hugh found for it all a rapid, abundant lucidity. "He was away from home at first, and I had to wait—but I crossed last week, found him and settled incoming home by Paris, where I had a grand four days' jaw with the fellows there and saw *their* great specimen of our master: all of which has given him time."

"And now his time's up?" the girl eagerly asked.

"It *must* be—and we shall see." But Hugh postponed that question to a matter of more moment still. "The thing is that at last I'm able to tell you how I feel the trouble I've brought you."

It made her, quickly colouring, rest grave eyes on him. "What do you know—when I haven't told you—about my 'trouble'?"

"Can't I have guessed, with a ray of intelligence?"—he had his answer ready. "You've sought asylum with this good friend from the effects of your father's resentment."

"'Sought asylum' is perhaps excessive," Lady Grace returned—"though it wasn't pleasant with him after that hour, no," she allowed. "And I couldn't go, you see, to Kitty."

"No indeed, you couldn't go to Kitty." He smiled at her hard as he added: "I should have liked to see you go to Kitty! Therefore exactly is it that I've set you adrift—that I've darkened and poisoned your days. You're paying with your comfort, with your peace, for having joined so gallantly in my grand remonstrance."

She shook her head, turning from him, but then turned back again—as if accepting, as if even relieved by, this version of the prime cause of her state. "Why do you talk of it as 'paying'—if it's all to come back to my *being* paid? I mean by your blest success—if you really do what you want."

"I have your word for it," he searchingly said, "that our really pulling it off together will make up to you——?"

"I should be ashamed if it didn't, for everything!"—she took the question from his mouth. "I believe in such a cause exactly as you do—and found a lesson, at Dedborough, in your frankness and your faith."

"Then you'll help me no end," he said all simply and sincerely.

"You've helped *me* already"—that she gave him straight back. And on it they stayed a moment, their strenuous faces more intensely communing.

"You're very wonderful—for a girl!" Hugh brought out.

"One *has* to be a girl, naturally, to be a daughter of one's house," she laughed; "and that's all I am of ours—but a true and a right and a straight one."

He glowed with his admiration. "You're splendid!"

That might be or not, her light shrug intimated; she gave it, at any rate, the go-by and more exactly stated her case. "I see our situation."

"So do I, Lady Grace!" he cried with the strongest emphasis. "And your father only doesn't."

"Yes," she said for intelligent correction—"he sees it, there's nothing in life he sees so much. But unfortunately he sees it all wrong."

Hugh seized her point of view as if there had been nothing of her that he wouldn't have seized. "He sees it all wrong then! My appeal the other day he took as a rude protest. And any protest——"

"Any protest," she quickly and fully agreed, "he takes as an offence, yes. It's his theory that he still has rights," she smiled, "though he *is* a miserable peer."

"How should he not have rights," said Hugh, "when he has really everything on earth?"

"Ah, he doesn't even *know* that—he takes it so much for granted." And she sought, though as rather sadly and despairingly, to explain. "He lives all in his own world."

"He lives all in his own, yes; but he does business all in ours—quite as much as the people who come up to the city in the Tube." With which Hugh had a still sharper recall of the stiff actual. "And he must be here to do business to-day."

"You know," Lady Grace asked, "that he's to meet Mr. Bender?"

"Lady Sandgate kindly warned me, and," her companion saw as he glanced at the clock on the chimney, "I've only ten minutes, at best. The 'Journal' won't have been good for him," he added—"you doubtless have seen the 'Journal'?"

"No"—she was vague. "We live by the 'Morning Post.'"

"That's why our friend here didn't speak then," Hugh said with a better light—"which, out of a dim consideration for her, I didn't do, either. But they've a leader this morning about Lady Lappington and her Longhi, and on Bender and his hauls, and on the certainty—if we don't do something energetic—of more and more Benders to come: such a conquering horde as invaded the old civilisation, only armed now with huge cheque-books instead of with spears and battle-axes. They refer to the rumour current—as too horrific to believe—of Lord Theign's putting up his Moretto; with the question of how properly to qualify any such sad purpose in him should the further report prove true of a new and momentous opinion about the picture entertained by several eminent authorities."

"Of whom," said the girl, intensely attached to this recital, "you're of course seen as not the least."

"Of whom, of course, Lady Grace, I'm as yet—however I'm 'seen'—the whole collection. But we've time"—he rested on that "The fat, if you'll allow me the expression, is on the fire—which, as I see the matter, is where this particular fat *should* be."

"Is the article, then," his companion appealed, "very severe?"

"I prefer to call it very enlightened and very intelligent—and the great thing is that it immensely 'marks,' as they say. It will have made a big public difference—from this day; though it's of course aimed not so much at persons as at conditions; which it calls upon us all somehow to tackle."

"Exactly"—she was full of the saving vision; "but as the conditions are directly embodied in persons——"

"Oh, of course it here and there bells the cat; which means that it bells three or four."

"Yes," she richly brooded—"Lady Lappington *is* a cat!"

"She will have been 'belled,' at any rate, with your father," Hugh amusedly went on, "to the certainty of a row; and a row can only be good for us—I mean for *us* in particular." Yet he had to bethink himself. "The case depends a good deal of course on how your father *takes* such a resounding rap."

"Oh, I know how he'll take it!"—her perception went all the way.

"In the very highest and properest spirit?"

"Well, you'll see." She was as brave as she was clear. "Or at least I shall!"

Struck with all this in her he renewed his homage. "You *are*, yes, splendid!"

"I even," she laughed, "surprise myself."

But he was already back at his calculations. "How early do the papers get to you?"

"At Dedborough? Oh, quite for breakfast—which isn't, however, very early."

"Then that's what has caused his wire to Bender."

"But how will such talk strike *him*?" the girl asked.

Hugh meanwhile, visibly, had not only followed his train of thought, he had let it lead him to certainty. "It will have moved Mr. Bender to absolute rapture."

"Rather," Lady Grace wondered, "than have put him off?"

"It will have put him prodigiously *on*! Mr. Bender—as he said to me at Dedborough of his noble host there," Hugh pursued—"is 'a very nice man'; but he's a product of the world of advertisment, and advertisement is all he sees and aims at. He lives in it as a saint in glory or a fish in water."

She took it from him as half doubting. "But mayn't advertisement, in so special a case, turn, on the whole, against him?"

Hugh shook a negative forefinger with an expression he might have caught from foreign comrades. "He rides the biggest whirlwind—he has got it saddled and bitted."

She faced the image, but cast about "Then where does our success come in?"

"In our making the beast, all the same, bolt with him and throw him." And Hugh further pointed the moral. "If in such proceedings all he knows is publicity the thing is to give him publicity, and it's only a question of giving him enough. By the time he has enough for himself, you see, he'll have too much for every one else—so that we shall 'up' in a body and slay him."

The girl's eyebrows, in her wondering face, rose to a question. "But if he has meanwhile got the picture?"

"We'll slay him before he gets it!" He revelled in the breadth of his view. "Our own policy must be to *organise* to that end the inevitable outcry. Organise Bender himself—organise him to scandal." Hugh had already even pity to spare for their victim. "He won't know it from a boom."

Though carried along, however, Lady Grace could still measure. "But that will be only if he wants and decides for the picture."

"We must make him then want and decide for it—decide, that is, for 'ours.' To save it we must work him up—he'll in that case want it so indecently much. Then *we* shall have to want it more!"

"Well," she anxiously felt it her duty to remind him, "you can take a horse to water——!"

"Oh, trust me to make him drink!"

There appeared a note in this that convinced her. "It's you, Mr. Crimble, who are 'splendid'!"

"Well, I shall be—with my jolly wire!" And all on that scent again, "May I come back to you from the club with Pappendick's news?" he asked.

"Why, rather, of course, come back!"

"Only not," he debated, "till your father has left."

Lady Grace considered too, but sharply decided. "Come when you *have* it. But tell me first," she added, "one thing." She hung fire a little while he waited, but she brought it out. "Was it you who got the 'Journal' to speak?"

"Ah, one scarcely 'gets' the 'Journal'!"

"Who then gave them their 'tip'?"

"About the Mantovano and its peril?" Well, he took a moment—but only not to say; in addition to which the butler had reappeared, entering from the lobby. "I'll tell you," he laughed, "when I come back!"

Gotch had his manner of announcement while the visitor was mounting the stairs. "Mr. Breckenridge Bender!"

"Ah then I go," said Lady Grace at once.

"I'll stay three minutes." Hugh turned with her, alertly, to the easier issue, signalling hope and cheer from that threshold as he watched her disappear; after which he faced about with as brave a smile and as ready for immediate action as if she had there within kissed her hand to him. Mr. Bender emerged at the same instant, Gotch withdrawing and closing the door behind him; and the former personage, recognising his young friend, threw up his hands for friendly pleasure.

III

"Ah, Mr. Crimble," he cordially inquired, "you've come with your great news?"

Hugh caught the allusion, it would have seemed, but after a moment. "News of the Moretto? No, Mr. Bender, I haven't news *yet.*" But he added as with high candour for the visitor's motion of disappointment: "I think I warned you, you know, that it would take three or four weeks."

"Well, in *my* country," Mr. Bender returned with disgust, "it would take three or four minutes! Can't you make 'em step more lively?"

"I'm expecting, sir," said Hugh good-humouredly, "a report from hour to hour."

"Then will you let me have it right off?"

Hugh indulged in a pause; after which very frankly: "Ah, it's scarcely for you, Mr. Bender, that I'm acting!"

The great collector was but briefly checked. "Well, can't you just act for Art?"

"Oh, you're doing that yourself so powerfully," Hugh laughed, "that I think I had best leave it to you!"

His friend looked at him as some inspector on circuit might look at a new improvement. "Don't you want to go round acting *with* me?"

"Go 'on tour,' as it were? Oh, frankly, Mr. Bender," Hugh said, "if I had any weight——!"

"You'd add it to your end of the beam? Why, what have I done that *you* should go back on me—after working me up so down there? The worst I've done," Mr. Bender continued, "is to refuse that Moretto."

"Has it deplorably been *offered* you?" our young man cried, unmistakably and sincerely affected. After which he went on, as his fellow-visitor only eyed him hard, not, on second thoughts, giving the owner of the great work away: "Then why are you—as if you were a banished Romeo—so keen for news from Verona?" To this odd mixture of business and literature Mr. Bender made no reply, contenting himself with but a large vague blandness that wore in him somehow the mark of tested utility; so that Hugh put him another question: "Aren't you here, sir, on the chance of the Mantovano?"

"I'm here," he then imperturbably said, "because Lord Theign has wired me to meet him. Ain't you here for that yourself?"

Hugh betrayed for a moment his enjoyment of a "big" choice of answers. "Dear, no! I've but been in, by Lady Sandgate's leave, to see that grand Lawrence."

"Ah yes, she's very kind about it—one does go 'in.'" After which Mr. Bender had, even in the atmosphere of his danger, a throb of curiosity. "Is any one *after* that grand Lawrence?"

"Oh, I hope not," Hugh laughed, "unless you again dreadfully are: wonderful thing as it is and so just in its right place there."

"You call it," Mr. Bender impartially inquired, "a *very* wonderful thing?"

"Well, as a Lawrence, it has quite bowled me over"—Hugh spoke as for the strictly aesthetic awkwardness of that. "But you know I take my pictures hard." He gave a punch to his hat, pressed for time in this connection as he was glad truly to appear to his friend. "I must make my little *rapport*." Yet before it he did seek briefly to explain. "We're a band of young men who care—and we watch the great things. Also—for I must give you the real truth about myself—we watch the great people."

"Well, I guess I'm used to being watched—if that's the worst you can do." To which Mr. Bender added in his homely way: "But you know, Mr. Crimble, what I'm *really* after."

Hugh's strategy on this would again have peeped out for us. "The man in this morning's 'Journal' appears at least to have discovered."

"Yes, the man in this morning's 'Journal' has discovered three or four weeks—as it appears to take you here for everything—after my beginning to talk. Why, they knew I was talking *that* time ago on the other side."

"Oh, they know things in the States," Hugh cheerfully agreed, "so independently of their happening! But you must have talked loud."

"Well, I haven't so much talked as raved," Mr. Bender conceded—"for I'm afraid that when I do want a thing I rave till I get it. You heard me at Ded-borough, and your enterprising daily press has at last caught the echo."

"Then they'll make up for lost time! But have you done it," Hugh asked, "to prepare an alibi?"

"An alibi?"

"By 'raving,' as you say, the saddle on the wrong horse. I don't think you at all believe you'll get the Sir Joshua—but meanwhile we shall have cleared up the question of the Moretto."

Mr. Bender, imperturbable, didn't speak till he had done justice to this picture of his subtlety. "Then, why on earth do you want to boom the Moretto?"

"You ask that," said Hugh, "because it's the boomed thing that's most in peril."

"Well, it's the big, the bigger, the biggest things, and if you drag their value to the light why shouldn't we want to grab them and carry them off—the same as all of *you* originally did?"

"Ah, not quite the same," Hugh smiled—"that I *will* say for you!"

"Yes, you stick it on now—you *have* got an eye for the rise in values. But I grant you your unearned increment, and you ought to be mighty glad that, to such a time, I'll pay it you."

Our young man kept, during a moment's thought, his eyes on his companion, and then resumed with all intensity and candour: "You may easily, Mr. Bender, be too much for me—as you appear too much for far greater people. But may I ask you, very earnestly, for your word on *this*, as to any case in which that happens—that when precious things, things we are to lose here, *are* knocked down to you, you'll let us at least take leave of them, let us have a sight of them in London, before they're borne off?"

Mr. Bender's big face fell almost with a crash. "Hand them over, you mean, to the sandwich men on Bond Street?"

"To one or other of the placard and poster men—I don't insist on the inserted human slice! Let the great values, as a compensation to us, be on view for three or four weeks."

"You ask me," Mr. Bender returned, "for a *general* assurance to that effect?"

"Well, a particular one—so it be particular enough," Hugh said—"will do just for now. Let me put in my plea for the issue—well, of the value that's actually in the scales."

"The Mantovano-Moretto?"

"The Moretto-Mantovano!"

Mr. Bender carnivorously smiled. "Hadn't we better know which it is first?"

Hugh had a motion of practical indifference for this. "The public interest—playing so straight on the question—may help to settle it. By which I mean that it will profit enormously—the question of probability, of identity itself will—by the discussion it will create. The discussion will promote certainty——"

"And certainty," Mr. Bender massively mused, "will kick up a row."

"*Of course* it will kick up a row!"—Hugh thoroughly guaranteed that. "You'll be, for the month, the best-abused man in England—if you venture to remain here at all; except, naturally, poor Lord Theign."

"Whom it won't be my interest, at the same time, to worry into backing down."

"But whom it will be exceedingly *mine* to practise on"—and Hugh laughed as at the fun before them—"if I may entertain the sweet hope of success. The only thing is—from my point of view," he went on—"that backing down before what he will call vulgar clamour isn't in the least in his traditions, nothing less so; and that if there should be really too much of it for his taste or his nerves he'll set his handsome face as a stone and never budge an inch. But at least again what I appeal to you for will have taken place—the picture will have been seen by a lot of people who'll care."

"It will have been seen," Mr. Bender amended—"on the mere contingency of my acquisition of it—only if its present owner consents."

"'Consents'?" Hugh almost derisively echoed; "why, he'll propose it himself, he'll insist on it, he'll put it through, once he's angry enough—as angry, I mean, as almost any public criticism of a personal act of his will be sure to make him; and I'm afraid the striking criticism, or at least animadversion, of this morning, will have blown on his flame of bravado."

Inevitably a student of character, Mr. Bender rose to the occasion. "Yes, I guess he's pretty mad."

"They've imputed to him"—Hugh but wanted to abound in that sense—"an intention of which after all he isn't guilty."

"So that"—his listener glowed with interested optimism—"if they don't look out, if they impute it to him again, I guess he'll just go and be guilty!"

Hugh might at this moment have shown to an initiated eye as fairly elated by the sense of producing something of the effect he had hoped. "You entertain the fond vision of lashing them up to that mistake, oh fisher in troubled waters?" And then with a finer art, as his companion, expansively bright but crudely acute, eyed him in turn as if to sound *him*: "The strongest thing in such a type—one does make out—is his resentment of a liberty taken; and the most natural furthermore is quite that he should feel almost anything you do take uninvited from the groaning board of his banquet of life to *be* such a liberty."

Mr. Bender participated thus at his perceptive ease in the exposed aristocratic illusion. "Yes, I guess he has always lived as he likes, the way those of you who have got things fixed for them *do*, over here; and to have to quit it on account of unpleasant remark—"

But he gave up thoughtfully trying to express what this must be; reduced to the mere synthetic interjection "My!"

"That's it, Mr. Bender," Hugh said for the consecration of such a moral; "he won't quit it without a hard struggle."

Mr. Bender hereupon at last gave himself quite gaily away as to his high calculation of impunity. "Well, I guess he won't struggle too hard for me to hold on to him if I *want* to!"

"In the thick of the conflict then, however that may be," Hugh returned, "don't forget what I've urged on you—the claim of our desolate country."

But his friend had an answer to this. "My natural interest, Mr. Crimble—considering what I do for it—is in the claim of ours. But I wish you were on my side!"

"Not so much," Hugh hungrily and truthfully laughed, "as I wish you were on mine!" Decidedly, none the less, he had to go. "Good-bye—for another look here!"

He reached the doorway of the second room, where, however, his companion, freshly alert at this, stayed him by a gesture. "How much is she really worth?"

"'She'?" Hugh, staring a moment, was miles at sea. "Lady Sandgate?"

"Her great-grandmother."

A responsible answer was prevented—the butler was again with them; he had opened wide the other door and he named to Mr. Bender the personage under his convoy. "Lord John!"

Hugh caught this from the inner threshold, and it gave him his escape. "Oh, ask *that* friend!" With which he sought the further passage to the staircase and street, while Lord John arrived in charge of Mr. Gotch, who, having remarked to the two occupants of the front drawing-room that her ladyship would come, left them together.

IV

"Then Theign's not yet here!" Lord John had to resign himself as he greeted his American ally. "But he told me I should find you."

"He has kept me waiting," that gentleman returned—"but what's the matter with him anyway?"

"The matter with him"—Lord John treated such ignorance as irritating—"must of course be this beastly thing in the 'Journal.'"

Mr. Bender proclaimed, on the other hand, his incapacity to seize such connections. "What's the matter with the beastly thing?"

"Why, aren't you aware that the stiffest bit of it is a regular dig at you?"

"If you call *that* a regular dig you can't have had much experience of the Papers. I've known them to dig much deeper."

"I've had *no* experience of such horrid attacks, thank goodness; but do you mean to say," asked Lord John with the surprise of his own delicacy, "that you don't unpleasantly feel it?"

"Feel it where, my dear sir?"

"Why, God bless me, such impertinence, everywhere!"

"All over me at once?"—Mr. Bender took refuge in easy humour. "Well, I'm a large man—so when I want to feel so much I look out for something good. But what, if he suffers from the blot on his ermine—ain't that what you wear?—does our friend propose to do about it?"

Lord John had a demur, which was immediately followed by the apprehension of support in his uncertainty. Lady Sandgate was before them, having reached them through the other room, and to her he at once referred the question. "What *will* Theign propose, do you think, Lady Sandgate, to do about it?"

She breathed both her hospitality and her vagueness. "To 'do'———?"

"Don't you know about the thing in the 'Journal'—awfully offensive all round?"

"There'd be even a little pinch for *you* in it," Mr. Bender said to her—"if you were bent on fitting the shoe!"

Well, she met it all as gaily as was compatible with a firm look at her elder guest while she took her place with them. "Oh, the shoes of such monsters as that are much too big for poor *me!*" But she was more specific for Lord John. "I know only what Grace has just told me; but since it's a question of footgear dear Theign will certainly—what you may call—take his stand!"

Lord John welcomed this assurance. "If I know him he'll take it splendidly!"

Mr. Bender's attention was genial, though rather more detached. "And what—while he's about it—will he take it particularly *on?*"

"Oh, we've plenty of things, thank heaven," said Lady Sandgate, "for a man in Theign's position to hold fast by!"

Lord John freely confirmed it. "Scores and scores—rather! And I will say for us that, with the rotten way things seem going, the fact may soon become a real convenience."

Mr. Bender seemed struck—and not unsympathetic. "I see that your system would be rather a fraud if you hadn't pretty well fixed *that!*"

Lady Sandgate spoke as one at present none the less substantially warned and convinced. "It doesn't, however, alter the fact that we've thus in our ears the first growl of an outcry."

"Ah," Lord John concurred, "we've unmistakably the first growl of an outcry!"

Mr. Bender's judgment on the matter paused at sight of Lord Theign, introduced and announced, as Lord John spoke, by Gotch; but with the result of his addressing directly the person so presenting himself. "Why, they tell me that what this means, Lord Theign, is the first growl of an outcry!"

The appearance of the most eminent figure in the group might have been held in itself to testify to some such truth; in the sense at least that a certain conscious radiance, a gathered light of battle in his lordship's aspect would have been explained by his having taken the full measure—an inner success with which he glowed—of some high provocation. He was flushed, but he bore it as the ensign of his house; he was so admirably, vividly dressed, for the morning hour and for his journey, that he shone as with the armour of a knight; and the whole effect of him, from head to foot, with every jerk of his unconcern and every flash of his ease, was to call attention to his being utterly unshaken and knowing perfectly what he was about. It was at this happy pitch that he replied to the prime upsetter of his peace.

"I'm afraid I don't know what anything means to *you*, Mr. Bender—but it's exactly to find out that I've asked you, with our friend John, kindly to meet me here. For a very brief conference, dear lady, by your good leave," he went on to Lady Sandgate; "at which I'm only too pleased that you yourself should assist. The 'first growl' of any outcry, I may mention to you all, affects me no more than the last will——!"

"So I'm delighted to gather"—Lady Sandgate took him straight up—"that you don't let go your inestimable Cure."

He at first quite stared superior—"'Let go'?"—but then treated it with a lighter touch. "Upon my honour I might, you know—that dose of the daily press has made me feel so fit! I arrive at any rate," he pursued to the others and in particular to Mr. Bender, "I arrive with my decision taken—which I've thought may perhaps interest you. If that tuppeny rot *is* an attempt at an outcry I simply nip it in the bud."

Lord John rejoicingly approved. "Absolutely the only way—with the least self-respect—to treat it!"

Lady Sandgate, on the other hand, sounded a sceptical note. "But are you sure it's so easy, Theign, to hush up a *real* noise?"

"It ain't what I'd call a real one, Lady Sandgate," Mr. Bender said; "you can generally distinguish a real one from the squeak of two or three mice! But granted mice do affect you, Lord Theign, it will interest me to hear what sort of a trap—by what you say—you propose to set for them."

"You must allow me to measure, myself, Mr. Bender," his lordship replied, "the importance of a gross freedom publicly used with my absolutely personal proceedings and affairs; to the cause and origin of any definite report of which—in such circles!—I'm afraid I rather wonder if you yourself can't give me a clue."

It took Mr. Bender a minute to do justice to these stately remarks. "You rather wonder if I've talked of how I feel about your detaining in your hands my Beautiful Duchess——?"

"Oh, if you've already published her as 'yours'—with your *power* of publication!" Lord Theign coldly laughed,—"of course I trace the connection!"

Mr. Benders acceptance of responsibility clearly cost him no shade of a pang. "Why, I haven't for quite a while talked of a blessed other thing—and I'm capable of growing more profane over my *not* getting her than I guess any one would dare to be if I did."

"Well, you'll certainly not 'get' her, Mr. Bender," Lady Sandgate, as for reasons of her own, bravely trumpeted; "and even if there were a chance of it don't you see that your way wouldn't be publicly to abuse our noble friend?"

Mr. Bender but beamed, in reply, upon that personage. "Oh, I guess our noble friend knows I *have* to talk big about big things. You understand, sir, the scream of the eagle!"

"I'll forgive you," Lord Theign civilly returned, "all the big talk you like if you'll now understand *me*. My retort to that hireling pack shall be at once to dispose of a picture."

Mr. Bender rather failed to follow. "But that's what you wanted to do before."

"Pardon me," said his lordship—"I make a difference. It's what you wanted me to do."

The mystification, however, continued. "And you were *not*—as you seemed then—willing?"

Lord Theign waived cross-questions. "Well, I'm willing *now*—that's all that need concern us. Only, once more and for the last time," he added with all authority, "you can't have our Duchess!"

"You can't have our Duchess!"—and Lord John, as before the altar of patriotism, wrapped it in sacrificial sighs.

"You can't have our Duchess!" Lady Sandgate repeated, but with a grace that took the sting from her triumph. And she seemed still all sweet sociability as she added: "I wish he'd tell you too, you dreadful rich thing, that you can't have anything at all!"

Lord Theign, however, in the interest of harmony, deprecated that rigour. "Ah, what then would become of my happy retort?"

"And what—as it *is*," Mr. Bender asked—"becomes of my unhappy grievance?"

"Wouldn't a really great capture make up to you for that?"

"Well, I take more interest in what I want than in what I have—and it depends, don't you see, on how you measure the size."

Lord John had at once in this connection a bright idea. "Shouldn't you like to go back there and take the measure yourself?"

Mr. Bender considered him as through narrowed eyelids. "Look again at that tottering Moretto?"

"Well, its size—as you say—isn't in *any* light a negligible quantity."

"You mean that—big as it is—it hasn't yet stopped growing?"

The question, however, as he immediately showed, resided in what Lord Theign himself meant "It's more to the purpose," he said to Mr. Bender, "that I should mention to you the leading feature, or in other words the very essence, of my plan of campaign—which is to put the picture at once on view." He marked his idea with a broad but elegant gesture. "On view as a thing definitely disposed of."

"I say, I say, I say!" cried Lord John, moved by this bold stroke to high admiration.

Lady Sandgate's approval was more qualified. "But on view, dear Theign, how?"

"With one of those pushing people in Bond Street." And then as for the crushing climax of his policy: "As a Mantovano pure and simple."

"But my dear man," she quavered, "if it *isn't* one?"

Mr. Bender at once anticipated; the wind had suddenly risen for him and he let out sail. "Lady Sand-gate, it's going, by all that's—well, interesting, to *be* one!"

Lord Theign took him up with pleasure. "You seize me? We *treat* it as one!"

Lord John eagerly borrowed the emphasis. "We *treat* it as one!"

Mr. Bender meanwhile fed with an opened appetite on the thought—he even gave it back larger. "As the long-lost Number Eight!"

Lord Theign happily seized *him*. "That will be it—to a charm!"

"It will make them," Mr. Bender asked, "madder than anything?"

His patron—if not his client—put it more nobly. "It will markedly affirm my attitude."

"Which will in turn the more markedly create discussion."

"It may create all it will!"

"Well, if *you* don't mind it, *I* don't!" Mr. Bender concluded. But though bathed in this high serenity he was all for the rapid application of it elsewhere. "You'll put the thing on view right off?"

"As soon as the proper arrangement——"

114

"You put off your journey to *make* it?" Lady Sand-gate at once broke in.

Lord Theign bethought himself—with the effect of a gracious confidence in the others. "Not if these friends will act."

"Oh, I guess we'll *act!*" Mr. Bender declared.

"Ah, *won't* we though!" Lord John re-echoed.

"You understand then I have an interest?" Mr. Bender went on to Lord Theign.

His lordship's irony met it. "I accept that complication—which so much simplifies!"

"And yet also have a liberty?"

"Where else would be those you've taken? The point is," said Lord Theign, "that *I* have a show."

It settled Mr. Bender. "Then I'll *fix* your show." He snatched up his hat. "Lord John, come right round!"

Lord John had of himself reached the door, which he opened to let the whirlwind tremendously figured by his friend pass out first. Taking leave of the others he gave it even his applause. "The fellow can do anything anywhere!" And he hastily followed.

V

Lady Sandgate, left alone with Lord Theign, drew the line at their companion's enthusiasm. "That may be true of Mr. Bender—for it's dreadful how he bears one down. But I simply find him a terror."

"Well," said her friend, who seemed disposed not to fatigue the question, "I dare say a terror will help me." He had other business to which he at once gave himself. "And now, if you please, for that girl."

"I'll send her to you," she replied, "if you can't stay to luncheon."

"I've three or four things to do," he pleaded, "and I lunch with Kitty at one."

She submitted in that case—but disappointedly. "With Berkeley Square then you've time. But I confess I don't quite grasp the so odd inspiration that you've set those men to carry out."

He showed surprise and regret, but even greater decision. "Then it needn't trouble you, dear—it's enough that I myself go straight."

"Are you so very convinced it's straight?"—she wouldn't be a bore to him, but she couldn't not be a blessing.

"What in the world else is it," he asked, "when, having good reasons, one acts on 'em?"

"You must have an immense array," she sighed, "to fly so in the face of Opinion!"

"'Opinion'?" he commented—"I fly in its face? Why, the vulgar thing, as I'm taking my quiet walk, flies in mine! I give it a whack with my umbrella and send it about its business." To which he added with more reproach: "It's enough to have been dished by Grace—without *your* falling away!"

Sadly and sweetly she defended herself. "It's only my great affection—and all that these years have been for us: *they* it is that make me wish you weren't so proud."

"I've a perfect sense, my dear, of what these years have been for us—a very charming matter. But 'proud' is it you find me of the daughter who does her best to ruin me, or of the one who does her best to humiliate?"

Lady Sandgate, not undiscernibly, took her choice of ignoring the point of this. "Your surrenders to Kitty are your own affair—but are you sure you can really bear to see Grace?"

"I seem expected indeed to bear much," he said with more and more of his parental bitterness, "but I don't know that I'm yet in a funk before my child. Doesn't she *want* to see me, with any contrition, after the trick she has played me?" And then as his companion's answer failed: "In spite of which trick you suggest that I should leave the country with no sign of her explaining—?"

His hostess raised her head. "She does want to see you, I know; but you must recall the sequel to that bad hour at Dedborough—when it was you who declined to see *her*."

"Before she left the house with you, the next day, for this?"—he was entirely reminiscent. "What I recall is that even if I had condoned—that evening—her deception of *me* in my folly, I still loathed, for my friend's sake, her practical joke on poor John."

Lady Sandgate indulged in the shrug conciliatory. "It was your very complaint that your own appeal to her *became* an appeal from herself."

"Yes," he returned, so well he remembered, "she was about as civil to me then—picking a quarrel with me on such a trumped-up ground!—as that devil of a fellow in the newspaper; the taste of whose elegant remarks, for that matter, she must now altogether enjoy!"

His good friend showily balanced and might have been about to reply with weight; but what she in fact brought out was only: "I see you're right about it: I must let her speak for herself."

"That I shall greatly prefer to her speaking—as she did so extraordinarily, out of the blue, at Dedborough, upon my honour—for the wonderful friends she picks up: the picture-man introduced by her (what was his name?) who regularly 'cheeked' me, as I suppose he'd call it, in my own house, and whom I hope, by the way, that under this roof she's not able to be quite so thick with!"

If Lady Sandgate winced at that vain dream she managed not to betray it, and she had, in any embarrassment on this matter, the support, as we know, of her own tried policy. "She leads her life under this roof very much as under yours; and she's not of an age, remember, for me to pretend either to watch her movements or to control her contacts." Leaving him however thus to perform his pleasure the charming woman had before she went an abrupt change of tone. "Whatever your relations with others, dear friend, don't forget that *I'm* still here."

Lord Theign accepted the reminder, though, the circumstances being such, it scarce moved him to ecstasy. "That you're here, thank heaven, is of course a comfort—or would be if you understood."

"Ah," she submissively sighed, "if I don't always 'understand' a spirit so much higher than mine and a situation so much more complicated, certainly, I at least always defer, I at least always—well, what can I say but worship?" And then as he remained not other than finely passive, "The old altar, Theign," she went on—"and a spark of the old fire!"

He had not looked at her on this—it was as if he shrank, with his preoccupations, from a tender passage; but he let her take his left hand. "So I feel!" he was, however, kind enough to answer.

"Do feel!" she returned with much concentration. She raised the hand to her pressed lips, dropped it and with a rich "Good-bye!" reached the threshold of the other room.

"May I smoke?" he asked before she had disappeared.

"Dear, yes!"

He had meanwhile taken out his cigarette case and was looking about for a match. But something else occurred to him. "You must come to Victoria."

"Rather!" she said with intensity; and with that she passed away.

VI

Left alone he had a moment's meditation where he stood; it found issue in an articulate "Poor dear thing!"—an exclamation marked at once with patience and impatience, with resignation and ridicule. After which, waiting for his daughter, Lord Theign slowly and absently roamed, finding matches at last and lighting his cigarette—all with an air of concern that had settled on him more heavily from the moment of his finding himself alone. His luxury of gloom—if gloom it was—dropped, however, on his taking heed of Lady Grace, who, arriving on the scene through the other room, had had just time to stand and watch him in silence.

"Oh!" he jerked out at sight of her—which she had to content herself with as a parental greeting after separation, his next words doing little to qualify its dryness. "I take it for granted that you know I'm within a couple of hours of leaving England under a necessity of health." And then as drawing nearer, she signified without speaking her possession of this fact: "I've thought accordingly that before I go I should—on this first possible occasion since that odious occurrence at Dedborough—like to leave you a little more food for meditation, in my absence, on the painfully false position in which you there placed me." He carried himself restlessly even perhaps with a shade of awkwardness, to which her stillness was a contrast; she just waited, wholly passive—possibly indeed a trifle portentous. "If you had plotted and planned it in advance," he none the less firmly pursued, "if you had acted from some uncanny or malignant motive, you couldn't have arranged more perfectly to incommode, to disconcert and, to all intents and purposes, make light of me and insult me." Even before this charge she made no sign; with her eyes now attached to the ground she let him proceed. "I had practically guaranteed to our excellent, our charming friend, your favourable view of his appeal—which you yourself too, remember, had left him in so little doubt of!—so that, having by your performance so egregiously failed him, I have the pleasure of their coming down on me for explanations, for compensations, and for God knows what besides."

Lady Grace, looking up at last, left him in no doubt of the rigour of her attention. "I'm sorry indeed, father, to have done you any wrong; but may I ask whom, in such a connection, you refer to as 'they'?"

"'They'?" he echoed in the manner of a man who has had handed back to his more careful eye, across the counter, some questionable coin that he has tried to pass. "Why, your own sister to begin with—whose interest in what may make for your happiness I suppose you decently recognise; and *his* people, one and all, the delightful old Duchess in particular, who only wanted to be charming to you, and who are as good people, and as pleasant and as clever, damn it, when all's said and done, as any others that are likely to come your way." It clearly did his lordship good to work out thus his case, which grew more and more coherent to him and glowed with irresistible colour. "Letting alone gallant John himself, most amiable of men, about whose merits and whose claims you appear to have pretended to agree with me just that you might, when he presumed, poor chap, ardently to urge them, deal him with the more cruel effect that calculated blow on the mouth!"

It was clear that in the girl's great gravity embarrassment had no share. "They so come down on you I understand then, father, that you're obliged to come down on *me?*"

"Assuredly—for some better satisfaction than your just moping here without a sign!"

"But a sign of what, father?" she asked—as helpless as a lone islander scanning the horizon for a sail.

"Of your appreciating, of your in some degree dutifully considering, the predicament into which you've put me!"

"Hasn't it occurred to you in the least that you've rather put *me* into one?"

He threw back his head as from exasperated nerves. "I put you certainly in the predicament of your receiving by my care a handsome settlement in life—which all the elements that would make for your enjoying it had every appearance of successfully commending to you." The perfect readiness of which on his lips had, like a higher wave, the virtue of lifting and dropping him to still more tangible ground. "And if I understand you aright as wishing to know whether I apologise for that zeal, why you take a most preposterous view of our relation as father and daughter."

"You understand me no better than I fear I understand you," Lady Grace returned, "if what you expect of me is really to take back my words to Lord John." And then as he didn't answer, while their breach gaped like a jostled wound, "Have you seriously come to propose—and from *him* again," she added—"that I shall reconsider my resolute act and lend myself to your beautiful arrangement?"

It had so the sound of unmixed ridicule that he could only, for his dignity, not give way to passion. "I've come, above all, for *this*, I may say, Grace: to remind you of whom you're addressing when you jibe at me, and to make of you assuredly a plain demand—exactly as to whether you judged us to have actively *incurred* your treatment of our unhappy friend, to have brought it upon us, he and I, by my refusal to discuss with you at such a crisis the question of my disposition of a particular item of my property. I've only to look at you, for that matter," Lord Theign continued—always with a finer point and a higher consistency as his rehearsal of his wrongs broadened—"to have my inquiry, as it seems to me, eloquently answered. You flounced away from poor John, you took, as he tells me, 'his head off,' just to repay me for what you chose to regard as my snub on the score of your challenging my entertainment of a possible purchaser; a rebuke launched at me, practically, in the presence of a most inferior person, a stranger and an intruder, from whom you had all the air of taking your cue for naming me the great condition on which you'd gratify my hope. Am I to understand, in other words,"—and his lordship mounted to a climax—"that you sent us about our business because I failed to gratify *your* hope: that of my knocking under to your sudden monstrous pretension to lay down the law for my choice of ways and means of raising, to my best convenience, a considerable sum of money? You'll be so good as to understand, once for all, that I recognise there no right of interference from any quarter—and also to let that knowledge govern your behaviour in my absence."

Lady Grace had thus for some minutes waited on his words—waited even as almost with anxiety for the safe conduct he might look to from some of the more extravagant of them. But he at least felt at the end—if it was an end—all he owed them; so that there was nothing for her but to accept as achieved his dreadful felicity. "You're very angry with me, and I hope you won't feel me simply 'aggravating' if I say that, thinking everything over, I've done my best to allow for that. But I *can* answer your question if I do answer it by saying that my discovery of your possible sacrifice of one of our most beautiful things didn't predispose me to decide in favour of a person—however 'backed' by you—for whose benefit the sacrifice was to take place. Frankly," the girl pushed on, "I did quite hate, for the moment, everything that might make for such a mistake; and took the darkest view, let me also confess, of every one, without exception, connected with it I interceded with you, earnestly, for our precious picture, and you wouldn't on any terms *have* my intercession. On top of that Lord John blundered in, without timeliness or tact—and I'm afraid that, as I hadn't been the least in love with him even before, he did have to take the consequence."

Lord Theign, with an elated swing of his person, greeted this as all he could possibly want. "You recognise then that your reception of him *was* purely vindictive!—the meaning of which is that unless my conduct of my private interests, of which you know nothing whatever, happens to square with your superior wisdom you'll put me under boycott all round! While you chatter about mistakes and blunders, and about our charming friend's lack of the discretion of which you yourself set so grand an example, what account have you to offer of the scene you made me there before that fellow—your confederate, as he had all the air of being!—by giving it me with such effrontery that, if I had eminently done with him after his remarkable display, you at least were but the more determined to see him keep it up?"

The girl's justification, clearly, was very present to her, and not less obviously the truth that to make it strong she must, avoiding every side-issue, keep it very simple, "The only account I can give you, I think, is that I could but speak at such a moment as I felt, and that I felt—well, how can I say how deeply? If you can really bear to know, I feel so still I care in fact more than ever that we shouldn't do such things. I care, if you like, to indiscretion—I care, if you like, to offence, to arrogance, to folly. But even as my last word to you before you leave England on the conclusion of such a step, I'm ready to cry out to you that you oughtn't, you oughtn't, you oughtn't!"

Her father, with wonder-moved, elevated brows and high commanding hand, checked her as in an act really of violence—save that, like an inflamed young priestess, she had already, in essence, delivered her message. "Hallo, hallo, hallo, my distracted daughter—no 'crying out,' if you please!" After which, while arrested but unabashed, she still kept her lighted eyes on him, he gave back her conscious stare for a minute, inwardly and rapidly turning things over, making connections, taking, as after some long and lamentable lapse of observation, a new strange measure of her: all to the upshot of his then speaking with a difference of tone, a recognition of still more of the odious than he had supposed, so that the case might really call for some coolness. "You keep bad company, Grace—it pays the devil with your sense of proportion. If you make this row when I sell a picture, what will be left to you when I forge a cheque?"

"If you had arrived at the necessity of forging a cheque," she answered, "I should then resign myself to that of your selling a picture."

"But not short of that!"

"Not short of that. Not one of ours."

"But I couldn't," said his lordship with his best and coldest amusement, "sell one of somebody else's!"

She was, however, not disconcerted. "Other people do other things—they appear to have done them, and to be doing them, all about us. But *we* have been so decently different—always and ever. We've never done anything disloyal."

"'Disloyal'?"—he was more largely amazed and even interested now.

Lady Grace stuck to her word. "That's what it seems to *me!*"

"It seems to you"—and his sarcasm here was easy—"more disloyal to sell a picture than to buy one? Because we didn't paint 'em all ourselves, you know!"

She threw up impatient hands. "I don't ask you either to paint or to buy——!"

"Oh, *that's* a mercy!" he interrupted, riding his irony hard; "and I'm glad to hear you at least let me off *such* efforts! However, if it strikes you as gracefully filial to apply to your father's conduct so invidious a word," he went on less scathingly, "you must take from him, in your turn, his quite other view of what makes disloyalty—understanding distinctly, by the same token, that he enjoins on you not to give an odious illustration of it, while he's away, by discussing and deploring with any *one* of your extraordinary friends any aspect or feature whatever of his walk and conversation. That—pressed as I am for time," he went on with a glance at his watch while she remained silent—"is the main sense of what I have to say to you; so that I count on your perfect conformity. When you have told me that I *may* so count"—and casting about for his hat he espied it and went to take it up—"I shall more cordially bid you good-bye."

His daughter looked as if she had been for some time expecting the law thus imposed upon her—had been seeing where he must come out; but in spite of this preparation she made him wait for his reply in such tension as he had himself created. "To Kitty I've practically said nothing—and she herself can tell you why: I've in fact scarcely seen her this fortnight. Putting aside then Amy Sandgate, the only person to whom I've spoken—of your 'sacrifice,' as I suppose you'll let me call it?—is Mr. Hugh Crimble, whom you talk of as my 'confederate' at Dedborough."

Lord Theign recovered the name with relief. "Mr. Hugh Crimble—that's it!—whom you so amazingly caused to be present, and apparently invited to be active, at a business that so little concerned him."

"He certainly took upon himself to be interested, as I had hoped he would. But it was because I had taken upon *my* self—"

"To act, yes," Lord Theign broke in, "with the grossest want of delicacy! Well, it's from that exactly that you'll now forbear; and 'interested' as he may be—for which I'm deucedly obliged to him!—you'll not speak to Mr. Crimble again."

"Never again?"—the girl put it as for full certitude.

"Never of the question that I thus exclude. You may chatter your fill," said his lordship curtly, "about any others."

"Why, the particular question you forbid," Grace returned with great force, but as if saying something very reasonable—"that question is *the* question we care about: it's our very ground of conversation."

"Then," her father decreed, "your conversation will please to *dispense* with a ground; or you'll perhaps, better still—if that's the only way!—dispense with your conversation."

Lady Grace took a moment as if to examine this more closely. "You require of me not to communicate with Mr. Crimble at all?"

"Most assuredly I require it—since it's to that you insist on reducing me." He didn't look reduced, the master of Dedborough, as he spoke—which was doubtless precisely because he held his head so high to affirm what he suffered. "Is it so essential to your comfort," he demanded, "to hear him, or to make him, abuse me?"

"'Abusing' you, father dear, has nothing whatever to do with it!"— his daughter had fairly lapsed, with a despairing gesture, to the tenderness involved in her compassion for his perversity. "We look at the thing in a much larger way," she pursued, not heeding that she drew from him a sound of scorn for her "larger." "It's of our Treasure itself we talk—and of what can be *done* in such cases; though with a close application, I admit, to the case that you embody."

"Ah," Lord Theign asked as with absurd curiosity, "I embody a case?"

"Wonderfully, father—as you do everything; and it's the fact of its being exceptional," she explained, "that makes it so difficult to deal with."

His lordship had a gape for it. "'To deal with'? You're undertaking to 'deal' with me?"

She smiled more frankly now, as for a rift in the gloom. "Well, how can we help it if you *will* be a case?" And then as her tone but visibly darkened his wonder: "What we've set our hearts on is saving the picture."

"What you've set your hearts on, in other words, is working straight against me?"

But she persisted without heat. "What we've set our hearts on is working for England."

"And pray who in the world's 'England,'" he cried in his stupefaction, "unless I am?"

"Dear, dear father," she pleaded, "that's all we *want* you to be! I mean"— she didn't fear firmly to force it home—"in the real, the right, the grand sense; the sense that, you see, is so intensely ours."

"'Ours'?"—he couldn't but again throw back her word at her. "Isn't it, damn you, just *in* ours—?"

"No, no," she interrupted—"not in *ours!*" She smiled at him still, though it was strained, as if he really ought to perceive.

But he glared as at a senseless juggle. "What and who the devil are you talking about? What are 'we,' the whole blest lot of us, pray, but the best and most English thing in the country: people walking—and riding!—straight; doing, disinterestedly, most of the difficult and all the thankless jobs; minding their own business, above all, and expecting others to mind theirs?" So he let her "have" the stout sound truth, as it were—and so the direct force of it clearly might, by his view, have made her reel. "You and I, my lady, and your two decent brothers, God be thanked for them, and mine into the bargain, and all the rest, the jolly lot of us, take us together—make us numerous enough without any foreign aid or mixture: if that's what I understand you to mean!"

"You don't understand me at all—evidently; and above all I see you don't want to!" she had the bravery to add, "By 'our' sense of what's due to the nation in such a case I mean Mr. Crimble's and mine—and nobody's else at all; since, as I tell you, it's only with him I've talked."

It gave him then, every inch of him showed, the full, the grotesque measure of the scandal he faced. "So that 'you and Mr. Crimble' represent the standard, for me, in your opinion, of the proprieties and duties of our house?"

Well, she was too earnest—as she clearly wished to let him see—to mind his perversion of it. "I express to you the way we feel."

"It's most striking to hear, certainly, what you express"—he had positively to laugh for it; "and you speak of him, with your insufferable 'we,' as if you were presenting him as your—God knows what! You've enjoyed a large exchange of ideas, I gather, to have arrived at such unanimity." And then, as if to fall into no trap he might somehow be laying for her, she dropped all eagerness and rebutted nothing: "You must see a great deal of your fellow-critic not to be able to speak of yourself without him!"

"Yes, we're fellow-critics, father"—she accepted this opening. "I perfectly adopt your term." But it took her a minute to go further. "I saw Mr. Crim-ble here half an hour ago."

"Saw him 'here'?" Lord Theign amazedly asked. "He *comes* to you here—and Amy Sandgate has been silent?"

"It wasn't her business to tell you—since, you see, she could leave it to me. And I quite expect," Lady Grace then produced, "that he'll come again."

It brought down with a bang all her father's authority. "Then I simply exact of you that you don't see him."

The pause of which she paid it the deference was charged like a brimming cup. "Is that what you *really* meant by your condition just now—that when I do see him I shall not speak to him?"

"What I 'really meant' is what I really mean—that you bow to the law I lay upon you and drop the man altogether."

"Have nothing to do with him at all?"

"Have nothing to do with him at all."

"In fact"—she took it in—"give him wholly up."

He had an impatient gesture. "You sound as if I asked you to give up a fortune!" And then, though she had phrased his idea without consternation—verily as if it had been in the balance for her—he might have been moved by something that gathered in her eyes. "You're so wrapped up in him that the precious sacrifice is like *that* sort of thing?"

Lady Grace took her time—but showed, as her eyes continued to hold him, what *had* gathered. "I like Mr. Crimble exceedingly, father—I think him clever, intelligent, good; I want what he wants—I want it, I think, really, as much; and I don't at all deny that he has helped to make me so want it. But that doesn't matter. I'll wholly cease to see him, I'll give him up forever, if—if—!" She faltered, however, she hung fire with a smile that anxiously, intensely appealed. Then she began and stopped again, "If—if—!" while her father caught her up with irritation.

"'If,' my lady? If *what*, please?"

"If you'll withdraw the offer of our picture to Mr. Bender—and never make another to any one else!"

He stood staring as at the size of it—then translated it into his own terms. "If I'll obligingly announce to the world that I've made an ass of myself you'll kindly forbear from your united effort—the charming pair of you—to show me up for one?"

Lady Grace, as if consciously not caring or attempting to answer this, simply gave the first flare of his criticism time to drop. It wasn't till a minute passed that she said: "You don't agree to my compromise?"

Ah, the question but fatally sharpened at a stroke the stiffness of his spirit. "Good God, I'm to 'compromise' on top of everything?—I'm to let you browbeat me, haggle and bargain with me, over a thing that I'm entitled to settle with you as things have ever *been* settled among us, by uttering to you my last parental word?"

"You don't care enough then for what you name?"—she took it up as scarce heeding now what he said.

"For putting an end to your odious commerce—? I give you the measure, on the contrary," said Lord Theign, "of how much I care: as you give me, very strangely indeed, it strikes me, that of what it costs you—!" But his other words were lost in the hard long look at her from which he broke off in turn as for disgust.

It was with an effect of decently shielding herself—the unuttered meaning came so straight—that she substituted words of her own. "Of what it costs me to redeem the picture?"

"To lose your tenth-rate friend"—he spoke without scruple now.

She instantly broke into ardent deprecation, pleading at once and warning. "Father, father, oh—! You hold the thing in your hands."

He pulled up before her again as to thrust the responsibility straight back. "My orders then are so much rubbish to you?"

Lady Grace held her ground, and they remained face to face in opposition and accusation, neither making the other the sign of peace. But the girl at least *had*, in her way, held out the olive-branch, while Lord Theign had but reaffirmed his will. It was for her acceptance of this that he searched her, her last word not having yet come. Before it had done so, however, the door from the lobby opened and Mr. Gotch had regained their presence. This appeared to determine in Lady Grace a view of the importance of delay, which she signified to her companion in a "Well—I must think!" For the butler positively resounded, and Hugh was there.

"Mr. Crimble!" Mr. Gotch proclaimed—with the further extravagance of projecting the visitor straight upon his lordship.

VII

Our young man showed another face than the face his friend had lately seen him carry off, and he now turned it distressfully from that source of inspiration to Lord Theign, who was flagrantly, even from this first moment, no such source at all, and then from his noble adversary back again, under pressure of difficulty and effort, to Lady Grace, whom he directly addressed. "Here I am again, you see—and I've got my news, worse luck!" But his manner to her father was the next instant more brisk. "I learned you were here, my lord; but as the case is important I told them it was all right and came up. I've been to my club," he added for the girl, "and found the tiresome thing—!" But he broke down breathless.

"And it isn't good?" she cried with the highest concern.

Ruefully, yet not abjectly, he confessed, "Not so good as I hoped. For I assure you, my lord, I counted—"

"It's the report from Pappendick about the picture at Verona," Lady Grace interruptingly explained.

Hugh took it up, but, as we should well have seen, under embarrassment dismally deeper; the ugly particular defeat he had to announce showing thus, in his thought, for a more awkward force than any reviving possibilities that he might have begun to balance against them. "The man I told *you* about also," he said to his formidable patron; "whom I went to Brussels to talk with and who, most kindly, has gone for us to Verona. He has been able to get straight at *their* Mantovano, but the brute horribly wires me that he doesn't quite see the thing; see, I mean"—and he gathered his two hearers together now in his overflow of chagrin, conscious, with his break of the ice, more exclusively of that—"my vivid vital point, the absolute screaming identity of the two persons represented. I still hold," he persuasively went on, "that our man is their man, but Pappendick decides that he isn't—and as Pappendick has so *much* to be reckoned with of course I'm awfully abashed."

Lord Theign had remained what he had begun by being, immeasurably and inaccessibly detached—only with his curiosity more moved than he could help and as, on second thought, to see what sort of a still more offensive fool the heated youth would really make of himself. "Yes—you seem indeed remarkably abashed!"

Hugh clearly was thrown again, by the cold "cut" of this, colder than any mere social ignoring, upon a sense of the damnably poor figure he did offer; so that, while he straightened himself and kept a mastery of his manner and a control of his reply, we should yet have felt his cheek tingle. "I backed my own judgment strongly, I know—and I've got my snub. But I don't in the least knock under."

"Only the first authority in Europe doesn't care, I suppose, whether you do or not!"

"He isn't *the* first authority in Europe, thank God," the young man returned—"though he is, I admit, one of the three or four first. And I mean to appeal—I've another shot in my locker," he went on with his rather painfully forced smile to Lady Grace. "I had already written, you see, to dear old Bardi."

"Bardi of Milan?"—she recognised, it was admirably manifest, the appeal of his directness to her generosity, awkward as their predicament was also for her herself, and spoke to him as she might have spoken without her father's presence.

It would have shown for beautiful, on the spot, had there been any one to perceive it, that he devoutly recorded her intelligence. "You know of him?—how delightful of you! For the Italians, I now feel," he quickly explained, "he must have *most* the instinct—and it has come over me since that he'd have been more our man. Besides of course his so knowing the Verona picture."

She had fairly hung on his lips. "But does he know ours?"

"No—not ours yet. That is"—he consciously and quickly took himself up—"not yours! But as Pap-pendick went to Verona for us I've asked Bardi to do us the great favour to come here—if Lord Theign will be so good," he said, bethinking himself with a turn, "as to let him examine the Moretto." He faced again to the personage he mentioned, who, simply standing off and watching, in concentrated interest as well as detachment, this interview of his cool daughter and her still cooler guest, had plainly "elected," as it were, to give them rope to hang themselves. Staring very hard at Hugh he met his appeal, but in a silence clearly calculated; against which, however, the young man, bearing up, made such head as he could. He offered his next word, that is, equally to the two companions. "It's not at all impossible—for such curious effects have been!—that the Dedborough picture seen *after* the Verona will point a different moral from the Verona seen after the Dedborough."

"And so awfully *long* after—wasn't it?" Lady Grace asked.

"Awfully long after—it was years ago that Pappen-dick, being in this country for such purposes, was kindly admitted to your house when none of you were there, or at least visible."

"Oh of course we don't see *every one!*"—she heroically kept it up.

"You don't see every one," Hugh bravely laughed, "and that makes it all the more charming that you did, and that you still do, see me. I shall really get Bardi," he pursued, "to go again to Verona——"

"The last thing before coming here?"—she had guessed before he could say it; and still she sustained it, so that he could shine at her for assent. "How happy they should like so to work for you!"

"Ah, we're a band of brothers," he returned—"'we few, we happy few'—from country to country"; to which he added, gaining more ease for an eye at Lord Theign: "though we do have our little rubs and disputes, like Pappendick and me now. The thing, you see, is the ripping *interest* of it all; since," he developed and explained, for his elder friend's benefit, with pertinacious cheer and an assurance superficially at least recovered, "when we're really 'hit' over a case we'll do almost anything in life."

Lady Grace, recklessly throbbing in the breath of it all, immediately appropriated what her father let alone. "It must be so lovely to *feel* so hit!"

"It does spoil one," Hugh laughed, "for milder joys. Of course what I have to consider is the chance—putting it at the *merest* chance—of Bardi's own wet blanket! But that's again so very small—though," he pulled up with a drop to the comparative dismal, which he offered as an almost familiar tribute to Lord Theign, "you'll retort upon me naturally that I promised you the possibility of Pappendick's veto would be: all on the poor dear old basis, you'll claim, of the wish father to the thought. Well, I do wish to be right as much as I believe I am. Only give me time!" he sublimely insisted.

"How can we prevent your using it?" Lady Grace again interrupted; "or the fact either that if the worst comes to the worst—"

"The thing"—he at once pursued—"will always be at the least the greatest of Morettos? Ah," he cried so cheerily that there was still a freedom in it toward any it might concern, "the worst sha'n't come to the worst, but the best to the best: my conviction of which it is that supports me in the deep regret I have to express"—and he faced Lord Theign again—"for any inconvenience I may have caused you by my abortive undertaking. That, I vow here before Lady Grace, I will yet more than make up!"

Lord Theign, after the longest but the blankest contemplation of him, broke hereupon, for the first time, that attitude of completely sustained and separate silence which he had yet made compatible with his air of having deeply noted every element of the scene—so that it was of this full view his participation had effectively consisted, "I haven't the least idea, sir, what you're talking about!" And he squarely turned his back, strolling toward the other room, the threshold of which he the next moment had passed, remaining scantily within, however, and in sight of the others, not to say of ourselves; even though averted and ostensibly lost in some scrutiny that might have had for its object the great enshrined Lawrence.

There ensued upon his words and movement a vivid mute passage, the richest of commentaries, between his companions; who, deeply divided by the width of the ample room, followed him with their eyes and then used for their own interchange these organs of remark, eloquent now over Hugh's unmistakable dismissal at short order, on which obviously he must at once act. Lady Grace's young arms conveyed to him by a despairing contrite motion of surrender that she had done for him all she could do in his presence and that, however sharply doubtful the result, he was to leave the rest to herself. They communicated thus, the strenuous pair, for their full moment, without speaking; only with the prolonged, the charged give and take of their gaze and, it might well have been imagined, of their passion. Hugh had for an instant a show of hesitation—of the arrested impulse, while he kept her father within range, to launch at that personage before going some final remonstrance. It was the girl's raised hand and gesture of warning that waved away for him such a mistake; he decided, under her pressure, and after a last searching and answering look at her reached the door and let himself out. The stillness was then prolonged a minute by the further wait of the two others, Lord Theign where he had been standing and his daughter on the spot from which she had not moved. It presently ended in his lordship's turn about as if inferring by the silence that the intruder had withdrawn.

"Is that young man your lover?" he said as he drew again near.

Lady Grace waited a little, but spoke as quietly as if she had been prepared. "Has the question a bearing on the promise you a short time ago demanded of me?"

"It has a bearing on the so extraordinary appearance of your intimacy with him!"

"You mean that if he *should* be—what you ask me about—your exaction would then be modified?"

"My request that you break it short off? That request would, on the contrary," Lord Theign pronounced, "rest on an immense new ground. Therefore I insist on your telling me the truth."

"Won't the truth be before you, father, if you'll *think* a moment—without extravagance?" After which, while, as stiffly as ever—and it probably seemed to her impatience as stupidly—he didn't rise to it, she went on: "If I *offered* you not again to see him, does that make for you the appearance—?"

"If you offered it, you mean, on your condition—my promising not to sell? I promised," said Lord Theign, "absolutely nothing at all!"

She took him up with all expression. "So I promised as little! But that I should have been able to say what I did sufficiently meets your curiosity."

She might, wronged as she held herself, have felt him stupid not to see *how* wronged; but he was in any case acute for an evasion. "You risked your offer for the great equivalent over which you've so wildly worked yourself up."

"Yes, I've worked myself—that, I grant you and don't blush for! But hardly so much as to renounce my 'lover'—if," she prodigiously smiled, "I were so fortunate as to have one!"

"You renounced poor John mightily easily—whom you were so fortunate as to have!"

Her brows rose as high as his own had ever done. "Do you call Lord John my lover?"

"He was your suitor most assuredly," Lord Theign inimitably said, though without looking at her; "and as strikingly encouraged as he was respectfully ardent!"

"Encouraged by *you*, dear father, beyond doubt!"

"Encouraged—er—by every one: because you were (yes, you *were!*) encouraging. And what I ask of you now is a word of common candour as to whether you didn't, on your honour, turn him off because of your just then so stimulated views on the person who has been with us."

Grace replied but after an instant, as moved by more things than she could say—moved above all, in her trouble and her pity for him, by other things than harshness: "Oh father, father, father——!"

He searched her through all the compassion of her cry, but appeared to give way to her sincerity. "Well then if I *have* your denial I take it as answering my whole question—in a manner that satisfies me. If there's nothing, on your word, of that sort between you, you can all the more drop him."

"But you said a moment ago that I should all the more in the other case—that of there *being* something!"

He brushed away her logic-chopping. "If you're so keen then for past remarks I take up your own words—I accept your own terms for your putting

135

an end to Mr. Crimble." To which, while, turning pale, she said nothing, he added: "You recognise that you profess yourself ready——"

"Not again to see him," she now answered, "if you tell me the picture's safe? Yes, I recognise that I *was* ready—as well as how scornfully little you then were!"

"Never mind what I then was—the question's of what I actually am, since I close with you on it The picture's therefore as safe as you please," Lord Theign pursued, "if you'll do what you just now engaged to."

"I engaged to do nothing," she replied after a pause; and the face she turned to him had grown suddenly tragic. "I've no word to take back, for none passed between us; but I *won't* do what I mentioned and what you at once laughed at Because," she finished, "the case is different."

"Different?" he almost shouted—"*how*, different?"

She didn't look at him for it, but she was none the less strongly distinct "He has *been* here—and that has done it He knows," she admirably emphasised.

"Knows what I think of him, no doubt—for a brazen young prevaricator! But what else?"

She still kept her eyes on a far-off point. "What he will have seen—that I feel we're too good friends."

"Then your denial of it's false," her father fairly thundered—"and you *are* infatuated?"

It made her the more quiet. "I like him very much."

"So that your row about the picture," he demanded with passion, "has been all a blind?" And then as her quietness still held her: "And his a blind as much—to help him to get *at* you?"

She looked at him again now. "He must speak for himself. I've said what I mean."

"But what the devil *do* you mean?" Lord Theign, taking in the hour, had reached the door as in supremely baffled conclusion and with a sense of time lamentably lost.

Their eyes met upon it all dreadfully across the wide space, and, hurried and incommoded as she saw him, she yet made him still stand a minute. Then she let everything go. "Do what you like with the picture!"

He jerked up his arm and guarding hand as before a levelled blow at his face, and with the other hand flung open the door, having done with her now and immediately lost to sight. Left alone she stood a moment looking before her; then with a vague advance, held apparently by a quickly growing sense of the implication of her act, reached a table where she remained a little, deep afresh in thought—only the next thing to fall into a chair close to it and there, with her elbows on it, yield to the impulse of covering her flushed face with her hands.

BOOK THIRD

I

HUGH CRIMBLE waited again in the Bruton Street drawing-room—this time at the afternoon hour; he restlessly shifted his place, looked at things about him without seeing them; all he saw, all he outwardly studied, was his own face and figure as he stopped an instant before a long glass suspended between two windows. Just as he turned from that brief and perhaps not wholly gratified inspection Lady Grace—that he had sent up his name to whom was immediately apparent—presented herself at the entrance from the other room. These young persons had hereupon no instant exchange of words; their exchange was mute—they but paused where they were; while the silence of each evidently tested the other for full confidence. A measure of this comfort came first, it would have appeared, to Hugh; though he then at once asked for confirmation of it.

"Am I right, Lady Grace, am I right?—to have *come*, I mean, after so many days of not hearing, not knowing, and perhaps, all too stupidly, not trying." And he went on as, still with her eyes on him, she didn't speak; though, only, we should have guessed, from her stress of emotion. "Even if I'm wrong, let me tell you, I don't care—simply because, whatever new difficulty I may have brought about for you here a fortnight ago, there's something that to-day adds to my doubt and my fear too great a pang, and that has made me feel I can scarce bear the suspense of them as they are."

The girl came nearer, and if her grave face expressed a pity it yet declined a dread. "Of what suspense do you speak? Your still being without the other opinion—?"

"Ah, that worries me, yes; and all the more, at this hour, as I say, that—" He dropped it, however: "I'll tell you in a moment! My *real* torment, all the while, has been not to know, from day to day, what situation, what complication that last scene of ours with your father here has let you in for; and yet at the same time—having no sign nor sound from you!—to see the importance of not making anything possibly worse by approaching you again, however discreetly. I've been in the dark," he pursued, "and feeling that I must leave *you* there; so that now—just brutally turning up once more under personal need and at any cost—I don't know whether I most want or most fear what I may learn from you."

Lady Grace, listening and watching, appeared to choose between different ways of meeting this appeal; she had a pacifying, postponing gesture, marked with a beautiful authority, a sign of the value for her of what she gave precedence to and which waved off everything else. "Have you had—first of all—any news yet of Bardi?"

"That I have is what has driven me straight *at* you again—since I've shown you before how I turn to you at a crisis. He has come as I hoped and like a regular good 'un," Hugh was able to state; "I've just met him at the station, but I pick him up again, at his hotel in Clifford Street, at five. He stopped, on his way from Dover this morning, to my extreme exasperation, to 'sample' Canterbury, and I leave him to a bath and a change and tea. Then swooping down I whirl him round to Bond Street, where his very first apprehension of the thing (an apprehension, oh I guarantee you, so quick and clean and fine and wise) will be the flash-light projected—well," said the young man, to wind up handsomely, but briefly and reasonably, "over the whole field of our question."

She panted with comprehension. "That of the two portraits being but the one sitter!"

"That of the two portraits being but the one sitter. With everything so to the good, more and more, that bangs in, up to the head, the golden nail of authenticity, and"—he quite glowed through his gloom for it—"we take our stand in glory on the last Mantovano in the world."

It was a presumption his friend visibly yearned for—but over which, too, with her eyes away from him, she still distinguished the shadow of a cloud. "That is if the flash-light comes!"

"That is if it comes indeed, confound it!"—he had to enlarge a little under the recall of past experience. "So now, at any rate, you see my tension!"

She looked at him again as with a vision too full for a waste of words. "While you on your side of course keep well in view Mr. Bender's."

"Yes, while I keep well in view Mr. Bender's; though he doesn't know, you see, of Bardi's being at hand."

"Still," said the girl, always all lucid for the case, "if the 'flash-light' does presently break——!"

"It will first take him in the eye?" Hugh had jumped to her idea, but he adopted it only to provide: "It might if he didn't now wear goggles, so to say!—clapped on him too hard by Pappendick's so damnably perverse opinion." With which, however, he quickly bethought himself. "Ah, of course, these wretched days, you haven't known of Pappendick's personal visit. After that wire from Verona I wired him back defiance—"

"And that brought him?" she cried.

"To do the honest thing, yes—I *will* say for him: to renew, for full assurance, his early memory of our picture."

She hung upon it. "But only to stick then to what he had telegraphed?"

"To declare that for *him*, lackaday! our thing's a pure Moretto—and to declare as much, moreover, with all the weight of his authority, to Bender himself, who of course made a point of seeing him."

"So that Bender"—she followed and wondered—"is, as a consequence, wholly off?"

It made her friend's humour play up in his acute-ness. "Bender, Lady Grace, is, by the law of his being, never 'wholly' off—or on!—anything. He lives, like the moon, in mid-air, shedding his silver light on earth; never quite gone, yet never *all* there—save for inappreciable moments. He *would* be in eclipse as a peril, I grant," Hugh went on—"if the question had struck him as really closed. But luckily the blessed Press—which is a pure heavenly joy and now quite immense on it—keeps it open as wide as Piccadilly."

"Which makes, however," Lady Grace discriminated, "for the danger of a grab."

"Ah, but all the more for the shame of a surrender! Of course I admit that when it's a question of a life spent, like his, in waiting, acquisitively, for the cat to jump, the only thing for one, at a given moment, as against that signal, is to be found one's self by the animal in the line of its trajectory. That's exactly," he laughed, "where we are!"

She cast about as intelligently to note the place. "Your great idea, you mean, *has* so worked—with the uproar truly as loud as it has seemed to come to us here?"

"All beyond my wildest hope," Hugh returned; "since the sight of the picture, flocked to every day by thousands, so beautifully *tells*. That we must at any cost keep it, that the nation must, and hang on to it tight, is the cry that fills the air—to the tune of ten letters a day in the Papers, with every three days a gorgeous leader; to say nothing of more and more passionate talk all over the place, some of it awfully wild, but all of it wind in our sails."

"I suppose it was that wind then that blew me round there to see the thing in its new light," Lady Grace said. "But I couldn't stay—for tears!"

"Ah," Hugh insisted on his side for comfort, "we'll crow loudest yet! And don't meanwhile, just *don't*, those splendid strange eyes of the fellow seem consciously to plead? The women, bless them, adore him, cling to him, and there's talk of a 'Ladies' League of Protest'—all of which keeps up the pitch."

"Poor Amy and I are a ladies' league," the girl joylessly joked—"as we now take in the 'Journal' regardless of expense."

"Oh then you practically *have* it all—since," Hugh, added after a brief hesitation, "I suppose Lord Theign himself doesn't languish uninformed."

"At far-off Salsomaggiore—by the papers? No doubt indeed he isn't spared even the worst," said Lady Grace—"and no doubt too it's a drag on his cure."

Her companion seemed struck with her lack of assurance. "Then you don't—if I may ask—hear from him?"

"I? Never a word."

"He doesn't write?" Hugh allowed himself to insist.

"He doesn't write. And I don't write either."

"And Lady Sandgate?" Hugh once more ventured.

"Doesn't *she* write?"

"Doesn't *she* hear?" said the young man, treating the other form of the question as a shade evasive.

"I've asked her not to tell me," his friend replied—"that is if he simply holds out."

"So that as she doesn't tell you"—Hugh was clear for the inference—"he of course does hold out." To which he added almost accusingly while his eyes searched her: "But your case is really bad."

She confessed to it after a moment, but as if vaguely enjoying it. "My case is really bad."

He had a vividness of impatience and contrition. 197

"And it's I who—all too blunderingly!—have made it so?"

"I've made it so myself," she said with a high head-shake, "and you, on the contrary—!" But here she checked her emphasis.

"Ah, I've so *wanted*, through our horrid silence, to help you!" And he pressed to get more at the truth. "You've so quite fatally displeased him?"

"To the last point—as I tell you. But it's not to that I refer," she explained; "it's to the ground of complaint I've given *you*." And then as this but left him blank, "It's time—it was at once time—that you should know," she pursued; "and yet if it's hard for me to speak, as you see, it was impossible for me to write. But there it is." She made her sad and beautiful effort. "The last thing before he left us I let the picture go."

"You mean—?" But he could only wonder—till, however, it glimmered upon him. "You gave up your protest?"

"I gave up my protest. I told him that—so far as I'm concerned!—he might do as he liked."

Her poor friend turned pale at the sharp little shock of it; but if his face thus showed the pang of too great a surprise he yet wreathed the convulsion in a gay grimace. "You leave me to struggle alone?"

"I leave you to struggle alone."

He took it in bewilderingly, but tried again, even to the heroic, for optimism. "Ah well, you decided, I suppose, on some new personal ground."

"Yes; a reason came up, a reason I hadn't to that extent looked for and which of a sudden—quickly, before he went—I *had* somehow to deal with. So to give him my word in the dismal sense I mention was my only way to meet the strain." She paused; Hugh waited for something further, and "I gave him my word I wouldn't help you," she wound up.

He turned it over. "To *act* in the matter—I see."

"To act in the matter"—she went through with it—"after the high stand I had taken."

Still he studied it. "I see—I see. It's between you and your father."

"It's between him and me—yes. An engagement not again to trouble him."

Hugh, from his face, might have feared a still greater complication; so he made, as he would probably have said, a jolly lot of this. "Ah, that was nice of you. And natural. *That's* all right!"

"No"—she spoke from a deeper depth—"it's altogether wrong. For whatever happens I must now accept it."

"Well, say you must"—he really declined not to treat it almost as rather a "lark"—"if we can at least go on talking."

"Ah, we *can* at least go on talking!" she perversely sighed. "I can say anything I like so long as I don't say it to *him*" she almost wailed. But she added with more firmness: "I can still hope—and I can still pray."

He set free again with a joyous gesture all his confidence. "Well, what more *could* you do, anyhow? So isn't that enough?"

It took her a moment to say, and even then she didn't. "Is it enough for *you*, Mr. Crimble?"

"What *is* enough for me"—he could for his part readily name it—"is the harm done you at our last meeting by my irruption; so that if you got his consent to see me——!"

"I didn't get his consent!"—she had turned away from the searching eyes, but she faced them again to rectify: "I see you against his express command."

"Ah then thank God I came!"—it was like a bland breath on a *feu de joie*: he flamed so much higher.

"Thank God you've come, yes—for my deplorable exposure." And to justify her name for it before he could protest, "I *offered* him here not to see you," she rigorously explained.

"'Offered him?'"—Hugh did drop for it. "Not to see me—ever again?"

She didn't falter. "Never again."

Ah then he understood. "But he wouldn't let that serve——?"

"Not for the price I put on it."

"His yielding on the picture?"

"His yielding on the picture."

Hugh lingered before it all. "Your proposal wasn't 'good enough'?"

"It wasn't good enough."

"I see," he repeated—"I see." But he was in that light again mystified. "Then why are you therefore not free?"

"Because—just after—you came back, and I *did* see you again!"

Ah, it was all present. "You found you were too sorry for me?"

"I found I was too sorry for you—as he himself found I was."

Hugh had got hold of it now. "And *that*, you mean, he couldn't stomach?"

"So little that when you had gone (and *how* you had to go you remember) he at once proposed, rather than that I should deceive you in a way so different from his own——"

"To do all we want of him?"

"To do all I did at least."

"And it was *then*," he took in, "that you wouldn't deal?"

"Well"—try though she might to keep the colour out, it all came straighter and straighter now—"those moments had brought you home to me as they had also brought *him*; making such a difference, I felt, for what he veered round to agree to."

"The difference"—Hugh wanted it so adorably definite—"that you didn't see your way to accepting——?"

"No, not to accepting the condition he named."

"Which was that he'd keep the picture for you if you'd treat me as too 'low'——?"

"If I'd treat you," said Lady Grace with her eyes on his fine young face, "as impossible."

He kept her eyes—he clearly liked so to make her repeat it. "And not even for the sake of the picture——?" After he had given her time, however, her silence, with her beautiful look in it, seemed to admonish him not to force her for his pleasure; as if what she had already told him didn't make him throb enough for the wonder of it. He *had* it, and let her see by his high flush how he made it his own—while, the next thing, as it was but part of her avowal, the rest of that illumination called for a different intelligence. "Your father's reprobation of me personally is on the ground that you're all such great people?"

145

She spared him the invidious answer to this as, a moment before, his eagerness had spared her reserve; she flung over the "ground" that his question laid bare the light veil of an evasion, "'Great people,' I've learned to see, mustn't—to remain great—do what my father's doing."

"It's indeed on the theory of their not so behaving," Hugh returned, "that we see them—all the inferior rest of us—in the grand glamour of their greatness!"

If he had spoken to meet her admirable frankness half-way, that beauty in her almost brushed him aside to make at a single step the rest of the journey. "You won't see them in it for long—if they don't now, under such tests and with such opportunities, begin to take care."

This had given him, at a stroke, he clearly felt, all freedom for the closer criticism. "Lord Theign perhaps recognises some such canny truth, but 'takes care,' with the least trouble to himself and the finest short cut—does it, if you'll let me say so, rather on the cheap—by finding 'the likes' of me, as his daughter's trusted friend, out of the question."

"Well, you won't mind that, will you?" Lady Grace asked, "if he finds his daughter herself, in any such relation to you, quite as much so."

"Different enough, from position to position and person to person," he brightly brooded, "is the view that gets itself *most* comfortably taken of the implications of Honour!"

"Yes," the girl returned; "my father, in the act of despoiling us all, all who are interested, without apparently the least unpleasant consciousness, keeps the balance showily even, to his mostly so fine, so delicate sense, by suddenly discovering that he's scandalised at my caring for your friendship."

Hugh looked at her, on this, as with the gladness verily of possession promised and only waiting—or as if from that moment forth he had her assurance of everything that most concerned him and that might most inspire. "Well, isn't the moral of it all simply that what his perversity of pride, as we can only hold it, will have most done for us is to bring us—and to keep us—blessedly together?"

She seemed for a moment to question his "simply." "Do you regard us as so much 'together' when you remember where, in spite of everything, I've put myself?"

"By telling him to do what he likes?" he recalled without embarrassment. "Oh, that wasn't in spite of 'everything'—it was only in spite of the Mantovano."

"'Only'?" she flushed—"when I've given the picture up?"

"Ah," Hugh cried, "I don't care a hang for the picture!" And then as she let him, closer, close to her with this, possess himself of her hands: "We both only care, don't we, that we're given to each other thus? We both only care, don't we, that nothing can keep us apart?"

"Oh, if you've forgiven me—!" she sighed into his fond face.

"Why, since you gave the thing up *for* me," he pleadingly laughed, "it isn't as if you had given *me* up——!"

"For anything, anything? Ah never, never!" she breathed.

"Then why aren't we all right?"

"Well, if you will——!"

"Oh for ever and ever and ever!"—and with this ardent cry of his devotion his arms closed in their strength and she was clasped to his breast and to his lips.

The next moment, however, she had checked him with the warning "Amy Sandgate!"—as if she had heard their hostess enter the other room. Lady Sand-gate was in fact almost already upon them—their disjunction had scarce been effected and she had reached the nearer threshold. They had at once put the widest space possible between them—a little of the flurry of which transaction agitated doubtless their clutch at composure. They gave back a shade awkwardly and consciously, on one side and the other, the speculative though gracious attention she for a few moments made them and their recent intimate relation the subject of; from all of which indeed Lady

Grace sought and found cover in a prompt and responsible address to Hugh. "Mustn't you go without more delay to Clifford Street?"

He came back to it all alert "At once!" He had recovered his hat and reached the other door, whence he gesticulated farewell to the elder lady. "Please pardon me"—and he disappeared.

Lady Sandgate hereupon stood for a little silently confronted with the girl. "Have you freedom of mind for the fact that your father's suddenly at hand?"

"He has come back?"—Lady Grace was sharply struck.

"He arrives this afternoon and appears to go straight to Kitty—according to a wire that I find downstairs on coming back late from my luncheon. He has returned with a rush—as," said his correspondent in the elation of triumph, "I was *sure* he would!"

Her young friend was more at sea. "Brought back, you mean, by the outcry—even though he so hates it?"

But she was more and more all lucidity—save in so far as she was now almost all authority. "Ah, hating still more to seem afraid, he has come back to face the music!"

Lady Grace, turning away as in vague despair for the manner in which the music might affect him, yet wheeled about again, after thought, to a positive recognition and even to quite an inconsequent pride. "Yes—that's dear old father!"

And what was Lady Sandgate moreover but mistress now of the subject? "At the point the row has reached he couldn't stand it another day; so he has thrown up his cure and—lest we should oppose him!—not even announced his start."

"Well," her companion returned, "now that I've *done* it all I shall never oppose him again!"

Lady Sandgate appeared to show herself as still under the impression she might have received on entering. "He'll only oppose *you!*"

"If he does," said Lady Grace, "we're at present two to bear it."

"Heaven save us then"—the elder woman was quick, was even cordial, for the sense of this—"your good friend *is* clever!"

Lady Grace honoured the remark. "Mr. Crim-ble's remarkably clever."

"And you've arranged——?"

"We haven't arranged—but we've understood. So that, dear Amy, if *you* understand—!" Lady Grace paused, for Gotch had come in from the hall.

"His lordship has arrived?" his mistress immediately put to him.

"No, my lady, but Lord John has—to know if he's expected *here*, and in that case, by your ladyship's leave, to come up."

Her ladyship turned to the girl. "May Lord John—as we do await your father—come up?"

"As suits *you*, please!"

"He may come up," said Lady Sandgate to Gotch. "His lordship's expected." She had a pause till they were alone again, when she went on to her companion: "You asked me just now if I understood. Well—I do understand!"

Lady Grace, with Gotch's withdrawal, which left the door open, had reached the passage to the other room. "Then you'll excuse me!"—she made her escape.

II

Lord John, reannounced the next instant from the nearest quarter and quite waiving salutations, left no doubt of the high pitch of his eagerness and tension as soon as the door had closed behind him. "What on earth then do you suppose he has come back to *do*—?" To which he added while his hostess's gesture impatiently disclaimed conjecture: "Because when a fellow really finds himself the centre of a cyclone——!"

"Isn't it just at the centre," she interrupted, "that you keep remarkably still, and only in the suburbs that you feel the rage? I count on dear Theign's doing nothing in the least foolish—!"

"Ah, but he can't have chucked everything for nothing," Lord John sharply returned; "and wherever you place him in the rumpus he can't not meet somehow, hang it, such an assault on his character as a great nobleman and good citizen."

"It's his luck to have become with the public of the newspapers the scapegoat-in-chief: for the sins, so-called, of a lot of people!" Lady Sandgate inconclusively sighed.

"Yes," Lord John concluded for her, "the mercenary millions on whose traffic in their trumpery values—when they're so lucky as to have any!—*this* isn't a patch!"

"Oh, there are cases *and* cases: situations and responsibilities so intensely differ!"—that appeared on the whole, for her ladyship, the moral to be gathered.

"Of course everything differs, all round, from everything," Lord John went on; "and who in the world knows anything of his own case but the victim of circumstances exposing himself, for the highest and purest motives, to be literally torn to pieces?"

"Well," said Lady Sandgate as, in her strained suspense, she freshly consulted her bracelet watch, "I hope he isn't already torn—if you tell me you've been to Kitty's."

"Oh, he was all right so far: he had arrived and gone out again," the young man explained, "as Lady Imber hadn't been at home."

"Ah cool Kitty!" his hostess sighed again—but diverted, as she spoke, by the reappearance of her butler, this time positively preceding Lord Theign, whom she met, when he presently stood before her, his garb of travel exchanged for consummate afternoon dress, with yearning tenderness and compassionate curiosity. "At last, dearest friend—what a joy! But with Kitty not at home to receive you?"

That young woman's parent made light of it for the indulged creature's sake. "Oh I knew my Kitty! I dressed and I find her at five-thirty." To which he added as he only took in further, without expression, Lord John: "But Bender, who came there before my arrival—he hasn't tried for me here?"

It was a point on which Lord John himself could at least be expressive. "I met him at the club at luncheon; he had had your letter—but for which chance, my dear man, I should have known nothing. You'll see him all right at this house; but I'm glad, if I may say so, Theign," the speaker pursued with some emphasis—"I'm glad, you know, to get hold of you first."

Lord Theign seemed about to ask for the meaning of this remark, but his other companion's apprehension had already overflowed. "You haven't come back, have you—to whatever it may be!—for *trouble* of any sort with Breckenridge?"

His lordship transferred his penetration to this fair friend, "Have you become so intensely absorbed—these remarkable days!—in 'Breckenridge'?"

She felt the shadow, you would have seen, of his claimed right, or at least privilege, of search—yet easily, after an instant, emerged clear. "I've thought and dreamt but of *you*—suspicious man!—in proportion as the clamour has spread; and Mr. Bender meanwhile, if you want to know, hasn't been near me once!"

Lord John came in a manner, and however unconsciously, to her aid. "You'd have seen, if he had been, what's the matter with him, I think—and what perhaps Theign has seen from his own letter: since," he went on to his fellow-visitor, "I understood him a week ago to have been much taken up with writing you."

Lord Theign received this without comment, only again with an air of expertly sounding the speaker; after which he gave himself afresh for a moment to Lady Sandgate. "I've not come home for any clamour, as you surely know me well enough to believe; or to notice for a minute the cheapest insolence and aggression—which frankly scarce reached me out there; or which, so far as it did, I was daily washed clean of by those blest waters. I returned on Mr. Bender's letter," he then vouchsafed to Lord John—"three extraordinarily vulgar pages about the egregious Pap-pendick!"

"About his having suddenly turned up in person, yes, and, as Breckenridge says, marked the picture down?"—the young man was clearly all-knowing. "That *has* of course weighed on Bender—being confirmed apparently, on the whole, by the drift of public opinion."

Lord Theign took, on this, with a frank show of reaction from some of his friend's terms, a sharp turn off; he even ironically indicated the babbler or at least the blunderer in question to Lady Sandgate. "He too has known me so long, and he comes here to talk to me of 'the drift of public opinion'!" After which he quite charged at his vain informant. "Am I to tell you again that I snap my fingers at the drift of public opinion?—which is but another name for the chatter of all the fools one doesn't know, in addition to all those (and plenty of 'em!) one damnably does."

Lady Sandgate, by a turn of the hand, dropped oil from her golden cruse. "Ah, you did *that*, in your own grand way, before you went abroad!"

"I don't speak of the matter, my dear man, in the light of its effect on *you*," Lord John importantly explained—"but in the light of its effect on Bender; who so consumedly wants the picture, if he *is* to have it, to be a Mantovano, but seems unable to get it taken at last for anything but the fine old Moretto that of course it has always been."

Lord Theign, in growing disgust at the whole beastly complication, betrayed more and more the odd pitch of the temper that had abruptly restored him with such incalculable weight to the scene of action. "Well, isn't a fine old Moretto good enough for him; confound him?"

It pulled up not a little Lord John, who yet made his point. "A fine old Moretto, you know, was exactly what he declined at Dedborough—for its comparative, strictly comparative, insignificance; and he only thought of the picture when the wind began to rise for the enormous rarity—"

"That that mendacious young cad who has bamboozled Grace," Lord Theign broke in, "tried to befool us, for his beggarly reasons, into claiming for it?"

Lady Sandgate renewed her mild influence. "Ah, the knowing people haven't had their last word—the possible Mantovano isn't exploded *yet*." Her noble friend, however, declined the offered spell. "I've had enough of the knowing people—the knowing people are serpents! My picture's to take or to leave—and it's what I've come back, if you please, John, to say to your man to his face."

This declaration had a report as sharp and almost as multiplied as the successive cracks of a discharged revolver; yet when the light smoke cleared Lady Sand-gate at least was still left standing and smiling. "Yes, why in mercy's name can't he choose *which?*—and why does he write him, dreadful Breckenridge, such tiresome argumentative letters?"

Lord John took up her idea as with the air of something that had been working in him rather vehemently, though under due caution too, as a consequence of this exchange, during which he had apprehensively watched his elder. "I don't think I quite see *how*, my dear Theign, the poor chap's letter was so offensive."

In that case his dear Theign could tell him. "Because it was a tissue of expressions that may pass current—over counters and in awful newspapers—in *his* extraordinary world or country, but that I decline to take time to puzzle out here."

"If he didn't make himself understood," Lord John took leave to laugh, "it must indeed have been an unusual production for Bender."

"Oh, I often, with the wild beauty, if you will, of so many of his turns, haven't a notion," Lady Sandgate confessed with an equal gaiety, "of what he's talking about."

"I think I never miss his weird sense," her younger guest again loyally contended—"and in fact as a general thing I rather like it!"

"I happen to like nothing that I don't enjoy," Lord Theign rejoined with some asperity—"and so far as I do follow the fellow he assumes on my part an interest in his expenditure of purchase-money that I neither feel nor pretend to. He doesn't want—by what I spell out—the picture he refused at Dedborough; he may possibly want—if one reads it so—the picture on view in Bond Street; and he yet appears to make, with great emphasis, the stupid ambiguous point that these two 'articles' (the greatest of Morettos an 'article'!) haven't been 'by now' proved different: as if I engaged with him that I myself would so prove them!"

Lord John indulged in a pause—but also in a suggestion. "He must allude to your hoping—when you allowed us to place the picture with Mackintosh—that it would show to all London in the most precious light conceivable."

"Well, if it hasn't so shown"—and Lord Theign stared as if mystified—"what in the world's the meaning of this preposterous racket?"

"The racket is largely," his young friend explained, "the vociferation of the people who contradict each other about it."

On which their hostess sought to enliven the gravity of the question. "Some—yes—shouting on the housetops that's a Mantovano of the Mantovanos, and others shrieking back at them that they're donkeys if not criminals."

"He may take it for whatever he likes," said Lord Theign, heedless of these contributions, "he may father it on Michael Angelo himself if he'll but clear out with it and let me alone!"

"What he'd *like* to take it for," Lord John at this point saw his way to remark, "is something in the nature of a Hundred Thousand."

"A Hundred Thousand?" cried his astonished friend.

"Quite, I dare say, a Hundred Thousand"—the young man enjoyed clearly handling even by the lips so round a sum.

Lady Sandgate disclaimed however with agility any appearance of having gaped. "Why, haven't you yet realised, Theign, that those are the American figures?"

His lordship looked at her fixedly and then did the same by Lord John, after which he waited a little. "I've nothing to do with the American figures—which seem to me, if you press me, you know, quite intolerably vulgar."

"Well, I'd be as vulgar as anybody for a Hundred Thousand!" Lady Sandgate hastened to proclaim.

"Didn't he let us know at Dedborough," Lord John asked of the master of that seat, "that he had no use, as he said, for lower values?"

"I've heard him remark myself," said their companion, rising to the monstrous memory, "that he wouldn't take a cheap picture—even though a 'handsome' one—as a present."

"And does he call the thing round the corner a cheap picture?" the proprietor of the work demanded.

Lord John threw up his arms with a grin of impatience. "All he wants to do, don't you see? is to prevent your *making* it one!"

Lord Theign glared at this imputation to him of a low ductility. "I offered the thing, as it was, at an estimate worthy of it—and of *me*."

"My dear reckless friend," his young adviser protested, "you named no figure *at all* when it came to the point——!"

"It *didn't* come to the point! Nothing came to the point but that I put a Moretto on view; as a thing, yes, perfectly"—Lord Theign accepted the reminding gesture—"on which a rich American had an eye and in which he had, so to speak, an interest. That was what I wanted, and so we left it—parting each of us ready but neither of us bound."

"Ah, Mr. Bender's bound, as he'd say," Lady Sand-gate interposed—"'bound' to make you swallow the enormous luscious plum that your appetite so morbidly rejects!"

"My appetite, as morbid as you like"—her old friend had shrewdly turned on her—"is my own affair, and if the fellow must deal in enormities I warn him to carry them elsewhere!"

Lord John, plainly, by this time, was quite exasperated at the absurdity of him. "But how can't you see that it's only a plum, as she says, for a plum and an eye for an eye—since the picture itself, with this huge ventilation, is now quite a different affair?"

"How the deuce a different affair when just what the man himself confesses is that, in spite of all the chatter of the prigs and pedants, there's no really established ground for treating it as anything but the same?" On which, as having so unanswerably spoken, Lord Theign shook himself free again, in his high petulance, and moved restlessly to where the passage to the other room appeared to offer his nerves an issue; all moreover to the effect of suggesting to us that something still other than what he had said might meanwhile work in him behind and beneath that quantity. The spectators of his trouble watched him, for the time, in uncertainty and with a mute but associated comment on the perversity and oddity he had so suddenly developed; Lord John giving a shrug of almost bored despair and Lady Sandgate signalling caution and tact for their action by a finger flourished to her lips, and in fact at once proceeding to apply these arts. The subject of her attention had still remained as in worried thought; he had even mechanically taken up a book from a table—which he then, after an absent glance at it, tossed down.

"You're so detached from reality, you adorable dreamer," she began— "and unless you stick to *that* you might as well have done nothing. What you call the pedantry and priggishness and all the rest of it is exactly what poor Breckenridge asked almost on his knees, wonderful man, to be *allowed* to pay you for; since even if the meddlers and chatterers haven't settled anything for those who know—though which of the elect themselves after all *does* seem to know?—it's a great service rendered him to have started such a hare to run!"

Lord John took freedom to throw off very much the same idea. "Certainly his connection with the whole question and agitation makes no end for his glory."

It didn't, that remark, bring their friend back to him, but it at least made his indifference flash with derision. "His 'glory'—Mr. Bender's glory? Why, they quite universally loathe him—judging by the stuff they print!"

"Oh, here—as a corrupter of our morals and a promoter of our decay, even though so many are flat on their faces to him—yes! But it's another affair over there where the eagle screams like a thousand steam-whistles and the newspapers flap like the leaves of the forest: *there* he'll be, if you'll only let him, the biggest thing going; since sound, in that air, seems to mean size, and size to be all that counts. If he said of the thing, as you recognise," Lord John went on, "'It's going to be a Mantovano,' why you can bet your life that it *is*—that it has *got* to be some kind of a one."

His fellow-guest, at this, drew nearer again, irritated, you would have been sure, by the unconscious infelicity of the pair—worked up to something quite openly wilful and passionate. "No kind of a furious flaunting one, under *my* patronage, that I can prevent, my boy! The Dedborough picture in the market—owing to horrid little circumstances that regard myself alone—is the Dedborough picture at a decent, sufficient, civilised Dedborough price, and nothing else whatever; which I beg you will take as my last word on the subject."

Lord John, trying whether he *could* take it, momentarily mingled his hushed state with that of their hostess, to whom he addressed a helpless look; after which, however, he appeared to find that he could only reassert himself. "May I nevertheless reply that I think you'll not be able to prevent *anything?*— since the discussed object will completely escape your control in New York!"

"And almost any discussed object"—Lady Sand-gate rose to the occasion also—"is in New York, by what one hears, easily *worth* a Hundred Thousand!"

Lord Theign looked from one of them to the other. "I sell the man a Hundred Thousand worth of swagger and advertisement; and of fraudulent swagger and objectionable advertisement at that?"

"Well"—Lord John was but briefly baffled—"when the picture's his you can't help its doing what it can and what it will for him anywhere!"

157

"Then it isn't his yet," the elder man retorted—"and I promise you never will be if he has *sent* you to me with his big drum!"

Lady Sandgate turned sadly on this to her associate in patience, as if the case were now really beyond them. "Yes, how indeed can it ever *become* his if Theign simply won't let him pay for it?"

Her question was unanswerable. "It's the first time in all my life I've known a man feel insulted, in such a piece of business, by happening *not* to be, in the usual way, more or less swindled!"

"Theign is unable to take it in," her ladyship explained, "that—as I've heard it said of all these money-monsters of the new type—Bender simply can't *afford* not to be cited and celebrated as the biggest buyer who ever lived."

"Ah, cited and celebrated at my *expense*—say it at once and have it over, that I may enjoy what you all want to do to me!"

"The dear man's inimitable—at his 'expense'!" It was more than Lord John could bear as he fairly flung himself off in his derisive impotence and addressed his wail to Lady Sandgate.

"Yes, at my expense is exactly what I mean," Lord Theign asseverated— "at the expense of my modest claim to regulate my behaviour by my own standards. There you perfectly *are* about the man, and it's precisely what I say—that he's to hustle and harry me *because* he's a money-monster: which I never for a moment dreamed of, please understand, when I let you, John, thrust him at me as a pecuniary resource at Dedborough. I didn't put my property on view that *he* might blow about it————!"

"No, if you like it," Lady Sandgate returned; "but you certainly didn't so arrange"—she seemed to think her point somehow would help—"that you might blow about it yourself!"

"Nobody wants to 'blow,'" Lord John more stoutly interposed, "either hot or cold, I take it; but I really don't see the harm of Bender's liking to be known for the scale of his transactions—actual or merely imputed even, if you will; since that scale is really so magnificent."

Lady Sandgate half accepted, half qualified this plea. "The only question perhaps is why he doesn't try for some precious work that somebody—less delicious than dear Theign—*can* be persuaded on bended knees to accept a hundred thousand for."

"'Try' for one?"—her younger visitor took it up while her elder more attentively watched him. "That was exactly what he did try for when he pressed you so hard in vain for the great Sir Joshua."

"Oh well, he mustn't come back to *that*—must he, Theign?" her ladyship cooed.

That personage failed to reply, so that Lord John went on, unconscious apparently of the still more suspicious study to which he exposed himself. "Besides which there *are* no things of that magnitude knocking about, don't you know?—they've *got* to be worked up first if they're to reach the grand publicity of the Figure! Would you mind," he continued to his noble monitor, "an agreement on some such basis as *this*?—that you shall resign yourself to the biggest equivalent you'll squeamishly consent to take, if it's at the same time the smallest he'll squeamishly consent to offer; but that, that done, you shall leave him free——"

Lady Sandgate took it up straight, rounding it off, as their companion only waited. "Leave him free to talk about the sum offered and the sum taken as practically one and the same?"

"Ah, you know," Lord John discriminated, "he doesn't 'talk' so much himself—there's really nothing blatant or crude about poor Bender. It's the rate at which—by the very way he's 'fixed': an awful way indeed, I grant you!—a perfect army of reporter-wretches, close at his heels, are always talking for him and of him."

Lord Theign spoke hereupon at last with the air as of an impulse that had been slowly gathering force. "*You* talk for him, my dear chap, pretty well. You urge his case, my honour, quite as if you were assured of a commission on the job—on a fine ascending scale! Has he put you up to that proposition, eh? *Do* you get a handsome percentage and *are* you to make a good thing of it?"

159

The young man coloured under this stinging pleasantry—whether from a good conscience affronted or from a bad one made worse; but he otherwise showed a bold front, only bending his eyes a moment on his watch. "As he's to come to you himself—and I don't know why the mischief he doesn't come!—he will answer you that graceful question."

"Will he answer it," Lord Theign asked, "with the veracity that the suggestion you've just made on his behalf represents him as so beautifully adhering to?" On which he again quite fiercely turned his back and recovered his detachment, the others giving way behind him to a blanker dismay.

Lord John, in spite of this however, pumped up a tone. "I don't see why you should speak as if I were urging some abomination."

"Then I'll tell you why!"—and Lord Theign was upon him again for the purpose. "Because I had rather give the cursed thing away outright and for good and all than that it should hang out there another day in the interest of such equivocations!"

Lady Sandgate's dismay yielded to her wonder, and her wonder apparently in turn to her amusement. "'Give it away,' my dear friend, to a man who only longs to smother you in gold?"

Her dear friend, however, had lost patience with her levity. "Give it away—just for a luxury of protest and a stoppage of chatter—to some cause as unlike as possible that of Mr. Bender's power of sound and his splendid reputation: to the Public, to the Authorities, to the Thingumbob, to the Nation!"

Lady Sandgate broke into horror while Lord John stood sombre and stupefied. "Ah, my dear creature, you've flights of extravagance——!"

"One thing's very certain," Lord Theign quite heedlessly pursued—"that the thought of my property on view there does give intolerably on my nerves, more and more every minute that I'm conscious of it; so that, hang it, if one thinks of it, why shouldn't I, for my relief, do again, damme, *what I like?*—that is bang the door in their faces, have the show immediately stopped?" He turned with the attraction of this idea from one of his listeners to the other. "It's *my* show—it isn't Bender's, surely!—and I can do just as I choose with it."

"Ah, but isn't that the very point?"—and Lady Sandgate put it to Lord John. "Isn't it Bender's show much more than his?"

Her invoked authority, however, in answer to this, made but a motion of disappointment and disgust at so much rank folly—while Lord Theign, on the other hand, followed up his happy thought. "Then if it's Bender's show, or if he claims it is, there's all the more reason!" And it took his lordship's inspiration no longer to flower. "See here, John—do this: go right round there this moment, please, and tell them from me to shut straight down!"

"'Shut straight down'?" the young man abhorrently echoed.

"Stop it *to-night*—wind it up and end it: see?" The more the entertainer of that vision held it there the more charm it clearly took on for him. "Have the picture removed from view and the incident closed."

"You seriously ask *that* of me!" poor Lord John quavered.

"Why in the world shouldn't I? It's a jolly lot less than you asked of me a month ago at Dedborough."

"What then am I to say to them?" Lord John spoke but after a long moment, during which he had only looked hard and—an observer might even then have felt—ominously at his taskmaster.

That personage replied as if wholly to have done with the matter. "Say anything that comes into your clever head. I don't really see that there's anything else *for* you!" Lady Sandgate sighed to the messenger, who gave no sign save of positive stiffness.

The latter seemed still to weigh his displeasing obligation; then he eyed his friend significantly—almost portentously. "Those are absolutely your sentiments?"

"Those are absolutely my sentiments"—and Lord Theign brought this out as with the force of a physical push.

"Very well then!" But the young man, indulging in a final, a fairly sinister, study of such a dealer in the arbitrary, made sure of the extent, whatever it was, of his own wrong. "Not one more day?"

Lord Theign only waved him away. "Not one more hour!"

He paused at the door, this reluctant spokesman, as if for some supreme protest; but after another prolonged and decisive engagement with the two pairs of eyes that waited, though differently, on his performance, he clapped on his hat as in the rage of his resentment and departed on his mission.

III

"He can't bear to do it, poor man!" Lady Sand-gate ruefully remarked to her remaining guest after Lord John had, under extreme pressure, dashed out to Bond Street.

"I dare say not!"—Lord Theign, flushed with the felicity of self-expression, made little of that. "But he goes too far, you see, and it clears the air—pouah! Now therefore"—and he glanced at the clock—"I must go to Kitty."

"Kitty—with what Kitty wants," Lady Sandgate opined—"won't thank you for *that!*"

"She never thanks me for anything"—and the fact of his resignation clearly added here to his bitterness. "So it's no great loss!"

"Won't you at any rate," his hostess asked, "wait for Bender?"

His lordship cast it to the winds. "What have I to do with him now?"

"Why surely if he'll accept your own price—!"

Lord Theign thought—he wondered; and then as if fairly amused at himself: "Hanged if I know what *is* my own price!" After which he went for his hat. "But there's one thing," he remembered as he came back with it: "where's my too, *too* unnatural daughter?"

"If you mean Grace and really want her I'll send and find out."

"Not now"—he bethought himself. "But does she *see* that chatterbox?"

"Mr. Crimble? Yes, she sees him."

He kept his eyes on her. "Then how far has it gone?"

Lady Sandgate overcame an embarrassment. "Well, not even yet, I think, so far as they'd like."

"They'd 'like'—heaven save the mark!—to marry?"

"I suspect them of it. What line, if it should come to that," she asked, "would you then take?"

He was perfectly prompt. "The line that for Grace it's simply ignoble."

The force of her deprecation of such language was qualified by tact. "Ah, darling, as dreadful as *that?*"

He could but view the possibility with dark resentment. "It lets us so down—from what we've always been and done; so down, down, down that I'm amazed you don't feel it!"

"Oh, I feel there's still plenty to keep you up!" she soothingly laughed.

He seemed to consider this vague amount—which he apparently judged, however, not so vast as to provide for the whole yearning of his nature. "Well, my dear," he thus more blandly professed, "I shall need all the extra *agrément* that your affection can supply."

If nothing could have been, on this, richer response, nothing could at the same time have bee more pleasing than her modesty. "Ah, my affectionate Theign, is, as I think you know, a fountain always in flood; but in any more worldly element than that—as you've ever seen for yourself—a poor strand with my own sad affairs, a broken reed; not 'great' as they used so finely to call it! You *are*—with the natural sense of greatness and, for supreme support, the instinctive grand man doing and taking things."

He sighed, none the less, he groaned, with his thoughts of trouble, for the strain he foresaw on these resolutions. "If you mean that I hold up my head, on higher grounds, I grant that I always have. But how much longer possible when my children commit such vulgarities? Why in the name of goodness are such children? What the devil has got into them, and is it really the case that when Grace offers as a proof of her license and a specimen of her taste a son-in-law as you tell me I'm in danger of helplessly to swallow the dose?"

"Do you find Mr. Crimble," Lady Sandgate as if there might really be something to say, "so utterly out of the question?"

"I found him on the two occasions before I went away in the last degree offensive and outrageous; but even if he charged one and one's poor dear decent old defences with less rabid a fury everything about him would forbid *that* kind of relation."

What kind of relation, if any, Hugh's deficiencies might still render thinkable Lord Theign was kept from going on to mention by the voice of Mr. Gotch, who had thrown open the door to the not altogether assured sound of "Mr. Breckenridge Bender." The guest in possession gave a cry of impatience, but Lady Sandgate said "Coming up?"

"If his lordship will see him."

"Oh, he's beyond his time," his lordship pronounced—"I can't see him now!"

"Ah, but *mustn't* you—and mayn't *I* then?" She waited, however, for no response to signify to her servant "Let him come," and her companion could but exhale a groan of reluctant accommodation as if he wondered at the point she made of it. It enlightened him indeed perhaps a little that she went on while Gotch did her bidding. "Does the kind of relation you'd be condemned to with Mr. Crimble let you down, down, down, as you say, more than the relation you've been having with Mr. Bender?"

Lord Theign had for it the most uninforming of stares. "Do you mean don't I hate 'em equally both?"

She cut his further reply short, however, by a "Hush!" of warning—Mr. Bender was there and his introducer had left them.

Lord Theign, full of his purpose of departure, sacrificed hereupon little to ceremony. "I've but a moment, to my regret, to give you, Mr. Bender, and if you've been unavoidably detained, as you great bustling people are so apt to be, it will perhaps still be soon enough for your comfort to hear from me that I've just given order to close our exhibition. From the present hour on, sir"—he put it with the firmness required to settle the futility of an appeal.

Mr. Bender's large surprise lost itself, however, promptly enough, in Mr. Bender's larger ease. "Why, do you really mean it, Lord Theign?—removing already from view a work that gives innocent gratification to thousands?"

"Well," said his lordship curtly, "if thousands have seen it I've done what I wanted, and if they've been gratified I'm content—and invite *you* to be."

Mr. Bender showed more keenness for this richer implication. "In other words it's I who may remove the picture?"

"Well—if you'll take it on my estimate."

"But what, Lord Theign, all this time," Mr. Bender almost pathetically pleaded, "*is* your estimate?"

The parting guest had another pause, which prolonged itself, after he had reached the door, in a deep solicitation of their hostess's conscious eyes. This brief passage apparently inspired his answer. "Lady Sandgate will tell you." The door closed behind him.

The charming woman smiled then at her other friend, whose comprehensive presence appeared now to demand of her some account of these strange proceedings. "He means that your own valuation is much too shockingly high."

"But how can I know *how* much unless I find out what he'll take?" The great collector's spirit had, in spite of its volume, clearly not reached its limit of expansion. "Is he crazily waiting for the thing to be proved *not* what Mr. Crimble claims?"

"No, he's waiting for nothing—since he holds that claim demolished by Pappendick's tremendous negative, which you wrote to tell him of."

Vast, undeveloped and suddenly grave, Mr. Bender's countenance showed like a barren tract under a black cloud. "I wrote to *report*, fair and square, on Pap-pendick, but to tell him I'd take the picture just the same, negative and all."

"Ah, but take it in that way not for what it is but for what it isn't."

"We know nothing about what it 'isn't,'" said Mr. Bender, "after all that has happened—we've only learned a little better every day what it is."

"You mean," his companion asked, "the biggest bone of artistic contention——?"

"Yes,"—he took it from her—"the biggest that has been thrown into the arena for quite a while. I guess I can do with it for *that*."

Lady Sandgate, on this, after a moment, renewed her personal advance; it was as if she had now made sure of the soundness of her main bridge. "Well, if it's the biggest bone I won't touch it; I'll leave it to be mauled by my betters. But since his lordship has asked me to name a price, dear Mr. Bender, I'll name one—and as you prefer big prices I'll try to make it suit you. Only it won't be for the portrait of a person nobody is agreed about. The whole world is agreed, you know, about my great-grandmother."

"Oh, shucks, Lady Sandgate!"—and her visitor turned from her with the hunch of overcharged shoulders.

But she apparently felt that she held him, or at least that even if such a conviction might be fatuous she must now put it to the touch. "You've been delivered into my hands—too charmingly; and you won't really pretend that you don't recognise that and in fact rather like it."

He faced about to her again as to a case of coolness unparalleled—though indeed with a quick lapse of real interest in the question of whether he had been artfully practised upon; an indifference to bad debts or peculation like that of some huge hotel or other business involving a margin for waste. He could afford, he could work waste too, clearly—and what was it, that term, you might have felt him ask, but a mean measure, anyway? quite as the "artful," opposed to his larger game, would be the hiding and pouncing of children at play. "Do I gather that those uncanny words of his were just meant to put me off?" he inquired. And then as she but boldly and smilingly shrugged, repudiating responsibility, "Look here, Lady Sandgate, ain't you honestly going to help me?" he pursued.

This engaged her sincerity without affecting her gaiety. "Mr. Bender, Mr. Bender, I'll help you if you'll help *me!*"

"You'll really get me something from him to go on with?"

"I'll get you something from him to go on with."

"That's all I ask—to get *that*. Then I can move the way I want. But without it I'm held up."

"You shall have it," she replied, "if I in turn may look to *you* for a trifle on account."

"Well," he dryly gloomed at her, "what do you call a trifle?"

"I mean"—she waited but an instant—"what you would feel as one."

"That won't do. You haven't the least idea, Lady Sandgate," he earnestly said, "*how* I feel at these foolish times. I've never got used to them yet."

"Ah, don't you understand," she pressed, "that if I give you an advantage I'm completely at your mercy?"

"Well, what mercy," he groaned, "do you deserve?"

She waited a little, brightly composed—then she indicated her inner shrine, the whereabouts of her precious picture. "Go and look at her again and you'll see."

His protest was large, but so, after a moment, was his compliance—his heavy advance upon the other room, from just within the doorway of which the great Lawrence was serenely visible. Mr. Bender gave it his eyes once more—though after the fashion verily of a man for whom it had now no freshness of a glamour, no shade of a secret; then he came back to his hostess. "Do you call giving me an advantage squeezing me by your sweet modesty for less than I may possibly bear?"

"How can I say fairer," she returned, "than that, with my backing about the other picture, which I've passed you my word for, thrown in, I'll resign myself to whatever you may be disposed—characteristically!—to give for this one."

"If it's a question of resignation," said Mr. Bender, "you mean of course what I may be disposed—characteristically!—*not* to give."

She played on him for an instant all her radiance. "Yes then, you dear sharp rich thing!"

"And you take in, I assume," he pursued, "that I'm just going to lean on you, for what I want, with the full weight of a determined man."

"Well," she laughed, "I promise you I'll thoroughly obey the direction of your pressure."

"All right then!" And he stopped before her, in his unrest, monumentally pledged, yet still more massively immeasurable. "How'll you have it?"

She bristled as with all the possible beautiful choices; then she shed her selection as a heaving fruit-tree might have dropped some round ripeness. It was for her friend to pick up his plum and his privilege. "Will you write a cheque?"

"Yes, if you want it right away." To which, however, he added, clapping vainly a breast-pocket: "But my cheque-book's down in my car."

"At the door?" She scarce required his assent to touch a bell. "I can easily send for it." And she threw off while they waited: "It's so sweet your 'flying round' with your cheque-book!"

He put it with promptitude another way. "It flies round pretty well with *Mr*——!"

"Mr. Bender's cheque-book—in his car," she went on to Gotch, who had answered her summons.

The owner of the interesting object further instructed him: "You'll find in the pocket a large red morocco case."

"Very good, sir," said Gotch—but with another word for his mistress. "Lord John would like to know—"

"Lord John's there?" she interrupted.

Gotch turned to the open door. "Here he is, my lady."

She accommodated herself at once, under Mr. Bender's eye, to the complication involved in his lordship's presence. "It's he who went round to Bond Street."

Mr. Bender stared, but saw the connection. "To stop the show?" And then as the young man was already there: "You've stopped the show?"

"It's 'on' more than ever!" Lord John responded while Gotch retired: a hurried, flurried, breathless Lord John, strikingly different from the backward messenger she had lately seen despatched. "But Theign should be here!"—he addressed her excitedly. "I announce you a call from the Prince."

"The Prince?"—she gasped as for the burden of the honour. "He follows you?"

Mr. Bender, with an eagerness and a candour there was no mistaking, recognised on behalf of his ampler action a world of associational advantage and auspicious possibility. "Is the Prince *after* the thing?"

Lord John remained, in spite of this challenge, conscious of nothing but his message. "He was there with Mackintosh—to see and admire the picture; which he thinks, by the way, a Mantovano pure and simple!—and did me the honour to remember me. When he heard me report to Mackintosh in his presence the sentiments expressed to me here by our noble friend and of which, embarrassed though I doubtless was," the young man pursued to Lady Sandgate, "I gave as clear an account as I could, he was so delighted with it that he declared they mustn't think then of taking the thing off, but must on the contrary keep putting it forward for all it's worth, and he would come round and congratulate and thank Theign and explain him his reasons."

Their hostess cast about for a sign. "Why Theign is at Kitty's, worse luck! The Prince calls on him *here?*"

"He calls, you see, on *you*, my lady—at five-forty-five; and graciously desired me so to put it you."

"He's very kind, but"—she took in her condition—"I'm not even *dressed!*"

"You'll have time"—the young man was a comfort—"while I rush to Berkeley Square. And pardon me, Bender—though it's so near—if I just bag your car."

"That's, that's it, take his car!"—Lady Sandgate almost swept him away.

"You may use my car all right," Mr. Bender contributed—"but what I want to know is what the man's *after.*"

"The man? what man?" his friend scarce paused to ask.

"The Prince then—if you allow he *is* a man! Is he after my picture?"

Lord John vividly disclaimed authority. "If you'll wait, my dear fellow, you'll see."

"Oh why should he 'wait'?" burst from their cautious companion—only to be caught up, however, in the next breath, so swift her gracious revolution. "Wait, wait indeed, Mr. Bender—I won't give you up for any Prince!" With which she appealed again to Lord John. "He wants to 'congratulate'?"

"On Theign's decision, as I've told you—which I announced to Mackintosh, by Theign's extraordinary order, under his Highness's nose, and which his Highness, by the same token, took up like a shot."

Her face, as she bethought herself, was convulsed as by some quick perception of what her informant must have done and what therefore the Prince's interest rested on; all, however, to the effect, given their actual company, of her at once dodging and covering that issue. "The decision to remove the picture?"

Lord John also observed a discretion. "He wouldn't hear of such a thing—says it must stay stock still. So there you are!"

This determined in Mr. Bender a not unnatural, in fact quite a clamorous, series of questions. "But *where* are we, and what has the Prince to do with Lord Theign's decision when that's all *I'm* here for? What in thunder *is* Lord Theign's decision—what was his 'extraordinary order'?"

Lord John, too long detained and his hand now on the door, put off this solicitor as he had already been put off. "Lady Sandgate, *you* tell him! I rush!"

Mr. Bender saw him vanish, but all to a greater bewilderment. "What the h—— then (I beg your pardon!) is he talking about, and what 'sentiments' did he report round there that Lord Theign had been expressing?"

His hostess faced it not otherwise than if she had resolved not to recognise the subject of his curiosity—for fear of other recognitions. "They put everything on *me*, my dear man—but I haven't the least idea."

He looked at her askance. "Then why does the fellow say you have?"

Much at a loss for the moment, she yet found her way. "Because the fellow's so agog that he doesn't know *what* he says!" In addition to which she was relieved by the reappearance of Gotch, who bore on a salver the object he had been sent for and to which he duly called attention.

"The large red morocco case."

Lady Sandgate fairly jumped at it. "Your blessed cheque-book. Lay it on my desk," she said to Gotch, though waiting till he had departed again before she resumed to her visitor: "Mightn't we conclude before he comes?"

"The Prince?" Mr. Bender's imagination had strayed from the ground to which she sought to lead it back, and it but vaguely retraced its steps. "Will *he* want your great-grandmother?"

"Well, he may when he sees her!" Lady Sandgate laughed. "And Theign, when he comes, will give you on his own question, I feel sure, every information. Shall I fish it out for you?" she encouragingly asked, beside him by her secretary-desk, at which he had arrived under her persuasive guidance and where she sought solidly to establish him, opening out the gilded crimson case for his employ, so that he had but to help himself. "What enormous cheques! *You* can never draw one for two-pound-ten!"

"That's exactly what you deserve I *should* do!" He remained after this solemnly still, however, like some high-priest circled with ceremonies; in consonance with which, the next moment, both her hands held out to him the open and immaculate page of the oblong series much as they might have presented a royal infant at the christening-font.

He failed, in his preoccupation, to receive it; so she placed it before him on the table, coming away with a brave gay "Well, I leave it to you!" She had not, restlessly revolving, kept her discreet distance for many minutes before she found herself almost face to face with the recurrent Gotch, upright at the door with a fresh announcement.

"Mr. Crimble, please—for Lady Grace."

"Mr. Crimble *again?*"—she took it discomposedly.

It reached Mr. Bender at the secretary, but to a different effect. "Mr. Crimble? Why he's just the man I want to see!"

Gotch, turning to the lobby, had only to make way for him. "Here he is, my lady."

"Then tell her ladyship."

"She has come down," said Gotch while Hugh arrived and his companion withdrew, and while Lady Grace, reaching the scene from the other quarter, emerged in bright equipment—in her hat, scarf and gloves.

IV

These young persons were thus at once confronted across the room, and the girl explained her preparation. "I was listening hard—for your knock and your voice."

"Then know that, thank God, it's all right!"—Hugh was breathless, jubilant, radiant.

"A Mantovano?" she delightedly cried.

"A Mantovano!" he proudly gave back.

"A Mantovano!"—it carried even Lady Sandgate away.

"A Mantovano—a sure thing?" Mr. Bender jumped up from his business, all gaping attention to Hugh.

"I've just left our blest Bardi," said that young man—"who hasn't the shadow of a doubt and is delighted to publish it everywhere."

"Will he publish it right here to *me?*" Mr. Bender hungrily asked.

"Well," Hugh smiled, "you can try him."

"But try him how, where?" The great collector, straining to instant action, cast about for his hat "Where *is* he, hey?"

"Don't you wish I'd tell you?" Hugh, in his personal elation, almost cynically answered.

"Won't you wait for the Prince?" Lady Sandgate had meanwhile asked of her friend; but had turned more inspectingly to Lady Grace before he could reply. "My dear child—though you're lovely!—are you sure you're ready for him?"

"For the Prince!"—the girl was vague. "Is he coming?"

"At five-forty-five." With which she consulted her bracelet watch, but only at once to wail for alarm. "Ah, it *is* that, and I'm not dressed!" She hurried off through the other room.

Mr. Bender, quite accepting her retreat, addressed himself again unabashed to Hugh: "It's your blest Bardi I want first—I'll take the Prince after."

The young man clearly could afford indulgence now. "Then I left him at Long's Hotel."

"Why, right near! I'll come back." And Mr. Bender's flight was on the wings of optimism.

But it all gave Hugh a quick question for Lady Grace. "Why does the Prince come, and what in the world's happening?"

"My father has suddenly returned—it may have to do with that."

The shadow of his surprise darkened visibly to that of his fear. "Mayn't it be more than anything else to give you and me his final curse?"

"I don't know—and I think I don't care. I don't care," she said, "so long as you're right and as the greatest light of all declares you are."

"He *is* the greatest"—Hugh was vividly of that opinion now: "I could see it as soon as I got there with him, the charming creature! There, *before* the holy thing, and with the place, by good luck, for those great moments, practically to ourselves—without Macintosh to take in what was happening or any one else at all to speak of—it was but a matter of ten minutes: he had come, he had seen, and *I* had conquered."

"Naturally you had!"—the girl hung on him for it; "and what was happening beyond everything else was that for your original dear divination, one of the divinations of genius—with every creature all these ages so stupid— you were being baptized on the spot a great man."

"Well, he did let poor Pappendick have it at least-he doesn't think *he's* one: that that eminent judge couldn't, even with such a leg up, rise to my level or seize my point. And if you really want to know," Hugh went on in his gladness, "what for *us* has most particularly and preciously taken place, it is that in his opinion, for my career—"

"Your reputation," she cried, "blazes out and your fortune's made?"

He did a happy violence to his modesty. "Well, Bardi adores intelligence and takes off his hat to me."

"Then you need take off yours to nobody!"—such was Lady Grace's proud opinion. "But I should like to take off mine to *him*," she added; "which I seem to have put on—to get out and away with you—expressly for that."

Hugh, as he looked her over, took it up in bliss. "Ah, we'll go forth together to him then—thanks to your happy, splendid impulse!—and you'll back him gorgeously up in the good he thinks of me."

His friend yet had on this a sombre second thought. "The only thing is that our awful American——!"

But he warned her with a raised hand. "Not to speak of our awful Briton!"

For the door had opened from the lobby, admitting Lord Theign, unattended, who, at sight of his daughter and her companion, pulled up and held them a minute in reprehensive view—all at least till Hugh undauntedly, indeed quite cheerfully, greeted him.

"Since you find me again in your path, my lord, it's because I've a small, but precious document to deliver you, if you'll allow me to do so; which I feel it important myself to place in your hand." He drew from his breast a pocket-book and extracted thence a small unsealed envelope; retaining the latter a trifle helplessly in his hand while Lord Theign only opposed to this demonstration an unmitigated blankness. He went none the less bravely on. "I mentioned to you the last time we somewhat infelicitously met that I intended to appeal to another and probably more closely qualified artistic authority on the subject of your so-called Moretto; and I in fact saw the picture half an hour ago with Bardi of Milan, who, there in presence of it, did absolute, did ideal justice, as I had hoped, to the claim I've been making. I then went with him to his hotel, close at hand, where he dashed me off this brief and rapid, but quite conclusive, Declaration, which, if you'll be so good as to read it, will enable you perhaps to join us in regarding the vexed question as settled."

His lordship, having faced this speech without a sign, rested on the speaker a somewhat more confessed intelligence, then looked hard at the offered note and hard at the floor—all to avert himself actively afterward and, with his head a good deal elevated, add to his distance, as it were, from every one and everything so indelicately thrust on his attention. This movement had an ambiguous makeshift air, yet his companions, under the impression of it, exchanged a hopeless look. His daughter none the less lifted her voice. "If you won't take what he has for you from Mr. Crimble, father, will you take it from me?" And then as after some apparent debate he appeared to decide to heed her, "It may be so long again," she said, "before you've a chance to do a thing I ask."

"The chance will depend on yourself!" he returned with high dry emphasis. But he held out his hand for the note Hugh had given her and with which she approached him; and though face to face they seemed more separated than brought near by this contact without commerce. She turned away on one side when he had taken the missive, as Hugh had turned away on the other; Lord Theign drew forth the contents of the envelope and broodingly and inexpressively read the few lines; after which, as having done justice to their sense, he thrust the paper forth again till his daughter became aware and received it. She restored it to her friend while her father dandled off anew, but coming round this time, almost as by a circuit of the room, and meeting Hugh, who took advantage of it to repeat by a frank gesture his offer of Bardi's attestation. Lord Theign passed with the young man on this a couple of mute minutes of the same order as those he had passed with Lady Grace in the same connection; their eyes dealt deeply with their eyes—but to the effect of his lordship's accepting the gift, which after another minute he had slipped into his breast-pocket. It was not till then that he brought out a curt but resonant "Thank you!" While the others awaited his further pleasure he again bethought himself—then he addressed Lady Grace. "I must let Mr. Bender know——"

"Mr. Bender," Hugh interposed, "does know. He's at the present moment with the author of that note at Long's Hotel."

"Then I must now write him"—and his lordship, while he spoke and from where he stood, looked in refined disconnectedness out of the window.

"Will you write *there?*"—and his daughter indicated Lady Sandgate's desk, at which we have seen Mr. Bender so importantly seated.

Lord Theign had a start at her again speaking to him; but he bent his view on the convenience awaiting him and then, as to have done with so tiresome a matter, took advantage of it. He went and placed himself, and had reached for paper and a pen when, struck apparently with the display of some incongruous object, he uttered a sharp "Hallo!"

"You don't find things?" Lady Grace asked—as remote from him in one quarter of the room as Hugh was in another.

"On the contrary!" he oddly replied. But plainly suppressing any further surprise he committed a few words to paper and put them into an envelope, which he addressed and brought away.

"If you like," said Hugh urbanely, "I'll carry him that myself."

"But how do you know what it consists of?"

"I don't know. But I risk it."

His lordship weighed the proposition in a high impersonal manner—he even nervously weighed his letter, shaking it with one hand upon the finger-tips of the other; after which, as finally to acquit himself of any measurable obligation, he allowed Hugh, by a surrender of the interesting object, to redeem his offer of service. "Then you'll learn," he simply said.

"And may *I* learn?" asked Lady Grace.

"You?" The tone made so light of her that it was barely interrogative.

"May I go *with* him?"

Her father looked at the question as at some cup of supreme bitterness—a nasty and now quite regular dose with which his lips were familiar, but before which their first movement was always tightly to close. "*With* me, my lord," said Hugh at last, thoroughly determined they should open and intensifying the emphasis.

He had his effect, and Lord Theign's answer, addressed to Lady Grace, made indifference very comprehensive. "You may do what ever you dreadfully like!"

At this then the girl, with an air that seemed to present her choice as absolutely taken, reached the door which Hugh had come across to open for her.

Here she paused as for another, a last look at her father, and her expression seemed to say to him unaidedly that, much as she would have preferred to proceed to her act without this gross disorder, she could yet find inspiration too in the very difficulty and the old faiths themselves that he left her to struggle with. All this made for depth and beauty in her serious young face—as it had indeed a force that, not indistinguishably, after an instant, his lordship lost any wish for longer exposure to. His shift of his attitude before she went out was fairly an evasion; if the extent of the levity of one of his daughter's made him afraid, what might have been his present strange sense but a fear of the other from the extent of her gravity? Lady Grace passes from us at any rate in her laced and pearled and plumed slimness and her pale concentration—leaving her friend a moment, however, with his hand on the door.

"You thanked me just now for Bardi's opinion after all," Hugh said with a smile; "and it seems to me that—after all as well—I've grounds for thanking you!" On which he left his benefactor alone.

"Tit for tat!" There broke from Lord Theign, in his solitude, with the young man out of earshot, that vague ironic comment; which only served his turn, none the less, till, bethinking himself, he had gone back to the piece of furniture used for his late scribble and come away from it again the next minute delicately holding a fair slip that we naturally recognise as Mr. Bender's forgotten cheque. This apparently surprising value he now studied at his ease and to the point of its even drawing from him an articulate "What in damnation—?" His speculation dropped before the return of his hostess, whose approach through the other room fell upon his ear and whom he awaited after a quick thrust of the cheque into his waistcoat.

Lady Sandgate appeared now in due—that is in the most happily adjusted—splendour; she had changed her dress for something smarter and more appropriate to the entertainment of Princes, "Tea will be downstairs," she said. "But you're alone?"

"I've just parted," her friend replied, "with Grace and Mr. Crimble."

"'Parted' with them?"—the ambiguity struck her.

"Well, they've gone out together to flaunt their monstrous connection!"

"You speak," she laughed, "as if it were too gross—I They're surely coming back?"

"Back to you, if you like—but not to me."

"Ah, what are you and I," she tenderly argued, "but one and the same quantity? And though you may not as yet absolutely rejoice in—well, whatever they're doing," she cheerfully added, "you'll get beautifully used to it."

"That's just what I'm afraid of—what such horrid matters make of one!"

"At the worst then, you see"—she maintained her optimism—"the recipient of royal attentions!"

"Oh," said her companion, whom his honour seemed to leave comparatively cold, "it's simply as if the gracious Personage were coming to condole!"

Impatient of the lapse of time, in any case, she assured herself again of the hour. "Well, if he only does come!"

"John—the wretch!" Lord Theign returned—"will take care of that: he has nailed him and will bring him."

"What was it then," his friend found occasion in the particular tone of this reference to demand, "what was it that, when you sent him off, John spoke of you in Bond Street as specifically intending?"

Oh he saw it now all lucidly—if not rather luridly—and thereby the more tragically. "He described me in his nasty rage as consistently—well, heroic!"

"His rage"—she pieced it sympathetically out—"at your destroying his cherished credit with Bender?"

Lord Theign was more and more possessed of this view of the manner of it. "I had come between him and some profit that he doesn't confess to, but that made him viciously and vindictively serve me up there, as he caught the chance, to the Prince—and the People!"

She cast about, in her intimate interest, as for some closer conception of it. "By saying that you had remarked here that you offered the People the picture—?"

"As a sacrifice—yes!—to morbid, though respectable scruples." To which he sharply added, as if struck with her easy grasp of the scene: "But I hope you've nothing to call a memory for any such extravagance?"

Lady Sandgate waited—then boldly took her line. "None whatever! You had reacted against Bender—but you hadn't gone so far as *that!*"

He had it now all vividly before him. "I had reacted—like a gentleman; but it didn't thereby follow that I acted—or spoke—like a demagogue; and my mind's a complete blank on the subject of my having done so."

"So that there only flushes through your conscience," she suggested, "the fact that he has forced your hand?"

Fevered with the sore sense of it his lordship wiped his brow. "He has played me, for spite, his damned impertinent trick!"

She found but after a minute—for it wasn't easy—the right word, or the least wrong, for the situation. "Well, even if he did so diabolically commit you, you still don't want—do you?—to back out?"

Resenting the suggestion, which restored all his nobler form, Lord Theign fairly drew himself up. "When did I ever in all my life back out?"

"Never, never in all your life of course!"—she dashed a bucketful at the flare. "And the picture after all——!"

"The picture after all"—he took her up in cold grim gallant despair—"has just been pronounced definitely priceless." And then to meet her gaping ignorance: "By Mr. Crimble's latest and apparently greatest adviser, who strongly stamps it a Mantovano and whose practical affidavit I now possess."

Poor Lady Sandgate gaped but the more—she wondered and yearned. "Definitely priceless?"

"Definitely priceless." After which he took from its place of lurking, considerably unfolding it, the goodly slip he had removed from her blotting-book. "Worth even more therefore than what Bender so blatantly offers."

Her attention fell with interest, from the distance at which she stood, on this confirmatory document, her recognition of which was not immediate. "And is that the affidavit?"

"This is a cheque to your order, my lady, for ten thousand pounds."

"Ten thousand?"—she echoed it with a shout.

"Drawn by some hand unknown," he went on quietly.

"Unknown?"—again, in her muffled joy, she let it sound out.

"Which I found there at your desk a moment ago, and thought best, in your interest, to rescue from accident or neglect; even though it be, save for the single stroke of a name begun," he wound up with his look like a playing searchlight, "unhappily unsigned."

"Unsigned?"—the exhibition of her design, of her defeat, kept shaking her. "Then it isn't good—?"

"It's a Barmecide feast, my dear!"—he had still, her kind friend, his note of grimness and also his penetration of eye. "But who is it writes you colossal cheques?"

"And then leaves them lying about?" Her case was so bad that you would have seen how she felt she must *do* something—something quite splendid. She recovered herself, she faced the situation with all her bright bravery of expression and aspect; conscious, you might have guessed, that she had never more strikingly embodied, on such lines, the elegant, the beautiful and the true. "Why, who can it have been but poor Breckenridge too?"

"'Breckenridge'—?" Lord Theign had *his* smart echoes. "What in the world does he owe you money for?"

It took her but an instant more—she performed the great repudiation quite as she might be prepared to sweep, in the Presence impending, her grandest curtsey. "*Not,* you sweet suspicious thing, for my great-grandmother!" And then as his glare didn't fade: "Bender makes my life a burden—for the love of my precious Lawrence."

"Which you're weakly letting him grab?"—nothing could have been finer with this than Lord Theign's reprobation unless it had been his surprise.

She shook her head as in bland compassion for such an idea. "It isn't a payment, you goose—it's a bribe! I've withstood him, these trying weeks, as a rock the tempest; but he wrote that and left it there, the fiend, to tempt me—to corrupt me!"

"Without putting his name?"—her companion again turned over the cheque.

She bethought herself, clearly with all her genius, as to this anomaly, and the light of reality broke. "He must have been interrupted in the artful act— he sprang up with such a bound at Mr. Crimble's news. At once then—for his interest in it—he hurried off, leaving the cheque forgotten and unfinished."

She smiled more intensely, her eyes attached, as from fascination, to the morsel of paper still handled by her friend. "But of course on his next visit he'll *add* his great signature."

"The devil he will!"—and Lord Theign, with the highest spirit, tore the crisp token into several pieces, which fluttered, as worthless now as pure snowflakes, to the floor.

"Ay, ay, ay!"—it drew from her a wail of which the character, for its sharp inconsequence, was yet comic.

This renewed his stare at her. "Do *you* want to back out? I mean from your noble stand."

As quickly, however, she had saved herself. "I'd rather do even what you're doing—offer my treasure to the Thingumbob!"

He was touched by this even to sympathy. "Will you then *join* me in setting the example of a great donation————?"

"To the What-do-you-call-it?" she extravagantly smiled.

"I call it," he said with dignity, "the 'National Gallery.'"

She closed her eyes as with a failure of breath. "Ah my dear friend—!"

"It would convince me," he went on, insistent and persuasive.

"Of the sincerity of my affection?"—she drew nearer to him.

"It would comfort me"—he was satisfied with his own expression. Yet in a moment, when she had come all rustlingly and fragrantly close, "It would captivate me," he handsomely added.

"It would captivate you?" It was for *her*, we should have seen, to be satisfied with his expression; and, with our more informed observation of all it was a question of her giving up, she would have struck us as subtly bargaining.

183

He gallantly amplified. "It would peculiarly—by which I mean it would so naturally—unite us!"

Well, that was all she wanted. "Then for a complete union with you—of fact as well as of fond fancy!" she smiled—"there's nothing, even to my one ewe lamb, I'm not ready to surrender."

"Ah, we don't surrender," he urged—"we enjoy!"

"Yes," she understood: "with the glory of our grand gift thrown in."

"We quite swagger," he gravely observed—"though even swaggering would after this be dull without you."

"Oh, I'll *swagger* with you!" she cried as if it quite settled and made up for everything; and then impatiently, as she beheld Lord John, whom the door had burst open to admit: "The Prince?"

"The Prince!"—the young man launched it as a call to arms.

They had fallen apart on the irruption, the pair discovered, but she flashed straight at her lover: "Then we can swagger now!"

Lord Theign had reached the open door. "I meet him below."

Demurring, debating, however, she stayed him a moment. "But oughtn't I—in my own house?"

His lordship caught her meaning. "You mean he may think—?" But he as easily pronounced. "He shall think the Truth!" And with a kiss of his hand to her he was gone.

Lord John, who had gazed in some wonder at these demonstrations, was quickly about to follow, but she checked him with an authority she had never before used and which was clearly the next moment to prove irresistible. "Lord John, be so good as to stop." Looking about at the condition of a room on the point of receiving so august a character, she observed on the floor the fragments of the torn cheque, to which she sharply pointed. "And please pick up that litter!"

THE END.

PICTURE AND TEXT

NOTE

Two of the following papers were originally published, with illustrations, in Harper's Magazine and the title of one of them—the first of titles has been altered from "Our Artists in Europe." The other, the article on Mr. Sargent, was accompanied by reproductions of several of his portraits. The notice of Mr. Abbey and that of Mr. Reinhart appeared in Harper's Weekly. That of Mr. Alfred Parsons figured as an introduction to the catalogue of an exhibition of his pictures. The sketch of Daumier was first contributed to *The Century*, and "After the Play" to *The New Review*.

BLACK AND WHITE

If there be nothing new under the sun there are some things a good deal less old than others. The illustration of books, and even more of magazines, may be said to have been born in our time, so far as variety and abundance are the signs of it; or born, at any rate, the comprehensive, ingenious, sympathetic spirit in which we conceive and practise it.

If the centuries are ever arraigned at some bar of justice to answer in regard to what they have given, of good or of bad, to humanity, our interesting age (which certainly is not open to the charge of having stood with its hands in its pockets) might perhaps do worse than put forth the plea of having contributed a fresh interest in "black and white." The claim may now be made with the more confidence from the very evident circumstance that this interest is far from exhausted. These pages are an excellent place for such an assumption. In Harper they have again and again, as it were, illustrated the illustration, and they constitute for the artist a series of invitations, provocations and opportunities. They may be referred to without arrogance in support of the contention that the limits of this large movement, with all its new and rare refinement, are not yet in sight.

I

It is on the contrary the constant extension that is visible, with the attendant circumstances of multiplied experiment and intensified research—circumstances that lately pressed once more on the attention of the writer of these remarks on his finding himself in the particular spot which history will perhaps associate most with the charming revival. A very old English village, lying among its meadows and hedges, in the very heart of the country, in a hollow of the green hills of Worcestershire, is responsible directly and indirectly for some of the most beautiful work in black and white with which I am at liberty to concern myself here; in other words, for much of the work of Mr. Abbey and Mr. Alfred Parsons. I do not mean that Broadway has told these gentlemen all they know (the name, from which the American reader has to brush away an incongruous association, may as well be written first as last); for Mr. Parsons, in particular, who knows everything that can be known about English fields and flowers, would have good reason to insist that the measure of his large landscape art is a large experience. I only suggest that if one loves Broadway and is familiar with it, and if a part of that predilection is that one has seen Mr. Abbey and Mr. Parsons at work there, the pleasant confusion takes place of itself; one's affection for the wide, long, grass-bordered vista of brownish gray cottages, thatched, latticed, mottled, mended, ivied, immemorial, grows with the sense of its having ministered to other minds and transferred itself to other recipients; just as the beauty of many a bit in many a drawing of the artists I have mentioned is enhanced by the sense, or at any rate by the desire, of recognition. Broadway and much of the land about it are in short the perfection of the old English rural tradition, and if they do not underlie all the combinations by which (in their pictorial accompaniments to rediscovered ballads, their vignettes to story or sonnet) these particular talents touch us almost to tears, we feel at least that they *would* have sufficed: they cover the scale.

In regard, however, to the implications and explications of this perfection of a village, primarily and to be just, Broadway is, more than any one else. Mr.

Frank Millet. Mr. Laurence Hutton discovered but Mr. Millet appropriated it: its sweetness was wasted until he began to distil and bottle it. He disinterred the treasure, and with impetuous liberality made us sharers in his fortune. His own work, moreover, betrays him, as well as the gratitude of participants, as I could easily prove if it did not perversely happen that he has commemorated most of his impressions in color. That excludes them from the small space here at my command; otherwise I could testify to the identity of old nooks and old objects, those that constitute both out-of-door and in-door furniture.

In such places as Broadway, and it is part of the charm of them to American eyes, the sky looks down on almost as many "things" as the ceiling, and "things" are the joy of the illustrator. Furnished apartments are useful to the artist, but a furnished country is still more to his purpose. A ripe midland English region is a museum of accessories and specimens, and is sure, under any circumstances, to contain the article wanted. This is the great recommendation of Broadway; everything in it is convertible. Even the passing visitor finds himself becoming so; the place has so much character that it rubs off on him, and if in an old garden—an old garden with old gates and old walls and old summer-houses—he lies down on the old grass (on an immemorial rug, no doubt), it is ten to one but that he will be converted. The little oblong sheaves of blank paper with elastic straps are fluttering all over the place. There is portraiture in the air and composition in the very accidents. Everything is a subject or an effect, a "bit" or a good thing. It is always some kind of day; if it be not one kind it is another. The garden walls, the mossy roofs, the open doorways and brown interiors, the old-fashioned flowers, the bushes in figures, the geese on the green, the patches, the jumbles, the glimpses, the color, the surface, the general complexion of things, have all a value, a reference and an application. If they are a matter of appreciation, that is why the gray-brown houses are perhaps more brown than gray, and more yellow than either. They are various things in turn, according to lights and days and needs. It is a question of color (all consciousness at Broadway is that), but the irresponsible profane are not called upon to settle the tint.

It is delicious to be at Broadway and to *be* one of the irresponsible profane—not to have to draw. The single street is in the grand style, sloping slowly upward to the base of the hills for a mile, but you may enjoy it without a carking care as to how to "render" the perspective. Everything is stone except the general greenness—a charming smooth local stone, which looks as if it had been meant for great constructions and appears even in dry weather to have been washed and varnished by the rain. Half-way up the road, in the widest place, where the coaches used to turn (there were many of old, but the traffic of Broadway was blown to pieces by steam, though the destroyer has not come nearer than half a dozen miles), a great gabled mansion, which was once a manor or a house of state, and is now a rambling inn, stands looking at a detached swinging sign which is almost as big as itself—a very grand sign, the "arms" of an old family, on the top of a very tall post. You will find something very like the place among Mr. Abbey's delightful illustrations to, "She Stoops to Conquer." When the September day grows dim and some of the windows glow, you may look out, if you like, for Tony Lumpkin's red coat in the doorway or imagine Miss Hardcastle's quilted petticoat on the stair.

II

It is characteristic of Mr. Frank Millet's checkered career, with opposites so much mingled in it, that such work as he has done for Harper should have had as little in common as possible with midland English scenery. He has been less a producer in black and white than a promoter and, as I may say, a protector of such production in others; but none the less the back volumes of Harper testify to the activity of his pencil as well as to the variety of his interests. There was a time when he drew little else but Cossacks and Orientals, and drew them as one who had good cause to be vivid. Of the young generation he was the first to know the Russian plastically, especially the Russian soldier, and he had paid heavily for his acquaintance. During the Russo-Turkish war he was correspondent in the field (with the victors) of the New York *Herald* and the London *Daily News*—a capacity in which he made many out-of-the-way, many precious, observations. He has seen strange countries—the East and the South and the West and the North—and practised many arts. To the London *Graphic*, in 1877 he sent striking sketches from the East, as well as capital prose to the journals I have mentioned. He has always been as capable of writing a text for his own sketches as of making sketches for the text of others. He has made pictures without words and words without pictures. He has written some very clever ghost-stories, and drawn and painted some very immediate realities. He has lately given himself up to these latter objects, and discovered that they have mysteries more absorbing than any others. I find in Harper, in 1885. "A Wild-goose Chase" through North Germany and Denmark, in which both pencil and pen are Mr. Millet's, and both show the natural and the trained observer.

He knows the art-schools of the Continent, the studios of Paris, the "dodges" of Antwerp, the subjects, the models of Venice, and has had much æsthetic as well as much personal experience. He has draped and distributed Greek plays at Harvard, as well as ridden over Balkans to post pressing letters, and given publicity to English villages in which susceptible Americans may get the strongest sensations with the least trouble to themselves. If the trouble in each case will have been largely his, this is but congruous with the fact that he has not only found time to have a great deal of history himself, but has suffered himself to be converted by others into an element—beneficent I should call it if discretion did not forbid me—of *their* history. Springing from a very old New England stock, he has found the practice of art a wonderful antidote, in his own language, "for belated Puritanism." He is very modern, in the sense of having tried many things and availed himself of all of the facilities of his time; but especially on this ground of having fought out for himself the battle of the Puritan habit and the æsthetic experiment. His experiment was admirably successful from the moment that the Puritan levity was forced to consent to its becoming a serious one. In other words, if Mr. Millet is artistically interesting to-day (and to the author of these remarks he is highly so), it is because he is a striking example of what the typical American quality can achieve.

He began by having an excellent pencil, because as a thoroughly practical man he could not possibly have had a weak one. But nothing is more remunerative to follow than the stages by which "faculty" in general (which is what I mean by the characteristic American quality) has become the particular faculty; so that if in the artist's present work one recognizes—recognizes even fondly—the national handiness, it is as handiness regenerate and transfigured. The American adaptiveness has become a Dutch finish. The only criticism I have to make is of the preordained paucity of Mr. Millet's drawings; for my mission is not to speak of his work in oils, every year more important (as was indicated by the brilliant interior with figures that greeted the spectator in so friendly a fashion on the threshold of the Royal Academy exhibition of 1888), nor to say that it is illustration too—illustration of any old-fashioned song or story that hums in the brain or haunts the memory—nor even to hint that the admirable rendering of the charming old objects with which it deals (among which I include the human face and figure in dresses unfolded from the lavender of the past), the old surfaces and tones, the stuffs and textures, the old mahogany and silver and brass—the old sentiment too, and the old picture-making vision—are in the direct tradition of Terburg and De Hoogh and Metzu.

III

There is no paucity about Mr. Abbey as a virtuoso in black and white, and if one thing more than another sets the seal upon the quality of his work, it is the rare abundance in which it is produced. It is not a frequent thing to find combinations infinite as well as exquisite. Mr. Abbey has so many ideas, and the gates of composition have been opened so wide to him, that we cultivate his company with a mixture of confidence and excitement. The readers of Harper have had for years a great deal of it, and they will easily recognize the feeling I allude to—the expectation of familiarity in variety. The beautiful art and taste, the admirable execution, strike the hour with the same note; but the figure, the scene, is ever a fresh conception. Never was ripe skill less mechanical, and never was the faculty of perpetual evocation less addicted to prudent economies. Mr. Abbey never saves for the next picture, yet the next picture will be as expensive as the last. His whole career has been open to the readers of Harper, so that what they may enjoy on any particular occasion is not only the talent, but a kind of affectionate sense of the history of the talent, That history is, from the beginning, in these pages, and it is one of the most interesting and instructive, just as the talent is one of the richest and the most sympathetic in the art-annals of our generation. I may as well frankly declare that I have such a taste for Mr. Abbey's work that I cannot affect a judicial tone about it. Criticism is appreciation or it is nothing, and an intelligence of the matter in hand is recorded more substantially in a single positive sign of such appreciation than in a volume of sapient objections for objection's sake—the cheapest of all literary commodities. Silence is the perfection of disapproval, and it has the great merit of leaving the value of speech, when the moment comes for it, unimpaired.

Accordingly it is important to translate as adequately as possible the positive side of Mr. Abbey's activity. None to-day is more charming, and none helps us more to take the large, joyous, observant, various view of the business of art. He has enlarged the idea of illustration, and he plays with it in a hundred spontaneous, ingenious ways. "Truth and poetry" is the motto legibly stamped upon his pencil-case, for if he has on the one side a singular sense of the familiar, salient, importunate facts of life, on the other they reproduce themselves in his mind in a delightfully qualifying medium. It is this medium that the fond observer must especially envy Mr. Abbey, and that a literary observer will envy him most of all.

Such a hapless personage, who may have spent hours in trying to produce something of the same result by sadly different means, will measure the difference between the roundabout, faint descriptive tokens of respectable prose and the immediate projection of the figure by the pencil. A charming story-teller indeed he would be who should write as Mr. Abbey draws. However, what is style for one art is style for other, so blessed is the fraternity that binds them together, and the worker in words may take a lesson from the picture-maker of "She Stoops to Conquer." It is true that what the verbal artist would like to do would be to find out the secret of the pictorial, to drink at the same fountain. Mr. Abbey is essentially one of those who would tell us if he could, and conduct us to the magic spring; but here he is in the nature of the case helpless, for the happy *ambiente* as the Italians call it, in which his creations move is exactly the thing, as I take it, that he can least give an account of. It is a matter of genius and imagination—one of those things that a man determines for himself as little as he determines the color of his eyes. How, for instance, can Mr. Abbey explain the manner in which he directly *observes* figures, scenes, places, that exist only in the fairy-land of his fancy? For the peculiar sign of his talent is surely this observation in the remote. It brings the remote near to us, but such a complicated journey as it must first have had to make! Remote in time (in differing degrees), remote in place, remote in feeling, in habit, and in their ambient air, are the images that spring from his pencil, and yet all so vividly, so minutely, so consistently seen! Where does he see them, where does he find them, how does he catch them, and in what language does he delightfully converse with them? In what mystic recesses of space does the revelation descend upon him?

The questions flow from the beguiled but puzzled admirer, and their tenor sufficiently expresses the claim I make for the admirable artist when I say that his truth is interfused with poetry. He spurns the literal and yet superabounds in the characteristic, and if he makes the strange familiar he makes the familiar just strange enough to be distinguished. Everything is so human, so humorous and so caught in the act, so buttoned and petticoated and gartered, that it might be round the corner; and so it is—but the corner is the corner of another world. In that other world Mr. Abbey went forth to dwell in extreme youth, as I need scarcely be at pains to remind those who have followed him in Harper. It is not important here to give a catalogue of his contributions to that journal: turn to the back volumes and you will meet him at every step. Every one remembers his young, tentative, prelusive illustrations to Herrick, in which there are the prettiest glimpses, guesses and foreknowledge of the effects he was to make completely his own. The Herrick was done mainly, if I mistake not, before he had been to England, and it remains, in the light of this fact, a singularly touching as well as a singularly promising performance. The eye of sense in such a case had to be to a rare extent the mind's eye, and this convertibility of the two organs has persisted.

From the first and always that other world and that qualifying medium in which I have said that the human spectacle goes on for Mr. Abbey have been a county of old England which is not to be found in any geography, though it borders, as I have hinted, on the Worcestershire Broadway. Few artistic phenomena are more curious than the congenital acquaintance of this perverse young Philadelphian with that mysterious locality. It is there that he finds them all—the nooks, the corners, the people, the clothes, the arbors and gardens and teahouses, the queer courts of old inns, the sun-warmed angles of old parapets. I ought to have mentioned for completeness, in addition to his pictures to Goldsmith and to the scraps of homely British song (this latter class has contained some of his most exquisite work), his delicate drawing's for Mr. William Black's *Judith Shakespeare*. And in relation to that distinguished name—I don't mean Mr. Black's—it is a comfort, if I may be allowed the expression, to know that (as, to the best of my belief, I violate no confidence in saying) he is even now engaged in the great work of illustrating the comedies. He is busy with "The Merchant of Venice;" he is up to his neck in studies, in rehearsals. Here again, while in prevision I admire the result, what I can least refrain from expressing is a sort of envy of the process, knowing what it is with Mr. Abbey and what explorations of the delightful it entails—arduous, indefatigable, till the end seems almost smothered in the means (such material complications they engender), but making one's daily task a thing of beauty and honor and beneficence.

IV

Even if Mr. Alfred Parsons were not a masterly contributor to the pages of Harper, it would still be almost inevitable to speak of him after speaking of Mr. Abbey, for the definite reason (I hope that in giving it I may not appear to invade too grossly the domain of private life) that these gentlemen are united in domestic circumstance as well as associated in the nature of their work. In London, in the relatively lucid air of Campden Hill, they dwell together, and their beautiful studios are side by side. However, there is a reason for commemorating Mr. Parsons' work which has nothing to do with the accidental—the simple fact that that work forms the richest illustration of the English landscape that is offered us to-day. Harper has for a long time past been full of Mr. Alfred Parsons, who has made the dense, fine detail of his native land familiar in far countries, amid scenery of a very different type. This is what the modern illustration can do when the ripeness of the modern sense is brought to it and the wood-cutter plays with difficulties as the brilliant Americans do to-day, following his original at a breakneck pace. An illusion is produced which, in its very completeness, makes one cast an uneasy eye over the dwindling fields that are still left to conquer. Such art as Alfred Parsons'— such an accomplished translation of local aspects, translated in its turn by cunning hands and diffused by a wonderful system of periodicity through vast and remote communities, has, I confess, in a peculiar degree, the effect that so many things have in this age of multiplication—that of suppressing intervals and differences and making the globe seem alarmingly small. Vivid and repeated evocations of English rural things—the meadows and lanes, the sedgy streams, the old orchards and timbered houses, the stout, individual, insular trees, the flowers under the hedge and in it and over it, the sweet rich country seen from the slope, the bend of the unformidable river, the actual romance of the castle against the sky, the place on the hill-side where the gray church begins to peep (a peaceful little grassy path leads up to it over a stile)—all this brings about a terrible displacement of the very objects that make pilgrimage a passion, and hurries forward that ambiguous advantage which I don't envy our grandchildren, that of knowing all about everything in advance, having trotted round the globe annually in the magazines and lost the bloom of personal experience. It is a part of the general abolition of mystery with which we are all so complacently busy today. One would like to retire to another planet with a box of Mr. Parsons' drawings, and be homesick there for the pleasant places they commemorate.

There are many things to be said about his talent, some of which are not the easiest in the world to express. I shall not, however, make them more difficult by attempting to catalogue his contributions in these pages. A turning of the leaves of Harper brings one constantly face to face with him, and a systematic search speedily makes one intimate. The reader will remember the beautiful Illustrations to Mr. Blackmore's novel of *Springhaven*, which were interspersed with striking figure-pieces from the pencil of that very peculiar pictorial humorist Mr. Frederick Barnard, who, allowing for the fact that he always seems a little too much to be drawing for Dickens and that the footlights are the illumination of his scenic world, has so remarkable a sense of English types and attitudes, costumes and accessories, in what may be called the great-coat-and-gaiters period—the period when people were stiff with riding and wicked conspiracies went forward in sanded provincial inn-parlors. Mr. Alfred Parsons, who is still conveniently young, waked to his first vision of pleasant material in the comprehensive county of Somerset—a capital centre of impression for a painter of the bucolic. He has been to America; he has even reproduced with remarkable discrimination and truth some of the way-side objects of that country, not making them look in the least like their English equivalents, if equivalents they may be said to have. Was it there that Mr. Parsons learned so well how Americans would like England to appear? I ask this idle question simply because the England of his pencil, and not less of his brush (of his eminent brush there would be much to say), is exactly the England that the American imagination, restricted to itself, constructs from the poets, the novelists, from all the delightful testimony it inherits. It was scarcely to have been supposed possible that the native point of view would embrace and observe so many of the things that the more or less famished outsider is, in vulgar parlance, "after." In other words (though I appear to utter a foolish paradox), the danger might have been that Mr. Parsons knew his subject too well to feel it—to feel it, I mean, *à l'Américaine*. He is as tender of it as if he were vague about it, and as certain of it as if he were *blasé*.

But after having wished that his country should be just so, we proceed to discover that it is in fact not a bit different. Between these phases of our consciousness he is an unfailing messenger. The reader will remember how often he has accompanied with pictures the text of some amiable paper describing a pastoral region—Warwickshire or Surrey. Devonshire or the Thames. He will remember his exquisite designs for certain of Wordsworth's sonnets. A sonnet of Wordsworth is a difficult thing to illustrate, but Mr. Parsons' ripe taste has shown him the way. Then there are lovely morsels from his hand associated with the drawings of his friend Mr. Abbey—head-pieces, tailpieces, vignettes, charming combinations of flower and foliage, decorative clusters of all sorts of pleasant rural emblems. If he has an inexhaustible feeling for the country in general, his love of the myriad English flowers is perhaps the fondest part of it. He draws them with a rare perfection, and always—little definite, delicate, tremulous things as they are—with a certain nobleness. This latter quality, indeed. I am prone to find in all his work, and I should insist on it still more if I might refer to his important paintings. So composite are the parts of which any distinguished talent is made up that we have to feel our way as we enumerate them; and yet that very ambiguity is a challenge to analysis and to characterization. This "nobleness" on Mr. Parsons' part is the element of style—something large and manly, expressive of the total character of his facts. His landscape is the landscape of the male vision, and yet his touch is full of sentiment, of curiosity and endearment. These things, and others besides, make him the most interesting, the most living, of the new workers in his line. And what shall I say of the other things besides? How can I take precautions enough to say that among the new workers, deeply English as he is, there is comparatively something French in his manner? Many people will like him because they see in him—or they think they do—a certain happy mean. Will they not fancy they catch him taking the middle way between the unsociable French *étude* and the old-fashioned English "picture"? If one of these extremes is a desert, the other, no doubt, is an oasis still more vain. I have a recollection of productions of Mr. Alfred Parsons' which might have come from a Frenchman who was in love with English river-sides. I call to mind no studies—if he has made any—of French scenery; but if I did they would doubtless appear English enough. It is the fashion among sundry to maintain that the English landscape is of no use for *la peinture sérieuse*, that it is wanting in technical accent and is in general too storytelling, too self-conscious and dramatic also too lumpish and stodgy, of a green—*d'un vert bête*—which, when reproduced, looks like that of the chromo. Certain it is that there are many hands which are not to be trusted with it, and taste and integrity have been known to go down before it. But Alfred Parsons may be pointed to as one who has made the luxuriant and lovable things of his own country almost as "serious" as those familiar objects—the pasture and the poplar—which, even when infinitely repeated by the great school across the Channel, strike us as but meagre morsels of France.

V

In speaking of Mr. George H. Boughton, A.R.A., I encounter the same difficulty as with Mr. Millet: I find the window closed through which alone almost it is just to take a view of his talent. Mr. Boughton is a painter about whom there is little that is new to tell to-day, so conspicuous and incontestable is his achievement, the fruit of a career of which the beginning was not yesterday. He is a draughtsman and an illustrator only on occasion and by accident. These accidents have mostly occurred, however, in the pages of Harper, and the happiest of them will still be fresh in the memory of its readers. In the *Sketching Rambles in Holland* Mr. Abbey was a participant (as witness, among many things, the admirable drawing of the old Frisian woman bent over her Bible in church, with the heads of the burghers just visible above the rough archaic pew-tops—a drawing opposite to page 112 in the handsome volume into which these contributions were eventually gathered together); but most of the sketches were Mr. Boughton's, and the charming, amusing text is altogether his, save in the sense that it commemorates his companion's impressions as well as his own—the delightful, irresponsible, visual, sensual, pictorial, capricious impressions of a painter in a strange land, the person surely whom at particular moments one would give most to be. If there be anything happier than the impressions of a painter, it is the impressions of two, and the combination is set forth with uncommon spirit and humor in this frank record of the innocent lust of the eyes. Mr. Boughton scruples little, in general, to write as well as to draw, when the fancy takes him; to write in the manner of painters, with the bold, irreverent, unconventional, successful brush. If I were not afraid of the patronizing tone I would say that there is little doubt that if as a painter he had not had to try to write in character, he would certainly have made a characteristic writer. He has the most enviable "finds," not dreamed of in timid literature, yet making capital descriptive prose. Other specimens of them may be encountered in two or three Christmas tales, signed with the name whose usual place is the corner of a valuable canvas.

If Mr. Boughton is in this manner not a simple talent, further complications and reversions may be observed in him, as, for instance, that having reverted from America, where he spent his early years, back to England, the land of his origin, he has now in a sense oscillated again from the latter to the former country. He came to London one day years ago (from Paris, where he had been eating nutritively of the tree of artistic knowledge), in order to re-embark on the morrow for the United States; but that morrow never came—it has never come yet. Certainly now it never *can* come, for the country that Mr. Boughton left behind him in his youth is no longer there; the "old New York" is no longer a port to sail to, unless for phantom ships. In imagination, however, the author of "The Return of the *Mayflower*" has several times taken his way back; he has painted with conspicuous charm and success various episodes of the early Puritan story. He was able on occasion to remember vividly enough the low New England coast and the thin New England air. He has been perceptibly an inventor, calling into being certain types of face and dress, certain tones and associations of color (all in the line of what I should call subdued harmonies if I were not afraid of appearing to talk a jargon), which people are hungry for when they acquire "a Boughton," and which they can obtain on no other terms. This pictorial element in which he moves is made up of divers delicate things, and there would be a roughness in attempting to unravel the tapestry. There is old English, and old American, and old Dutch in it, and a friendly, unexpected new Dutch too—an ingredient of New Amsterdam—a strain of Knickerbocker and of Washington Irving. There is an admirable infusion of landscape in it, from which some people regret that Mr. Boughton should ever have allowed himself to be distracted by his importunate love of sad-faced, pretty women in close-fitting coifs and old silver-clasped cloaks. And indeed, though his figures are very "tender," his landscape is to my sense tenderer still. Moreover, Mr. Boughton bristles, not aggressively, but in the degree of a certain conciliatory pertinacity, with contradictious properties. He lives in one of the prettiest and most hospitable houses in London, but the note of his work is the melancholy of rural things, of lonely people and of quaint, far-off legend and refrain. There is a delightful ambiguity of period and even of clime in him, and he rejoices in that inability to depict the modern which is the most convincing sign of the contemporary.

He has a genius for landscape, yet he abounds in knowledge of every sort of ancient fashion of garment; the buckles and button-holes, the very shoe-ties, of the past are dear to him. It is almost always autumn or winter in his pictures. His horizons are cold, his trees are bare (he does the bare tree beautifully), and his draperies lined with fur; but when he exhibits himself directly, as in the fantastic "Rambles" before mentioned, contagious high spirits are the clearest of his showing. Here he appears as an irrepressible felicitous sketcher, and I know no pleasanter record of the joys of sketching, or even of those of simply looking. Théophile Gautier himself was not more inveterately addicted to this latter wanton exercise. There ought to be a pocket edition of Mr. Boughton's book, which would serve for travellers in other countries too, give them the point of view and put them in the mood. Such a blessing, and such a distinction too, is it to have an eye. Mr. Boughton's, in his good-humored Dutch wanderings, holds from morning till night a sociable, graceful revel. From the moment it opens till the moment it closes, its day is a round of adventures. His jolly pictorial narrative, reflecting every glint of October sunshine and patch of russet shade, tends to confirm us afresh in the faith that the painter's life is the best life, the life that misses fewest impressions.

VI

Mr. Du Maurier has a brilliant history, but it must be candidly recognized that it is written or drawn mainly in an English periodical. It is only during the last two or three years that the most ironical of the artists of *Punch* has exerted himself for the entertainment of the readers of Harper; but I seem to come too late with any commentary on the nature of his satire or the charm of his execution. When he began to appear in Harper he was already an old friend, and for myself I confess I have to go through rather a complicated mental operation to put into words what I think of him. What does a man think of the language he has learned to speak? He judges it only while he is learning. Mr. Du Maurier's work, in regard to the life it embodies, is not so much a thing we see as one of the conditions of seeing. He has interpreted for us for so many years the social life of England that the interpretation has become the text itself. We have accepted his types, his categories, his conclusions, his sympathies and his ironies, It is not given to all the world to thread the mazes of London society, and for the great body of the disinherited, the vast majority of the Anglo-Saxon public. Mr. Du Maurier's representation is the thing represented. Is the effect of it to nip in the bud any remote yearning for personal participation? I feel tempted to say yes, when I think of the follies, the flatnesses, the affectations and stupidities that his teeming pencil has made vivid. But that vision immediately merges itself in another—a panorama of tall, pleasant, beautiful people, placed in becoming attitudes, in charming gardens, in luxurious rooms, so that I can scarcely tell which is the more definite, the impression satiric or the impression plastic.

This I take to be a sign that Mr. Du Maurier knows how to be general and has a conception of completeness. The world amuses him, such queer things go on in it; but the part that amuses him most is certain lines of our personal structure. That amusement is the brightest; the other is often sad enough. A sharp critic might accuse Mr. Du Maurier of lingering too complacently on the lines in question; of having a certain ideal of "lissome" elongation to which the promiscuous truth is sometimes sacrificed. But in fact this artist's P truth never pretends to be promiscuous; it is avowedly select and specific. What he depicts is so preponderantly the "tapering" people that the remainder of the picture, in a notice as brief as the present, may be neglected. If his *dramatis personæ* are not all the tenants of drawing-rooms, they are represented at least in some relation to these. 'Arry and his friends at the fancy fair are in society for the time; the point of introducing them is to show how the contrast intensifies them. Of late years Mr. Du Maurier has perhaps been a little too docile to the muse of elegance; the idiosyncrasies of the "masher" and the high girl with elbows have beguiled him into occasional inattention to the doings of the short and shabby. But his career has been long and rich, and I allude, in such words, but to a moment of it.

The moral of it—I refer to the artistic one—seen altogether, is striking and edifying enough. What Mr. Du Maurier has attempted to do is to give, in a thousand interrelated drawings, a general satiric picture of the social life of his time and country. It is easy to see that through them "an increasing purpose runs;" they all hang together and refer to each other—complete, confirm, correct, illuminate each other. Sometimes they are not satiric: satire is not pure charm, and the artist has allowed himself to "go in" for pure charm. Sometimes he has allowed himself to go in for pure fantasy, so that satire (which should hold on to the mane of the real) slides off the other side of the runaway horse. But he remains, on the whole, pencil in hand, a wonderfully copious and veracious historian of his age and his civilization.

VII

I have left Mr. Reinhart to the last because of his importance, and now this very importance operates as a restriction and even as a sort of reproach to me. To go well round him at a deliberate pace would take a whole book. With Mr. Abbey, Mr. Reinhart is the artist who has contributed most abundantly to Harper; his work, indeed, in quantity, considerably exceeds Mr. Abbey's. He is the observer of the immediate, as Mr. Abbey is that of the considerably removed, and the conditions he asks us to accept are less expensive to the imagination than those of his colleague. He is, in short, the vigorous, racy *prosateur* of that human comedy of which Mr. Abbey is the poet. He illustrates the modern sketch of travel, the modern tale—the poor little "quiet," psychological, conversational modern tale, which I often think the artist invited to represent it to the eye must hate, unless he be a very intelligent master, little, on a superficial view, would there appear to be in it to represent. The superficial view is, after all, the natural one for the picture-maker. A talent of the first order, however, only wants to be set thinking, as a single word will often make it. Mr. Reinhart at any rate, triumphs; whether there be life or not in the little tale itself, there is unmistakable life in his version of it. Mr. Reinhart deals in that element purely with admirable frankness and vigor. He is not so much suggestive as positively and sharply representative. His facility, his agility, his universality are a truly stimulating sight. He asks not too many questions of his subject, but to those he does ask he insists upon a thoroughly intelligible answer. By his universality I mean perhaps as much as anything else his admirable drawing; not precious, as the æsthetic say, nor pottering, as the vulgar, but free, strong and secure, which enables him to do with the human figure at a moment's notice anything that any occasion may demand. It gives him an immense range, and I know not how to express (it is not easy) my sense of a certain capable indifference that is in him otherwise than by saying that he would quite as soon do one thing as another.

For it is true that the admirer of his work rather misses in him that intimation of a secret preference which many strong draughtsmen show, and which is not absent, for instance (I don't mean the secret, but the intimation), from the beautiful doings of Mr. Abbey. It is extremely present in Mr. Du Maurier's work, just as it was visible, less elusively, in that of John Leech, his predecessor in *Punch*. Mr. Abbey has a haunting type; Du Maurier has a haunting type. There was little perhaps of the haunted about Leech, but we know very well how he wanted his pretty girls, his British swell, and his "hunting men" to look. He betrayed a predilection; he had his little ideal. That an artist may be a great force and not have a little ideal, the scarcely too much to be praised Charles Keene is there (I mean he is in *Punch*) to show us. He has not a haunting type—not he—and I think that no one has yet discovered how he would have liked his pretty girls to look. He has kept the soft conception too much to himself—he has not trifled with the common truth by letting it appear. This common truth, in its innumerable combinations, is what Mr. Rein-hart also shows us (with of course infinitely less of a *parti pris* of laughing at it), though, as I must hasten to add, the female face and form in his hands always happen to take on a much lovelier cast than in Mr. Keene's. These things with him, however, are not a private predilection, an artist's dream. Mr. Reinhart is solidly an artist, but I doubt whether as yet he dreams, and the absence of private predilections makes him seem a little hard. He is sometimes rough with our average humanity, and especially rough with the feminine portion of it. He usually represents American life, in which that portion is often spoken of as showing to peculiar advantage. But Mr. Reinhart sees it generally, as very *bourgeois*. His good ladies are apt to be rather thick and short, rather huddled and plain. I shouldn't mind it so much if they didn't look so much alive. They are incontestably possible. The long, brilliant series of drawings he made to accompany Mr. Charles Dudley Warner's papers on the American watering-places form a rich *bourgeois* epic, which imaginations haunted by a type must accept with philosophy, for the sketches in question will have carried the tale, and all sorts of irresistible illusion with it, to the four corners of the earth. Full of observation and reality, of happy impressionism, taking all things as they come, with many a charming picture of youthful juxtaposition, they give us a sense, to which nothing need be added, of the energy of Mr. Reinhart's pencil. They are a final collection of pictorial notes on the manners and customs, the aspects and habitats, in July and August, of the great American democracy; of which, certainly, taking one thing with another, they give a very comfortable, cheerful account. But they confirm that analytic view of which I have ventured to give a hint—the view of Mr. Reinhart as an artist of immense capacity who yet somehow doesn't care. I must add that this aspect of him is modified, in the one case very gracefully, in the other by the operation of a sort of constructive humor, remarkably strong, in his illustrations of Spanish life and his sketches of the Berlin political world.

His fashion of remaining outside, as it were, makes him (to the analyst) only the more interesting, for the analyst, if he have any critical life in him, will be prone to wonder *why* he doesn't care, and whether matters may not be turned about in such a way as that he should, with the consequence that his large capacity would become more fruitful still. Mr. Reinhart is open to the large appeal of Paris, where he lives—as is evident from much of his work—where he paints, and where, in crowded exhibitions, reputation and honors have descended upon him. And yet Paris, for all she may have taught him, has not given him the mystic sentiment—about which I am perhaps writing nonsense. Is it nonsense to say that, being very much an incarnation of the modern international spirit (he might be a Frenchman in New York were he not an American in Paris), the moral of his work is possibly the inevitable want of finality, of intrinsic character, in that sweet freedom? Does the cosmopolite necessarily pay for his freedom by a want of function—the impersonality of not being representative? Must one be a little narrow to have a sentiment, and very local to have a quality, or at least a style; and would the missing type, if I may mention it yet again, haunt our artist—who is somehow, in his rare instrumental facility, outside of quality and style—a good deal more if he were not, amid the mixture of associations and the confusion of races, liable to fall into vagueness as to what types are? He can do anything he likes; by which I mean he can do wonderfully even the things he doesn't like. But he strikes me as a force not yet fully used.

EDWIN A. ABBE

Nothing is more interesting in the history of an artistic talent than the moment at which its "elective affinity" declares itself, and the interest is great in proportion as the declaration is unmistakable. I mean by the elective affinity of a talent its climate and period of preference, the spot on the globe or in the annals of mankind to which it most fondly attaches itself, to which it reverts incorrigibly, round which it revolves with a curiosity that is insatiable, from which in short it draws its strongest inspiration. A man may personally inhabit a certain place at a certain time, but in imagination he may be a perpetual absentee, and to a degree worse than the worst Irish landlord, separating himself from his legal inheritance not only by mountains and seas, but by centuries as well. When he is a man of genius these perverse predilections become fruitful and constitute a new and independent life, and they are indeed to a certain extent the sign and concomitant of genius. I do not mean by this that high ability would always rather have been born in another country and another age, but certainly it likes to choose, it seldom fails to react against imposed conditions. If it accepts them it does so because it likes them for themselves; and if they fail to commend themselves it rarely scruples to fly away in search of others. We have witnessed this flight in many a case; I admit that if we have sometimes applauded it we have felt at other moments that the discontented, undomiciled spirit had better have stayed at home.

Mr. Abbey has gone afield, and there could be no better instance of a successful fugitive and a genuine affinity, no more interesting example of selection—selection of field and subject—operating by that insight which has the precocity and certainty of an instinct. The domicile of Mr. Abbey's genius is the England of the eighteenth century; I should add that the palace of art which he has erected there commands—from the rear, as it were—various charming glimpses of the preceding age. The finest work he has yet done is in his admirable illustrations, in Harper's Magazine, to "She Stoops to Conquer," but the promise that he would one day do it was given some years ago in his delightful volume of designs to accompany Herrick's poems; to which we may add, as supplementary evidence, his drawings for Mr. William Black's novel of *Judith Shakespeare.*

Mr. Abbey was born in Philadelphia in 1852, and manifesting his brilliant but un-encouraged aptitudes at a very early age, came in 1872 to New York to draw for Harper's WEEKLY. Other views than this, if I have been correctly Informed, had been entertained for his future—a fact that provokes a smile now that his manifest destiny has been, or is in course of being, so very neatly accomplished. The spirit of modern aesthetics did not, at any rate, as I understand the matter, smile upon his cradle, and the circumstance only increases the interest of his having had from the earliest moment the clearest artistic vision.

It has sometimes happened that the distinguished draughtsman or painter has been born in the studio and fed, as it were, from the palette, but in the great majority of cases he has been nursed by the profane, and certainly, on the doctrine of mathematical chances, a Philadelphia genius would scarcely be an exception. Mr. Abbey was fortunate, however, in not being obliged to lose time; he learned how to swim by jumping into deep water. Even if he had not known by instinct how to draw, he would have had to perform the feat from the moment that he found himself attached to the "art department" of a remarkably punctual periodical. In such a periodical the events of the day are promptly reproduced; and with the morrow so near the day is necessarily a short one—too short for gradual education. Such a school is not, no doubt, the ideal one, but in fact it may have a very happy influence. If a youth is to give an account of a scene with his pencil at a certain hour—to give it, as it were, or perish—he will have become conscious, in the first place, of a remarkable incentive to observe it. so that the roughness of the foster-mother who imparts the precious faculty of quick, complete observation is really a blessing in disguise. To say that it was simply under this kind of pressure that Mr. Abbey acquired the extraordinary refinement which distinguishes his work in black and white is doubtless to say too much; but his admirers may be excused, in view of the beautiful result, for almost wishing, on grounds of patriotism, to make the training, or the absence of training, responsible for as much as possible. For as no artistic genius that our country has produced is more delightful than Mr. Abbey's, so, surely, nothing could be more characteristically American than that it should have formed itself in the conditions that happened to be nearest at hand, with the crowds, streets and squares, the railway stations and telegraph poles, the wondrous sign-boards and triumphant bunting, of New York for the source of its inspiration, and with a big hurrying printing-house for its studio. If to begin the practice of art in these conditions was to incur the danger of being crude, Mr. Abbey braved it with remarkable success. At all events, if he went neither I through the mill of Paris nor through that of Munich, the writer of these lines more than consoles himself for the accident. His talent is unsurpassably fine, and yet we reflect with complacency that he picked it up altogether at home. If he is highly distinguished he is irremediably native, and (premising always that I speak mainly of his work in black and white) it is difficult to see, as we look, for instance, at the admirable series of his drawings for "She Stoops to Conquer," what more Paris or Munich could have done for him. There is a certain refreshment in meeting an American artist of the first order who is not a pupil of Gérôme or of Cabanel.

Of course, I hasten to add, we must make our account with the fact that, as I began with remarking, the great development of Mr. Abbey's powers has taken place amid the brown old accessories of a country where that eighteenth century which he presently marked for his own are more profusely represented than they have the good-fortune to be in America, and consequently limit our contention to the point that his talent itself was already formed when this happy initiation was opened to it. He went to England for the first time in 1878. but it was not all at once that he fell into the trick, so irresistible for an artist doing his special work, of living there, I must forbid myself every impertinent conjecture, but it may be respectfully assumed that Mr. Abbey rather drifted into exile than committed himself to it with malice prepense. The habit, at any rate, to-day appears to be confirmed, and, to express it roughly, he is surrounded by the utensils and conveniences that he requires. During these years, until the recent period when he began to exhibit at the water-color exhibitions, his work has been done principally for Harper's Magazine, and the record of it is to be found in the recent back volumes. I shall not take space to tell it over piece by piece, for the reader who turns to the Magazine will have no difficulty in recognizing it. It has a distinction altogether its own; there is always poetry, humor, charm, in the idea, and always infinite grace and security in the execution.

As I have intimated, Mr. Abbey never deals with the things and figures of to-day; his imagination must perform a wide backward journey before it can take the air. But beyond this modern radius it breathes with singular freedom and naturalness. At a distance of fifty years it begins to be at home; it expands and takes possession; it recognizes its own. With all his ability, with all his tact, it would be impossible to him, we conceive, to illustrate a novel of contemporary manners; he would inevitably throw it back to the age of hair-powder and post-chaises. The coats and trousers, the feminine gear, the chairs and tables of the current year, the general aspect of things immediate and familiar, say nothing to his mind, and there are other interpreters to whom he is quite content to leave them. He shows no great interest even in the modern face, if there be a modern face apart from a modern setting; I am not sure what he thinks of its complications and refinements of expression, but he has certainly little relish for its *banal*, vulgar mustache, its prosaic, mercantile whisker, surmounting the last new thing in shirt-collars. Dear to him is the physiognomy of clean-shaven periods, when cheek and lip and chin, abounding in line and surface, had the air of soliciting the pencil. Impeccable as he is in drawing, he likes a whole face, with reason, and likes a whole figure; the latter not to the exclusion of clothes, in which he delights, but as the clothes of our great-grandfathers helped it to be seen. No one has ever understood breeches and stockings better than he, or the human leg, that delight of the draughtsman, as the costume of the last century permitted it to be known. The petticoat and bodice of the same period have as little mystery for him, and his women and girls have altogether the poetry of a by-gone manner and fashion. They are not modern heroines, with modern nerves and accomplishments, but figures of remembered song and story, calling up visions of spinet and harpsichord that have lost their music today, high-walled gardens that have ceased to bloom, flowered stuffs that are faded, locks of hair that are lost, love-letters that are pale. By which I don't mean that they are vague and spectral, for Mr. Abbey has in the highest degree the art of imparting life, and he gives it in particular to his well-made, blooming maidens. They live in a world in which there is no question of their passing Harvard or other examinations, but they stand very firmly on their quaintly-shod feet. They are exhaustively "felt," and eminently qualified to attract the opposite sex, which is not the case with ghosts, who, moreover, do not wear the most palpable petticoats of quilted satin, nor sport the most delicate fans, nor take generally the most ingratiating attitudes.

The best work that Mr. Abbey has done is to be found in the succession of illustrations to "She Stoops to Conquer;" here we see his happiest characteristics and—till he does something still more brilliant—may take his full measure. No work in black and white in our time has been more truly artistic, and certainly no success more unqualified. The artist has given us an evocation of a social state to its smallest details, and done it with an unsurpassable lightness of touch. The problem was in itself delightful—the accidents and incidents (granted a situation *de comédie*) of an old, rambling, wainscoted, out-of-the-way English country-house, in the age of Goldsmith. Here Mr. Abbey is in his element—given up equally to unerring observation and still more infallible divination. The whole place, and the figures that come and go in it, live again, with their individual look, their peculiarities, their special signs and oddities. The spirit of the dramatist has passed completely into the artist's sense, but the spirit of the historian has done so almost as much. Tony Lumpkin is, as we say nowadays, a document, and Miss Hardcastle embodies the results of research. Delightful are the humor and quaintness and grace of all this, delightful the variety and the richness of personal characterization, and delightful, above all, the drawing. It is impossible to represent with such vividness unless, to begin with, one sees; and it is impossible to see unless one wants to very much, or unless, in other words, one has a great love. Mr. Abbey has evidently the tenderest affection for just the old houses and the old things, the old faces and voices, the whole irrevocable human scene which the genial hand of Goldsmith has passed over to him, and there is no inquiry about them that he is not in a position to answer. He is intimate with the buttons of coats and the buckles of shoes: he knows not only exactly what his people wore, but exactly how they wore it, and how they felt when they had it on. He has sat on the old chairs and sofas, and rubbed against the old wainscots, and leaned over the old balusters. He knows every mended place in Tony Lumpkin's stockings, and exactly how that ingenuous youth leaned back on the spinet, with his thick, familiar thumb out, when he presented his inimitable countenance, with a grin, to Mr. Hastings, after he had set his fond mother a-whimpering. (There is nothing in the whole series, by-the-way, better indicated than the exquisitely simple, half-bumpkin, half-vulgar expression of Tony's countenance and smile in this scene, unless it be the charming arch yet modest face of Miss Hardcastle, lighted by the candle she carries, as, still holding the door by which she comes in, she is challenged by young Mar-low to relieve his bewilderment as to where he really is and what *she* really is.) In short, if we have all seen "She Stoops to Conquer" acted, Mr. Abbey has had the better fortune of seeing it off the stage; and it is noticeable how happily he has steered clear of the danger of making his people theatrical types—mere masqueraders and wearers of properties. This is especially the case with his women, who have not a hint of the conventional paint and patches, simpering with their hands in the pockets of aprons, but are taken from the same originals from which Goldsmith took them.

If it be asked on the occasion of this limited sketch of Mr. Abbey's powers where, after all, he did learn to draw so perfectly, I know no answer but to say that he learned it in the school in which he learned also to paint (as he has been doing in these latest years, rather tentatively at first, but with greater and greater success)—the school of his own personal observation. His drawing is the drawing of direct, immediate, solicitous study of the particular case, without tricks or affectations or any sort of cheap subterfuge, and nothing can exceed the charm of its delicacy, accuracy and elegance, its variety and freedom, its clear, frank solution of difficulties. If for the artist it be the foundation of every joy to know exactly what he wants (as I hold it is indeed), Mr. Abbey is, to all appearance, to be constantly congratulated. And I apprehend that he would not deny that it is a good-fortune for him to have been able to arrange his life so that his eye encounters in abundance the particular cases of which I speak. Two or three years ago, at the Institute of Painters in Water-colors, in London, he exhibited an exquisite picture of a peaceful old couple sitting in the corner of a low, quiet, ancient room, in the waning afternoon, and listening to their daughter as she stands up in the middle and plays the harp to them. They are Darby and Joan, with all the poetry preserved; they sit hand in hand, with bent, approving heads, and the deep recess of the window looking into the garden (where we may be sure there are yew-trees clipped into the shape of birds and beasts), the panelled room, the quaintness of the fireside, the old-time provincial expression of the scene, all belong to the class of effects which Mr. Abbey understands supremely well. So does the great russet wall and high-pitched mottled roof of the rural almshouse which figures in the admirable water-color picture that he exhibited last spring. A group of remarkably pretty countrywomen have been arrested in front of it by the passage of a young soldier—a raw recruit in scarlet tunic and white ducks, somewhat prematurely conscious of military glory. He gives them the benefit of the goose-step as he goes; he throws back his head and distends his fingers, presenting to the ladies a back expressive of more consciousness of his fine figure than of the lovely mirth that the artist has depicted in their faces. Lovely is their mirth indeed, and lovely are they altogether. Mr. Abbey has produced nothing more charming than this bright knot of handsome, tittering daughters of burghers, in their primeval pelisses and sprigged frocks. I have, however, left myself no space to go into the question of his prospective honors as a painter, to which everything now appears to point, and I have mentioned the two pictures last exhibited mainly because they illustrate the happy opportunities with which he has been able to surround himself. The sweet old corners he appreciates, the russet walls of moss-grown charities, the lowbrowed nooks of manor, cottage and parsonage, the fresh complexions that flourish in green, pastoral countries where it rains not a little—every item in this line that seems conscious of its pictorial use appeals to Mr. Abbey not in vain. He might have been a grandson of Washington Irving, which is a proof of what I have already said, that none of the young American workers in the same field have so little as he of that imperfectly assimilated foreignness of suggestion which is sometimes regarded as the strength, but which is also in some degree the weakness, of the pictorial effort of the United States. His execution is as sure of itself as if it rested upon infinite Parisian initiation, but his feeling can best be described by saying that it is that of our own dear mother-tongue. If the writer speaks when he writes, and the draughtsman speaks when he draws. Mr. Abbey, in expressing himself with his pencil, certainly speaks pure English, He reminds us to a certain extent of Meissonier, especially the Meissonier of the illustrations to that charming little volume of the *Conies Rémois*, and the comparison is highly to his advantage in the matter of freedom, variety, ability to represent movement (Meissonier's figures are stock-still), and facial expression—above all, in the handling of the female personage, so rarely attempted by the French artist. But he differs from the latter signally in the fact that though he shares his sympathy as to period and costume, his people are of another race and tradition, and move in a world locally altogether different. Mr. Abbey is still young, he is full of ideas and intentions, and the work he has done may, in view of his time of life, of his opportunities and the singular completeness of his talent, be regarded really as a kind of foretaste and prelude. It can hardly fail that he will do better things still, when everything is so favorable. Life itself is his subject, and that is always at his door. The only obstacle, therefore, that can be imagined in Mr. Abbey's future career is a possible embarrassment as to what to choose. He has hitherto chosen so well, however, that this obstacle will probably not be insuperable.

CHARLES S. REINHART

We Americans are accused of making too much ado about our celebrities, of being demonstratively conscious of each step that we take in the path of progress; and the accusation has its ground doubtless in this sense, that it is possible among us to-day to become a celebrity on unprecedentedly easy terms. This, however, at the present hour is the case all the world over, and it is difficult to see where the standard of just renown remains so high that the first stone may be cast. It is more and more striking that the machinery of publicity is so enormous, so constantly growing and so obviously destined to make the globe small, in relation of the objects, famous or obscure, which cover it, that it procures for the smallest facts and the most casual figures a reverberation to be expected only in the case of a world-conqueror. The newspaper and the telegram constitute a huge sounding-board, which has, every day and every hour, to be made to vibrate, to be fed with items, and the diffusion of the items takes place on a scale out of any sort of proportion to their intrinsic importance. The crackle of common things is transmuted into thunder—a thunder perhaps more resounding in America than elsewhere for the reason that the sheet of tin shaken by the Jupiter of the Press has been cut larger. But the difference is only of degree, not of kind; and if the system we in particular have brought to perfection would seem to be properly applied only to Alexanders and Napoleons, it is not striking that these adequate subjects present themselves even in other countries. The end of it all surely no man can see, unless it be that collective humanity is destined to perish from a rupture of its tympanum. That is a theme for a later hour, and meanwhile perhaps it is well not to be too frightened. Some of the items I just spoke of are, after all, larger than others; and if, as a general thing, it is a mistake to pull up our reputations to see how they are growing, there are some so well grown that they will bear it, and others of a hardy stock even while they are tender. We may feel, for instance, comparatively little hesitation in extending an importunate hand towards the fine young sapling of which Mr. Reinhart is one of the branches. It is a plant of promise, which has already flowered profusely and the fragrance of which it would be affectation not to to notice. Let us notice it, then, with candor, for it has all the air of being destined to make the future sweeter. The plant in question is of course simply the art of illustration in black and white, to which American periodical literature has, lately given such an impetus and which has returned the good office by conferring a great distinction on our magazines. In its new phase the undertaking has succeeded; and it is not always that fortune descends upon so deserving a head. Two or three fine talents in particular have helped it to succeed, and Mr. Reinhart is not the least conspicuous of these. It would be idle for a writer in Harper to pretend to any diffidence of appreciation of his work: for the pages are studded, from many years back, with the record of his ability. Mr. Rein-hart took his first steps and made his first hits in Harper, which owes him properly a portrait in return for so much portraiture. I may exaggerate the charm and the importance of the modern illustrative form, may see in it a capacity of which it is not yet itself wholly conscious, but if I do so Mr. Reinhart is partly responsible for the aberration. Abundant, intelligent, interpretative work in black and white is, to the sense of the writer of these lines, one of the pleasantest things of the time, having only to rise to the occasion to enjoy a great future. This idea, I confess, is such as to lead one to write not only sympathetically but pleadingly about the artists to whom one looks for confirmation of it. If at the same time as we commemorate what they have done we succeed in enlarging a little the conception of what they may yet do, we shall be repaid even for having exposed ourselves as fanatics— fanatics of the general manner, I mean, not of particular representatives of it.

May not this fanaticism, in a particular case, rest upon a sense of the resemblance between the general chance, as it may be called, of the draughtsman in black and white, with contemporary life for his theme, and the opportunity upon which the literary artist brings another form to bear? The forms are different, though with analogies; but the field is the same—the immense field of contemporary life observed for an artistic purpose. There is nothing so interesting as that, because it is ourselves; and no artistic problem is so charming as to arrive, either in a literary or a plastic form, at a close and direct notation of what we observe. If one has attempted some such exploit in a literary form, one cannot help having a sense of union and comradeship with those who have approached the question with the other instrument. This will be especially the case if we happen to have appreciated that instrument even to envy. We may as well say it outright, we envy it quite unspeakably in the hands of Mr. Reinhart and in those of Mr. Abbey. There is almost no limit to the service to which we can imagine it to be applied, and we find ourselves wishing that these gentlemen may be made adequately conscious of all the advantages it represents. We wonder whether they really *are* so; we are disposed even to assume that they are not, in order to join the moral, to insist on the lesson. The master whom we have mentally in view Mr. Reinhart is a near approach to him may be, if he will only completely know it, so prompt, so copious, so universal—so "all there," as we say nowadays, and indeed so all everywhere. There is only too much to see, too much to do, and his process is the one that comes nearest to minimizing the quantity. He can touch so many things, he can go from one scene to another, he can sound a whole concert of notes while the painter is setting up his easel. The painter is majestic, dignified, academic, important, superior, anything you will; but he is, in the very nature of the case, only occasional. He is "serious," but he is comparatively clumsy: he is a terrible time getting under way, and he has to sacrifice so many subjects while he is doing one. The illustrator makes one immense sacrifice, of course—that of color; but with it he purchases a freedom which enables him to attack ever so many ideas. It is by variety and numerosity that he commends himself to his age, and it is for these qualities that his age commends him to the next. The twentieth century, the latter half of it, will, no doubt, have its troubles, but it will have a great compensatory luxury, that of seeing the life of a hundred years before much more vividly than we—even happy we—see the life of a hundred years ago. But for this our illustrators must do their best, appreciate the endless capacity of their form. It is to the big picture what the short story is to the novel.

It is doubtless too much, I hasten to add, to ask Mr. Reinhart, for instance, to work to please the twentieth century. The end will not matter if he pursues his present very prosperous course of activity, for it is assuredly the fruitful vein, the one I express the hope to see predominant, the portrayal of the manners, types and aspects that surround us. Mr. Reinhart has reached that happy period of life when a worker is in full possession of his means, when he has done for his chosen instrument everything he can do in the way of forming it and rendering it complete and flexible, and has the fore only to apply it with freedom, confidence and success. These, to our sense, are the golden hours of an artist's life; happier even than the younger time when the future seemed infinite in the light of the first rays of glory, the first palpable hits. The very sense that the future is *not* unlimited and that opportunity is at its high-water-mark gives an intensity to the enjoyment of maturity. Then the acquired habit of "knowing how" must simplify the problem of execution and leave the artist free to think only of his purpose, as befits a real creator. Mr. Reinhart is at the enviable stage of knowing in perfection how; he has arrived at absolute facility and felicity. The machine goes of itself; it is no longer necessary to keep lifting the cover and pouring in the oil of fond encouragement: all the attention may go to the idea and the subject. It may, however, remain very interesting to others to know how the faculty was trained, the pipe was tuned. The early phases of such a process have a relative importance even when, at the lime (so gradual are many beginnings and so obscure man a morrow) they may have appeared neither delightful nor profitable. They are almost always to be summed up in the single precious word practice. This word represents, at any rate, Mr. Reinhart's youthful history, and the profusion in which, though no doubt occasionally disguised, the boon was supplied to him in the offices of Harper's Magazine. There is nothing so innate that it has not also to be learned, for the best part of any aptitude is the capacity to increase it.

Mr. Reinhart's experience began to accumulate very early, for at Pittsburgh, where he was born, he was free to draw to his heart's content. There was no romantic attempt, as I gather, to nip him in the bud. On the contrary, he was despatched with almost prosaic punctuality to Europe, and was even encouraged to make himself at home in Munich. Munich, in his case, was a *pis-aller* for Paris, where it would have been his preference to study when he definitely surrendered, as it were, to his symptoms. He went to Paris, but Paris seemed blocked and complicated, and Munich presented advantages which, if not greater, were at least easier to approach. Mr. Reinhart passe through the mill of the Bavarian school, and when it had turned him out with its characteristic polish he came back to America with a very substantial stock to dispose of. It would take a chapter by itself if we were writing a biography, this now very usual episode of the return of the young American from the foreign conditions in which he has learned his professional language, and his position in face of the community that he addresses in a strange idiom. There has to be a prompt adjustment between ear and voice, if the interlocutor is not to seem to himself to be intoning in the void. There is always an inner history in all this, as well as an outer one—such, however, as it would take much space to relate. Mr. Reinhart's more or less alienated accent fell, by good-fortune, on a comprehending listener. He had made a satirical drawing, in the nature of the "cartoon" of a comic journal, on a subject of the hour, and addressed it to the editor of *Harper's Weekly*. The drawing was not published—the satire was perhaps not exactly on the right note—but the draughtsman was introduced. Thus began, by return of post, as it were, and with preliminaries so few that they could not well have been less, a connection of many years. If I were writing a biography another chapter would come in here—a curious, almost a pathetic one; for the course of things is so rapid in this country that the years of Mr. Reinhart's apprenticeship to pictorial journalism, positively recent as they are, already are almost prehistoric. To-morrow, at least, the complexion of that time, its processes, ideas and standards, together with some of the unsophisticated who carried them out, will belong to old New York. A certain mollifying dimness rests upon them now, and their superseded brilliancy gleams through it but faintly. It is a lively span for Mr. Reinhart to have been at once one of the unsophisticated and one of the actually modern.

That portion of his very copious work to which, more particularly. I apply the latter term, has been done for Harper's Magazine. During these latter years it has come, like so much of American work to-day, from beyond the seas. Whether or not that foreign language of which I just spoke never became, in New York, for this especial possessor of it, a completely convenient medium of conversation, is more than I can say; at any rate Mr. Reinhart eventually reverted to Europe and settled in Paris. Paris had seemed rather inhospitable to him in his youth, but he has now fitted his key to the lock. It would be satisfactory to be able to express scientifically the reasons why, as a general thing, the American artist, as well as his congener of many another land, carries on his function with less sense of resistance in that city than elsewhere. He likes Paris best, but that is not scientific. The difference is that though theoretically the production of pictures is recognized in America and in England, in Paris it is recognized both theoretically and practically. And I do not mean by this simply that pictures are bought—for they are not, predominantly, as it happens—but that they are more presupposed. The plastic is implied in the French conception of things, and the studio is as natural a consequence of it as the post-office is of letter-writing. Vivid representation is the genius of the French language and the need of the French mind. The people have invented more aids to it than any other, and as these aids make up a large part of the artist's life, he feels his best home to be in the place where he finds them most. He may begin to quarrel with that home on the day a complication is introduced by the question of *what* he shall represent—a totally different consideration from that of the method; but for Mr. Reinhart this question has not yet offered insoluble difficulties. He represents everything—he has accepted so general an order. So long as his countrymen flock to Paris and pass in a homogeneous procession before his eyes, there is not the smallest difficulty in representing *them*. When the case requires that they shall be taken in connection with their native circumstances and seen in their ambient air, he is prepared to come home and give several months to the task, as on the occasion of Mr. Dudley Warner's history of a tour among the watering-places, to which he furnished so rich and so curious a pictorial accompaniment. Sketch-book in hand, he betakes himself, according to need, to Germany, to England, to Italy, to Spain. The readers of Harper will have forgotten his admirable pictorial notes on the political world at Berlin, so rich and close in characterization. To the *Spanish Vistas* of Mr. G. P. Lathrop he contributed innumerable designs, delightful notes of an artist's quest of the sketchable, many of which are singularly full pictures. The "Soldiers Playing Dominoes" at a café is a powerful page of life. Mr. Reinhart has, of course, interpreted many a fictive scene—he has been repeatedly called upon to make the novel and the story visible. This he energetically and patiently does; though of course we are unable to say whether the men and women he makes us see are the very people whom the authors have seen. That is a thing that, in any case, one will never know; besides, the authors who don't see vaguely are apt to see perversely. The story-teller has, at any rate, the comfort with Mr. Reinhart that his drawings are constructive and have the air of the actual. He likes to represent character—he rejoices in the specifying touch.

The evidence of this is to be found also in his pictures, for I ought already to have mentioned that, for these many years (they are beginning to be many), he has indulged in the luxury of color. It is not probable that he regards himself in the first place as an illustrator, in the sense to which the term is usually restricted. He is a very vigorous and various painter, and at the Salon a constant and conspicuous exhibitor. He is fond of experiments, difficulties and dangers, and I divine that it would be his preference to be known best by his painting, in which he handles landscape with equal veracity. It is a pity that the critic is unable to contend with him on such a point without appearing to underestimate that work. Mr. Reinhart has so much to show for his preference that I am conscious of its taking some assurance to say that I am not sure he is right. This would be the case even if he had nothing else to show than the admirable picture entitled "Washed Ashore" ("Un Epave ") which made such an impression in the Salon of 1887. It represents the dead body of an unknown man whom the tide has cast up, lying on his back, feet forward, disfigured, dishonored by the sea. A small group of villagers are collected near it, divided by the desire to look and the fear to see. A gendarme, official and responsible, his uniform contrasting with the mortal disrepair of the victim, takes down in his note-book the *procès-verbal* of the incident, and an old sailor, pointing away with a stiffened arm, gives him the benefit of what *he* knows about the matter. Plain, pitying, fish-wives, hushed, with their shawls in their mouths, hang back, as if from a combination too solemn—the mixture of death and the law. Three or four men seem to be glad it isn't they. The thing is a masterpiece of direct representation, and has wonderfully the air of something seen, found without being looked for. Excellently composed but not artificial, deeply touching but not sentimental, large, close and sober, this important work gives the full measure of Mr. Reinhart's great talent and constitutes a kind of pledge. It may be perverse on my part to see in it the big banknote, as it were, which may be changed into a multitude of gold and silver pieces. I cannot, however, help doing so. "Washed Ashore" is painted as only a painter paints, but I irreverently translate it into its equivalent in "illustrations"—half a hundred little examples, in black and white, of the same sort of observation. For this observation, immediate, familiar, sympathetic, human, and not involving a quest of style for which color is really indispensable, is a mistress at whose service there is no derogation in placing one's self. To do little things instead of big *may* be a derogation; a great deal will depend upon the way the little things are done. Besides, no work of art is absolutely little. I grow bold and even impertinent as I think of the way Mr. Rein-hart might scatter the smaller coin. At any rate, whatever proportion his work in this line may bear to the rest, it is to be hoped that nothing will prevent him from turning out more and more to play the rare faculty that produces it. His studies of American *moeurs* in association with Mr. Warner went so far on the right road that we would fain see him make all the rest of the journey. They made us ask straightway for more, and were full of intimations of what was behind. They showed what there is to see—what there is to guess. Let him carry the same inquiry further, let him carry it all the way. It would be serious work and would abound in reality; it would help us, as it were, to know what we are talking about. In saying this I feel how much I confirm the great claims I just made for the revival of illustration.

ALFRED PARSONS

It would perhaps be extravagant to pretend, in this embarrassed age, that Merry England is still intact; but it would be strange if the words "happy England" should not rise to the lips of the observer of Mr. Alfred Parsons' numerous and delightful studies of the gardens, great and small, of his country. They surely have a representative value in more than the literal sense, and might easily minister to the quietest complacency of patriotism. People whose criticism is imaginative will see in them a kind of compendium of what, in home things, is at once most typical and most enviable; and, going further, they will almost wish that such a collection might be carried by slow stages round the globe, to kindle pangs in the absent and passions in the alien. As it happens to be a globe the English race has largely peopled, we can measure the amount of homesickness that would be engendered on the way. In fact, one doubts whether the sufferer would even need to be of English strain to attach the vision of home to the essentially lovable places that Mr. Parsons depicts. They seem to generalize and typify the idea, so that every one may feel, in every case, that he has a sentimental property in the scene. The very sweetness of its reality only helps to give it that story-book quality which persuades us we have known it in youth.

And yet such scenes may well have been constructed for the despair of the Colonial; for they remind us, at every glance, of that perfection to which there is no short cut—not even "unexampled prosperity "—and to which time is the only guide. Mr. Parsons' pictures speak of many complicated things, but (in what they tell us of his subjects) they speak most of duration. Such happy nooks have grown slowly, such fortunate corners have had a history; and their fortune has been precisely that they have had time to have it comfortably, have not been obliged to try for character without it.

Character is their strong point and the most expensive of all ingredients. Mr. Parsons' portraiture seizes every shade of it, seizes it with unfailing sympathy. He is doubtless clever enough to paint rawness when he must, but he has an irrepressible sense of ripeness. Half the ripeness of England—half the religion, one might almost say—is in its gardens; they are truly pious foundations. It is doubtless because there are so many of them that the country seems so finished, and the sort of care they demand is an intenser deliberation, which passes into the national temper. One must have lived in other lands to observe fully how large a proportion of this one is walled in for growing flowers. The English love of flowers is inveterate; it is the most, unanimous protest against the grayness of some of the conditions, and it should receive justice from those who accuse the race of taking its pleasure too sadly. A good garden is an organized revel, and there is no country in which there are so many.

Mr. Parsons had therefore only to choose, at his leisure, and one might heartily have envied him the process, scarcely knowing which to prefer of all the pleasant pilgrimages that would make up such a quest. He had, fortunately, the knowledge which could easily lead to more, and a career of discovery behind him. He knew the right times for the right things, and the right things for the right places. He had innumerable memories and associations; he had painted up and down the land and looked over many walls. He had followed the bounty of the year from month to month and from one profusion to another. To follow it with him, in this admirable series, is to see that he is master of the subject. There will be no lack of confidence on the part of those who have already perceived, in much of Mr. Parsons' work, a supreme illustration of all that is widely nature-loving in the English interest in the flower. No sweeter submission to mastery can be imagined than the way the daffodils, under his brush (to begin at the beginning), break out into early April in the lovely drawings of Stourhead. One of the most charming of these—a corner of an old tumbled-up place in Wiltshire, where many things have come and gone—represents that moment of transition in which contrast is so vivid as to make it more dramatic than many plays—the very youngest throb of spring, with the brown slope of the foreground coming back to consciousness in pale lemon-colored patches and, on the top of the hill, against the still cold sky, the equally delicate forms of the wintry trees. By the time these forms have thickened, the expanses of daffodil will have become a mass of bluebells. All the daffodil pictures have a rare loveliness, but especially those that deal also with the earlier fruit-blossom, the young plum-trees in Berkshire orchards. Here the air is faintly pink, and the painter makes us feel the little *blow* in the thin blue sky. The spring, fortunately, is everybody's property and, in the language of all the arts, the easiest word to conjure with. It is therefore partly Mr. Parsons' good-luck that we enjoy so his rendering of these phases; but on the other hand we look twice when it's a case of meddling with the exquisite, and if he inspires us with respect it is because we feel that he has been deeply initiated. No one knows better the friendly reasons for our stopping, when chatting natives pronounce the weather "foine," at charming casual corners of old villages, where grassy ways cross each other and timbered houses bulge irregularly and there are fresh things behind crooked palings; witness the little vision of Blewbury, in Berkshire, reputedly of ancient British origin, with a road all round it and only footways within. No one, in the Herefordshire orchards, masses the white cow-parsley in such profusion under the apple blossoms; or makes the whitewashed little damson-trees look so innocently responsible and charming on the edge of the brook over which the planks are laid for the hens. Delightful, in this picture, is the sense of the clean spring day, after rain, with the blue of the sky washed faint. Delightful is the biggish view (one of the less numerous oil-pictures) of the Somersetshire garden, where that peculiarly English look of the open-air room is produced by the stretched carpet of the turf and the firm cushions of the hedges, and a pair of proprietors, perhaps happier than they know, are putting in an afternoon among their tulips, under the flushed apple-trees whose stems are so thin and whose brims so heavy. Are the absorbed couple, at any rate, aware of the surprising degree to which the clustered ruddy roofs of the next small town, over the hedge, off at the left, may remind the fanciful spectator of the way he has seen little dim Italian cities look on their hill-tops? The whole thing, in this subject, has the particular English note to which Mr. Parsons repeatedly testifies, the nook quality, the air of a land and a life so infinitely subdivided that they produce a thousand pleasant privacies. The painter moves with the months and finds, after the earliest things, the great bed of pansies in the angle of the old garden at Sutton, in which, for felicity of position and perfect pictorial service rendered—to say nothing of its polygonal, pyramidal roof—the ancient tool-house, or tea-house, is especially to be commended.

Very far descended is such a corner as this, very full of reference to vanished combinations and uses; and the artist communicates to us a feeling for it that makes us wish disinterstedly it may be still as long preserved.

He finds in June, at Blackdown, the blaze of the yellow azalea-bush, or in another spot the strong pink of the rhododendron, beneath the silver firs that deepen the blue of the sky. He finds the Vicarage Walk, at King's Langley, a smother of old-fashioned flowers—a midsummer vista for the figures of a happy lady and a lucky dog. He finds the delicious huddle of the gabled, pigeon-haunted roof of a certain brown old building at Frame, with poppies and gladiolus and hollyhock crowding the beautiful foreground. He finds—apparently in the same place—the tangle of the hardy flowers that come while the roses are still in bloom, with the tall blue larkspurs standing high among them. He finds the lilies, white and red, at Broadway, and the poppies, which have dropped most of their petals—apparently to let the roses, which are just coming out, give *their* grand party. Their humility is rewarded by the artist's admirable touch in the little bare poppy-heads that nod on their flexible pins.

But I cannot go on to say everything that such a seeker, such a discoverer, as Mr. Parsons finds—the less that the purpose of these limited remarks is to hint at our own *trouvailles*. A view of the field, at any rate, would be incomplete without such specimens as the three charming oil-pictures which commemorate Holme Lacey. There are gardens and gardens, and these represent the sort that are always spoken of in the plural and most arrogate the title. They form, in England, a magnificent collection, and if they abound in a quiet assumption of the grand style it must be owned that they frequently achieve it. There are people to be found who enjoy them, and it is not, at any rate, when Mr. Parsons deals with them that we have an opening for strictures. As we look at the blaze of full summer in the brilliantly conventional parterres we easily credit the tale of the 40,000 plants it takes to fill the beds. More than this, we like the long paths of turf that stretch between splendid borders, recalling the frescoed galleries of a palace; we like the immense hedges, whose tops are high against the sky. While we are liking, we like perhaps still better, since they deal with a very different order, the two water-colors from the dear little garden at Winchelsea—especially the one in which the lady takes he ease in her hammock (on a sociable, shady terrace, from which the ground drops), and looks at red Rye, across the marshes. Another garden where a contemplative hammock would be in order is the lovely canonical plot at Salisbury, with the everlasting spire above it tinted in the summer sky—unless, in the same place, you should choose to hook yourself up by the grassy bank of the Avon, at the end of the lawn, with the meadows, the cattle, the distant willows across the river, to look at.

Three admirable water-colors are devoted by Mr. Parsons to the perceptible dignity of Gravetye, in Sussex, the dignity of very serious gardens, entitled to ceremonious consideration, Few things in England can show a greater wealth of bloom than the wide flowery terrace immediately beneath the gray, gabled house, where tens of thousands of tea-roses, in predominant possession, have, in one direction, a mass of high yews for a background. They divide their province with the carnations and pansies: a wilder ness of tender petals ignorant of anything rougher than the neighborhood of the big unchanged medley of tall yuccas and saxifrage, with miscellaneous filling-in, in the picture which presents the charming house in profile. The artist shows us later, in September, at Gravetye, the pale violet multitude of the Michaelmas daisies; another I great bunch, or bank, of which half masks and greatly beautifies the rather bare yellow cottage at Broadway. This brings us on to the autumn, if I count as autumnal the admirable large water-color of a part of a garden at Shiplake, with the second bloom of the roses and a glimpse of a turn of the Thames. This exquisite picture expresses to perfection the beginning of the languor of the completed season—with its look of warm rest, of doing nothing, in the cloudless sky. To the same or a later moment belongs the straight walk at Fladbury—the old rectory garden by the Avon, with its Irish yews and the red lady in her chair; also the charming water-color of young, slim apple-trees, full of fruit (this must be October), beneath an admirable blue and white sky. Still later comes the big pear-tree that has turned, among barer boughs, to flame-color, and, in another picture, the very pale russet of the thinned cherry-trees, standing, beneath a grayish sky, above a foreshortened slope. Last of all we have, in oils, December and a hard frost in a bare apple-orchard, indented with a deep gully which makes the place somehow a subject and which, in fact, three or four years ago, made it one for a larger picture by Mr. Parsons, full of truth and style.

This completes his charming story of the life of the English year, told in a way that convinces us of his intimate acquaintance with it. Half the interest of Mr. Parsons' work is in the fact that he paints from a full mind and from a store of assimilated knowledge. In every touch of nature that he communicates to us we feel something of the thrill of the whole—we feel the innumerable relations, the possible variations of the particular objects. This makes his manner serious and masculine—rescues it from the thinness of tricks and the coquetries of *chic*. We walk with him on a firm earth, we taste the tone of the air and seem to take nature and the climate and all the complicated conditions by their big general hand. The painter's manner, in short, is one with the study of things—his talent is a part of their truth. In this happy series we seem to see still more how that talent was formed, how his rich motherland has been, from the earliest observation, its nurse and inspirer. He gives back to her all the good she has done him.

JOHN S. SARGENT

I was on the point of beginning this sketch of the work of an artist to whom distinction has come very early in life by saying, in regard to the degree to which the subject of it enjoys the attention of the public, that no American painter has hitherto won himself such recognition from the expert; but I find myself pausing at the start as on the edge of a possible solecism. Is Mr. Sargent in very fact an American painter? The proper answer to such a question is doubtless that we shall be well advised to pretend it, and the reason of this is simply that we have an excellent opportunity. Born in Europe, he has also spent his life in Europe, but none the less the burden of proof would rest with those who should undertake to show that he is a European. Moreover he has even on the face of it this great symptom of an American origin, that in the line of his art he might easily be mistaken for a Frenchman. It sounds like a paradox, but it is a very simple truth, that when to-day we look for "American art" we find it mainly in Paris. When we find it out of Paris, we at least find a great deal of Paris in it. Mr. Sargent came up to the irresistible city in his twentieth year, from Florence, where in 1856 he had been born of American parents and where his fortunate youth had been spent. He entered immediately the studio of Caro-lus Duran, and revealed himself in 1877, at the age of twenty-two, in the portrait of that master—-a fine model in more than one sense of the word. He was already in possession of a style; and if this style has gained both in finish and in assurance, it has not otherwise varied. As he saw and "rendered" ten years ago, so he sees and renders to-day; and I may add that there is no present symptom of his passing into another manner.

Those who have appreciated his work most up to the present time articulate no wish for a change, so completely does that work seem to them, in its kind, the exact translation of his thought, the exact "fit" of his artistic temperament. It is difficult to imagine a young painter less in the dark about his own ideal, more lucid and more responsible from the first about what he desires. In an altogether exceptional degree does he give us the sense that the intention and the art of carrying it out are for him one and the same thing. In the brilliant portrait of Carolus Duran, which he was speedily and strikingly to surpass, he gave almost the full measure of this admirable peculiarity, that perception with him is already by itself a kind of execution. It is likewise so, of course, with many another genuine painter; but in Sargent's case the process by which the object seen resolves itself into the object pictured is extraordinarily immediate. It is as if painting were pure tact of vision, a simple manner of feeling.

From the time of his first successes at the Salon he was hailed, I believe, as a recruit of high value to the camp of the Impressionists, and to-day he is for many people most conveniently pigeon-holed under that head. It is not necessary to protest against the classification if this addition always be made to it, that Mr. Sargent's impressions happen to be worthy of record. This is by no means inveterately the case with those of the ingenuous artists who most rejoice in the title in question. To render the impression of an object may be a very fruitful effort, but it is not necessarily so; that will depend upon what, I won't say the object, but the impression, may have been. The talents engaged in this school lie, not unjustly, as it seems to me under the suspicion of seeking the solution of their problem exclusively in simplification. If a painter works for other eyes as well as his own he courts a certain danger in this direction—that of being arrested by the cry of the spectator: "Ah! but excuse me; I myself take more impressions than that" We feel a synthesis not to be an injustice only when it is rich. Mr. Sargent simplifies, I think, but he simplifies with style, and his impression is the finest form of his energy.

His work has been almost exclusively in portraiture, and it has been his fortune to paint more women than men; therefore he has had but a limited opportunity to reproduce that generalized grand air with which his view of certain figures of gentlemen invests the model, which is conspicuous in the portrait of Carolus Duran and of which his splendid "Docteur Pozzi," the distinguished Paris surgeon (a work not sent to the Salon), is an admirable example. In each of these cases the model has been of a gallant pictorial type, one of the types which strike us as made for portraiture (which is by no means the way of all), as especially appears, for instance, in the handsome hands and frilled wrists of M. Carolus, whose cane rests in his fine fingers as if it were the hilt of a rapier. The most brilliant of all Mr. Sargent's productions is the portrait of a young lady, the magnificent picture which he exhibited in 1881; and if it has mainly been his fortune since to commemorate the fair faces of women, there is no ground for surprise at this sort of success on the part of one who had given so signal a proof of possessing the secret of the particular aspect that the contemporary lady (of any period) likes to wear in the eyes of posterity. Painted when he was but four-and-twenty years of age, the picture by which Mr. Sargent was represented at the Salon of 1881 is a performance which may well have made any critic of imagination rather anxious about his future. In common with the superb group of the children of Mr. Edward Boit, exhibited two years later, it offers the slightly "uncanny" spectacle of a talent which on the very threshold of its career has nothing more to learn. It is not simply precocity in the guise of maturity—a phenomenon we very often meet, which deceives us only for an hour; it is the freshness of youth combined with the artistic experience, really felt and assimilated, of generations. My admiration for this deeply distinguished work is such that I am perhaps in danger of overstating its merits; but it is worth taking into account that to-day, after several years' acquaintance with them, these merits seem to me more and more to justify enthusiasm. The picture has this sign of productions of the first order, that its style clearly would save it if everything else should change—our measure of its value of resemblance, its expression of character, the fashion of dress, the particular associations it evokes. It is not only a portrait, but a picture, and it arouses even in the profane spectator something of the painter's sense, the joy of engaging also, by sympathy, in the solution of the artistic problem. There are works of which it is sometimes said that they are painters' pictures (this description is apt to be intended invidiously), and the production of which I speak has the good-fortune at once to belong to this class and to give the "plain man" the kind of pleasure that the plain man looks for.

The young lady, dressed in black satin, stands upright, with her right hand bent back, resting on her waist, while the other, with the arm somewhat extended, offers to view a single white flower. The dress. stretched at the hips over a sort of hoop, and ornamented in front, where it opens on a velvet petticoat with large satin bows, has an old-fashioned air, as if it had been worn by some demure princess who might have sat for Velasquez. The hair, of which the arrangement is odd and charming, is disposed in two or three large curls fastened at one side over the temple with a comb. Behind the figure is the vague faded sheen, exquisite in tone, of a silk curtain, light, undefined, and losing itself at the bottom. The face is young, candid and peculiar. Out of these few elements the artist has constructed a picture which it is impossible to forget, of which the most striking characteristic is its simplicity, and yet which overflows with perfection. Painted with extraordinary breadth and freedom, so that surface and texture are interpreted by the lightest hand, it glows with life, character and distinction, and strikes us as the most complete—with one exception perhaps—of the author's productions. I know not why this representation of a young girl in black, engaged in the casual gesture of holding up a flower, should make so ineffaceable an impression and tempt one to become almost lyrical in its praise; but I remember that, encountering the picture unexpectedly in New York a year or two after it had been exhibited in Paris, it seemed to me to have acquired an extraordinary general value, to stand for more artistic truth than it would be easy to formulate. The language of painting, the tongue in which, exclusively, Mr. Sargent expresses himself, is a medium into which a considerable part of the public, for the simple an excellent reason that they don't understand it, will doubtless always be reluctant and unable to follow him.

Two years before he exhibited the young lady in black, in 1879, Mr. Sargent had spent several months in Spain, and here, even more than he had already been, the great Velasquez became the god of his idolatry. No scenes are more delightful to the imagination than those in which we figure youth and genius confronted with great examples, and if such matters did not belong to the domain of private life we might entertain ourselves with reconstructing the episode of the first visit to the museum of Madrid, the shrine of the painter of Philip IV., of a young Franco-American worshipper of the highest artistic sensibility, expecting a supreme revelation and prepared to fall on his knees. It is evident that Mr. Sargent fell on his knees and that in this attitude he passed a considerable part of his sojourn in Spain. He is various and experimental; if I am not mistaken, he sees each work that he produces in a light of its own, not turning off successive portraits according to some well-tried receipt which has proved useful in the case of their predecessors; nevertheless there is one idea that pervades them all, in a different degree, and gives them a family resemblance—the idea that it would be inspiring to know just how Velasquez would have treated the theme. We can fancy that on each occasion Mr. Sargent, as a solemn preliminary, invokes him as a patron saint. This is not, in my intention, tantamount to saying that the large canvas representing the contortions of a dancer in the lamp-lit room of a *posada*, which he exhibited on his return from Spain, strikes me as having come into the world under the same star as those compositions of the great Spaniard which at Madrid alternate with his royal portraits. This singular work, which has found an appreciative home in Boston, has the stamp of an extraordinary energy and facility—of an actual scene, with its accidents and peculiarities caught, as distinguished from a composition where arrangement and invention have played their part. It looks like life, but it looks also, to my view, rather like a perversion of life, and has the quality of an enormous "note" or memorandum, rather than of a representation. A woman in a voluminous white silk dress and a black mantilla pirouettes in the middle of a dusky room, to the accompaniment of her own castanets and that of a row of men and women who sit in straw chairs against the whitewashed wall and thrum upon guitar and tambourine or lift other castanets into the air. She appears almost colossal, and the twisted and inflated folds of her long dress increase her volume. She simpers, in profile, with a long chin, while she slants back at a dangerous angle, and the lamplight (it proceeds from below, as if she were on a big platform) makes a strange play in her large face. In the background the straight line of black-clad, black-hatted, white-shirted musicians projects shadows against the wall, on which placards, guitars, and dirty finger-marks display themselves. The merit of this production is that the air of reality is given in it with remarkable breadth and boldness; its defect it is difficult to express save by saying that it makes the spectator vaguely uneasy and even unhappy—an accident the more to be regretted as a lithe, inspired female figure, given up to the emotion of the dance, is not intrinsically a displeasing object. "El Jaleo" sins, in my opinion, in the direction of ugliness, and, independently of the fact that the heroine is circling round incommoded by her petticoats, has a want of serenity.

This is not the defect of the charming, dusky, white-robed person who, in the Tangerine subject exhibited at the Salon of 1880 (the fruit of an excursion to the African coast at the time of the artist's visit to Spain), stands on a rug, under a great white Moorish arch, and from out of the shadows of the large drapery, raised pentwise by her hands, which covers her head, looks down, with painted eyes and brows showing above a bandaged mouth, at the fumes of a beautiful censer or chafing-dish placed on the carpet. I know not who this stately Mahometan may be, nor in what mysterious domestic or religious rite she may be engaged; but in her muffled contemplation and her pearl-colored robes, under her plastered arcade which shines in the Eastern light, she transports and torments us. The picture is exquisite, a radiant effect of white upon white, of similar but discriminated tones. In dividing the honor that Mr. Sargent has won by his finest work between the portrait of the young lady of 1881 and the group of four little girls which was painted in 1882 and exhibited with the success it deserved the following year, I must be careful to give the latter picture not too small a share. The artist has done nothing more felicitous and interesting than this view of a rich dim, rather generalized French interior (the perspective of a hall with a shining floor, where screens and tall Japanese vases shimmer and loom), which encloses the life and seems to form the happy play-world of a family of charming children. The treatment is eminently unconventional, and there is none of the usual symmetrical balancing of the figures in the foreground. The place is regarded as a whole; it is a scene, a comprehensive impression; yet none the less do the little figures in their white pinafores (when was the pinafore ever painted with that power and made so poetic?) detach themselves and live with a personal life. Two of the sisters stand hand in hand at the back, in the delightful, the almost equal, company of a pair of immensely tall emblazoned jars, which overtop them and seem also to partake of the life of the picture; the splendid porcelain and the aprons of the children shine together, while a mirror in the brown depth behind them catches the light. Another little girl presents herself, with abundant tresses and slim legs, her hands behind her, quite to the left; and the youngest, nearest to the spectator, sits on the floor and plays with her doll. The naturalness of the composition, the loveliness of the complete effect, the light, free' security of the execution, the sense it gives us as of assimilated secrets and of instinct and knowledge playing together—all this makes the picture as astonishing a work on the part of a young man of twenty-six as the portrait of 1881 was astonishing on the part of a young man of twenty-four.

It is these remarkable encounters that justify us in writing almost prematurely of a career which is not yet half unfolded. Mr. Sargent is sometimes accused of a want of "finish," but if finish means the last word of expressiveness of touch, "The Hall with the Four Children," as we may call it, may-stand as a permanent reference on this point. If the picture of the Spanish dancer illustrates, as it seems to me to do, the latent dangers of the Impressionist practice, so this finer performance shows what victories it may achieve. And in relation to the latter I must repeat what I said about the young lady with the flower, that this is the sort of work which, when produced in youth, leads the attentive spectator to ask unanswerable questions. He finds himself murmuring, "Yes, but what is left?" and even wondering whether it be an advantage to an artist to obtain early in life such possession of his means that the struggle with them, discipline, *tâtonnement,* cease to exist for him. May not this breed an irresponsibility of cleverness, a wantonness, an irreverence—what is vulgarly termed a "larkiness"—on the part of the youthful genius who has, as it were, all his fortune in his pocket? Such are the possibly superfluous broodings of those who are critical even in their warmest admirations and who sometimes suspect that it may be better for an artist to have a certain part of his property invested in unsolved difficulties. When this is not the case, the question with regard to his future simplifies itself somewhat portentously. "What will he do with it?" we ask, meaning by the pronoun the sharp, completely forged weapon. It becomes more purely a question of responsibility, and we hold him altogether to a higher account. This is the case with Mr. Sargent; he knows so much about the art of painting that he perhaps does not fear emergencies quite enough, and that having knowledge to spare he may be tempted to play with it and waste it. Various, curious, as we have called him, he occasionally tries experiments which seem to arise from the mere high spirits of his brush, and runs risks little courted by the votaries of the literal, who never expose their necks to escape from the common. For the literal and the common he has the smallest taste; when he renders an object into the language of painting his translation is a generous paraphrase.

As I have intimated, he has painted little but portraits; but he has painted very many of these, and I shall not attempt in so few pages to give a catalogue of his works. Every canvas that has come from his hands has not figured at the Salon; some of them have seen the light at other exhibitions in Paris; some of them in London (of which city Mr. Sargent is now an inhabitant), at the Royal Academy and the Grosvenor Gallery. If he has been mainly represented by portraits there are two or three little subject-pictures of which I retain a grateful memory. There stands out in particular, as a pure gem, a small picture exhibited at the Grosvenor, representing a small group of Venetian girls of the lower class, sitting in gossip together one summer's day in the big, dim hall of a shabby old palazzo. The shutters let in a clink of light; the scagliola pavement gleams faintly in it; the whole place is bathed in a kind of transparent shade. The girls are vaguely engaged in some very humble household work; they are counting turnips or stringing onions, and these small vegetables, enchantingly painted, look as valuable as magnified pearls. The figures are extraordinarily natural and vivid; wonderfully light and fine is the touch by which the painter evokes the small familiar Venetian realities (he has handled them with a vigor altogether peculiar in various other studies which I have not space to enumerate), and keeps the whole thing free from that element of humbug which has ever attended most attempts to reproduce the idiosyncrasies of Italy. I am, however, drawing to the end of my remarks without having mentioned a dozen of those brilliant triumphs in the field of portraiture with which Mr. Sargent's name is preponderantly associated. I jumped from his "Carolus Duran" to the masterpiece of 1881 without speaking of the charming "Madame Pailleron" of 1879, or the picture of this lady's children the following year. Many, or rather most, of Mr. Sargent's sitters have been French, and he has studied the physiognomy of this nation so attentively that a little of it perhaps remains in the brush with which to-day, more than in his first years, he represents other types. I have alluded to his superb "Docteur Pozzi," to whose very handsome, still youthful head and slightly artificial posture he has given so fine a French cast that he might be excused if he should, even on remoter pretexts, find himself reverting to it. This gentleman stands up in his brilliant red dressing-gown with the *prestance* of a princely Vandyck. I should like to commemorate the portrait of a lady of a certain age and of an equally certain interest of appearance—a lady in black, with black hair, a black hat and a vast feather, which was displayed at that entertaining little annual exhibition of the "Mirlitons," in the Place Vendôme. With the exquisite modelling of its face (no one better than Mr. Sargent understands the beauty that resides in exceeding fineness), this head remains in my mind as a masterly rendering of the look of experience—such experience as may be attributed to a woman slightly faded and eminently distinguished. Subject and treatment in this valuable piece are of an equal interest, and in the latter there is an element of positive sympathy which is not always in a high degree the sign of Mr. Sargent's work. What shall I say of the remarkable canvas which, on the occasion of the Salon of 1884, brought the critics about our artist's ears, the already celebrated portrait of "Madame G.?" It is an experiment of a highly original kind, and the painter has had in the case, in regard to what Mr. Ruskin would call the "rightness" of his attempt, the courage of his opinion. A contestable beauty, according to Parisian fame, the lady stands upright beside a table on which her right arm rests, with her body almost fronting the spectator and her face in complete profile. She wears an entirely sleeveless dress of black satin, against which her admirable left arm detaches itself; the line of her harmonious profile has a sharpness which Mr. Sargent does not always seek, and the crescent of Diana, an ornament in diamonds, rests on her singular head. This work had not the good-fortune to please the public at large, and I believe it even excited a kind of unreasoned scandal—an idea sufficiently amusing in the light of some of the manifestations of the plastic effort to which, each year, the Salon stands sponsor. This superb picture, noble in conception and masterly in line, gives to the figure represented something of the high relief of the profiled images on great friezes. It is a work to take or to leave, as the phrase is, and one in regard to which the question of liking or disliking comes promptly to be settled. The author has never gone further in being boldly and consistently himself.

Two of Mr. Sargent's recent productions have been portraits of American ladies whom it must have been a delight to paint; I allude to those of Lady

Playfair and Mrs. Henry White, both of which were seen in the Royal Academy of 1885, and the former subsequently in Boston, where it abides. These things possess, largely, the quality which makes Mr. Sargent so happy as a painter of women—a quality which can best be expressed by a reference to what it is not, to the curiously literal, prosaic, sexless treatment to which, in the commonplace work that looks down at us from the walls of almost all exhibitions, delicate feminine elements have evidently so often been sacrificed. Mr. Sargent handles these elements with a special feeling for them, and they borrow a kind of noble intensity from his brush. This intensity is not absent from the two portraits I just mentioned, that of Lady Playfair and that of Mrs. Henry White; it looks out at us from the erect head and frank animation of the one, and the silvery sheen and shimmer of white satin and white lace which form the setting of the slim tall-ness of the other. In the Royal Academy of 1886 Mr. Sargent was represented by three important canvases, all of which reminded the spectator of how much the brilliant effect he produces in an English exhibition arises from a certain appearance that he has of looking down from a height, a height of cleverness, a sensible giddiness of facility, at the artistic problems of the given case. Sometimes there is even a slight impertinence in it; that, doubtless, was the impression of many of the people who passed, staring, with an ejaculation, before the triumphant group of the three Misses V. These young ladies, seated in a row, with a room much foreshortened for a background, and treated with a certain familiarity of frankness, excited in London a chorus of murmurs not dissimilar to that which it had been the fortune of the portrait exhibited in 1884 to elicit in Paris, and had the further privilege of drawing forth some prodigies of purblind criticism. Works of this character are a genuine service; after the short-lived gibes of the profane have subsided, they are found to have cleared the air. They remind people that the faculty of taking a direct, independent, unborrowed impression is not altogether lost.

In this very rapid review I have accompanied Mr. Sargent to a very recent date. If I have said that observers encumbered with a nervous temperament may at any moment have been anxious about his future, I have it on my conscience to add that the day has not yet come for a complete extinction of this anxiety. Mr. Sargent is so young, in spite of the place allotted to him in these pages, so often a record of long careers and uncontested triumphs that, in spite also of the admirable works he has already produced, his future is the most valuable thing he has to show. We may still ask ourselves what he will do with it, while we indulge the hope that he will see fit to give successors to the two pictures which I have spoken of emphatically as his finest. There is no greater work of art than a great portrait—a truth to be constantly taken to heart by a painter holding in his hands the weapon that Mr. Sargent wields. The gift that he possesses he possesses completely—the immediate perception of the end and of the means. Putting aside the question of the subject (and to a great portrait a common sitter will doubtless not always contribute), the highest result is achieved when to this element of quick perception a certain faculty of brooding reflection is added. I use this name for want of a better, and I mean the quality in the light of which the artist sees deep into his subject, undergoes it, absorbs it, discovers in it new things that were not on the surface, becomes patient with it, and almost reverent, and, in short, enlarges and humanizes the technical problem.

HONORÉ DAUMIER

AS we attempt, at the present day, to write the history of everything, it would be strange if we had happened to neglect the annals of caricature; for the very essence of the art of Cruikshank and Gavarni, of Daumier and Leech, is to be historical; and every one knows how addicted is this great science to discoursing about itself. Many industrious seekers, in England and France, have ascended the stream of time to the source of the modern movement of pictorial satire. The stream of time is in this case mainly the stream of journalism; for social and political caricature, as the present century has practised it, is only journalism made doubly vivid.

The subject indeed is a large one, if we reflect upon it, for many people would tell us that journalism is the greatest invention of our age. If this rich affluent has shared the great fortune of the general torrent, so, on other sides, it touches the fine arts, touches manners, touches morals. All this helps to account for its inexhaustible life; journalism is the criticism of the moment *at* the moment, and caricature is that criticism at once simplified and intensified by a plastic form. We know the satiric image as periodical, and above all as punctual—the characteristics of the printed sheet with which custom has at last inveterately associated it.

This, by-the-way, makes us wonder considerably at the failure of caricature to achieve, as yet, a high destiny in America—a failure which might supply an occasion for much explanatory discourse, much searching of the relations of things. The newspaper has been taught to flourish among us as it flourishes nowhere else, and to flourish moreover on a humorous and irreverent basis; yet it has never taken to itself this helpful concomitant of an unscrupulous spirit and a quick periodicity. The explanation is probably that it needs an old society to produce ripe caricature. The newspaper thrives in the United States, but journalism languishes; for the lively propagation of news is one thing and the large interpretation of it is another. A society has to be old before it becomes critical, and it has to become critical before it can take pleasure in the reproduction of its incongruities by an instrument as impertinent as the indefatigable crayon. Irony, scepticism, pessimism are, in any particular soil, plants of gradual growth, and it is in the art of caricature that they flower most aggressively. Furthermore they must be watered by education—I mean by the education of the eye and hand—all of which things take time. The soil must be rich too, the incongruities must swarm. It is open to doubt whether a pure democracy is very liable to make this particular satiric return upon itself; for which it would seem tha' certain social complications are indispensable. These complications are supplied from the moment a democracy becomes, as we may say, impure from its own point of view; from the moment variations and heresies, deviations or perhaps simple affirmations of taste and temper begin to multiply within it. Such things afford a *point d'appui*; for it is evidently of the essence of caricature to be reactionary. We hasten to add that its satiric force varies immensely in kind and in degree according to the race, or to the individual talent, that takes advantage of it.

I used just now the term pessimism; but that was doubtless in a great measure because I have been turning over a collection of the extraordinarily vivid drawings of Honoré Daumier. The same impression would remain with me, no doubt, if I had been consulting an equal quantity of the work of Gavarni the wittiest, the most literary and most acutely profane of all chartered mockers with the pencil. The feeling of disrespect abides in all these things, the expression of the spirit for which humanity is definable primarily by its weaknesses. For Daumier these weaknesses are altogether ugly and grotesque, while for Gavarni they are either basely graceful or touchingly miserable; but the vision of them in both cases is close and direct. If, on the other hand, we look through a dozen volumes of the collection of *Punch* we get an equal impression of hilarity, but we by no means get an equal impression of irony. Certainly the pages of *Punch* do not reek with pessimism; their "criticism of life" is gentle and forbearing. Leech is positively optimistic; there is at any rate nothing infinite in his irreverence; it touches bottom as soon as it approaches the pretty woman or the nice girl. It is such an apparition as this that really, in Gavarni, awakes the scoffer. Du Maurier is as graceful as Gavarni, but his sense of beauty conjures away almost everything save our minor vices. It is in the exploration of our major ones that Gavarni makes his principal discoveries of charm or of absurdity of attitude. None the less, of course, the general inspiration of both artists is the same: the desire to try the innumerable different ways in which the human subject may *not* be taken seriously.

If this view of that subject, in its plastic manifestations, makes history of a sort, it will not in general be of a kind to convert those persons who find history sad reading. The writer of the present lines remained unconverted, lately, on an occasion on which many cheerful influences were mingled with his impression. They were of a nature to which he usually does full justice, even overestimating perhaps their charm of suggestion; but, at the hour I speak of, the old Parisian quay, the belittered print-shop, the pleasant afternoon, the glimpse of the great Louvre on the other side of the Seine, in the interstices of the sallow *estampes* suspended in window and doorway— all these elements of a rich actuality availed only to mitigate, without transmuting, that general vision of a high, cruel pillory which pieced itself together as I drew specimen after specimen from musty portfolios. I had been passing the shop when I noticed in a small *vitrine*, let into the embrasure of the doorway, half a dozen soiled, striking lithographs, which it took no more than a first glance to recognize as the work of Daumier. They were only old pages of the *Charivari*, torn away from the text and rescued from the injury of time; and they were accompanied with an inscription to the effect that many similar examples of the artist were to be seen within. To become aware of this circumstance was to enter the shop and to find myself promptly surrounded with bulging; *cartons* and tattered relics. These relics—crumpled leaves of the old comic journals of the period from 1830 to 1855—are neither rare nor expensive; but I happened to have lighted on a particularly copious collection, and I made the most of my small good-fortune, in order to transmute it, if possible, into a sort of compensation for my having missed unavoidably, a few months before, the curious exhibition "de la Caricature Moderne" held for several weeks just at hand, in the École des Beaux-Arts.

Daumier was said to have appeared there in considerable force; and it was a loss not to have had that particular opportunity of filling one's mind with him.

There was perhaps a perversity in having wished to do so, strange, indigestible stuff of contemplation as he might appear to be; but the perversity had had an honorable growth. Daumier's great days were in the reign of Louis-Philippe; but in the early years of the Second Empire he still plied his coarse and formidable pencil. I recalled, from a juvenile consciousness, the last failing strokes of it. They used to impress me in Paris, as a child, with their abnormal blackness as well as with their grotesque, magnifying movement, and there was something in them that rather scared a very immature admirer. This small personage, however, was able to perceive later, when he was unfortunately deprived of the chance of studying them, that there were various things in them besides the power to excite a vague alarm. Daumier was perhaps a great artist; at all events unsatisfied curiosity increased in proportion to that possibility.

The first complete satisfaction of it was really in the long hours that I spent in the little shop on the quay. There I filled my mind with him, and there too, at no great cost, I could make a big parcel of these cheap reproductions of his work. This work had been shown in the Ecole des Beaux-Arts as it came from his hand; M. Champfleury, his biographer, his cataloguer and devotee, having poured forth the treasures of a precious collection, as I suppose they would be called in the case of an artist of higher flights. It was only as he was seen by the readers of the comic journals of his day that I could now see him; but I tried to make up for my want of privilege by prolonged immersion. I was not able to take home all the portfolios from the shop on the quay, but I took home what I could, and I went again to turn over the superannuated piles. I liked looking at them on the spot; I seemed still surrounded by the artist's vanished Paris and his extinct Parisians. Indeed no quarter of the delightful city probably shows, on the whole, fewer changes from the aspect it wore during the period of Louis-Philippe, the time when it will ever appear to many of its friends to have been most delightful. The long line of the quay is unaltered, and the rare charm of the river. People came and went in the shop: it is a wonder how many, in the course of an hour, may lift the latch even of an establishment that pretends to no great business. What was all this small, sociable, contentious life but the great Daumier's subject-matter? He was the painter of the Parisian bourgeois, and the voice of the bourgeois was in the air.

M. Champfleury has given a summary of Daumier's career in his smart little *Histoire e la Caricature Moderne*, a record not at all abundant in personal detail. The biographer has told his story better perhaps in his careful catalogue of the artist's productions, the first sketch of which is to be found in *L'Art* for 1878. This copious list is Daumier's real history; his life cannot have been a very different business from his work. I read in the interesting publication of M. Grand-Carteret (*Les Moeurs et la Caricature en France* 1888) that our artist produced nearly 4000 lithographs and a thousand drawings on wood, up to the time when failure of eyesight compelled him to rest. This is not the sort of activity that leaves a man much time for independent adventures, and Daumier was essentially of the type, common in France, of the specialist so immersed in his specialty that he can be painted in only one attitude—a general circumstance which perhaps helps to account for the paucity, in that country, of biography, in our English sense of the word, in proportion to the superabundance of criticism.

Honoré Daumier was born at Marseilles February 26th, 1808; he died on the 11th of the same month, 1879. His main activity, however, was confined to the earlier portion of a career of almost exactly seventy-one years, and I find it affirmed in Vapereau's *Dictionnaire des Contemporains* that he became completely blind between 1850 and 1860. He enjoyed a pension from the State of 2400 francs; but what relief from misery could mitigate a quarter of a century of darkness for a man who had looked out at the world with such vivifying eyes? His father had followed the trade of a glazier, but was otherwise vocal than in the emission of the rich street-cry with which we used all to be familiar, and which has vanished with so many other friendly pedestrian notes. The elder Daumier wrought verses as well as window-panes, and M. Champfleury has disinterred a small volume published by him in 1823. The merit of his poetry is not striking; but he was able to transmit the artistic nature to his son, who, becoming promptly conscious of it, made the inevitable journey to Paris in search of fortune.

The young draughtsman appeared to have missed at first the way to this boon; inasmuch as in the year 1832 he found himself condemned to six months' imprisonment for a lithograph disrespectful to Louis-Philippe. This drawing had appeared in the *Caricature*, an organ of pictorial satire founded in those days by one Philipon, with the aid of a band of young mockers to whom he gave ideas and a direction, and several others, of whom Gavarni, Henry Monnier, Decamps, Grandville, were destined to make themselves a place. M. Eugène Montrosier, in a highly appreciative article on Daumier in *L'Art* for 1878, says that this same Philipon was *le journalisme fait homme*; which did not prevent him—rather in fact fostered such a result—from being perpetually in delicate relations with the government. He had had many horses killed under him, and had led a life of attacks, penalties, suppressions and resurrections. He subsequently established the *Charivari* and launched a publication entitled *L'Association Lithographique Mensuelle*, which brought to light much of Daumier's early work. The artist passed rapidly from seeking his way to finding it, and from an ineffectual to a vigorous form.

In this limited compass and in the case of such a quantity of production it is almost impossible to specify—difficult to pick dozens of examples out of thousands. Daumier became more and more the political spirit of the *Charivari*, or at least the political pencil, for M. Philipon, the breath of whose nostrils was opposition—one perceives from here the little bilious, bristling, ingenious, insistent man—is to be credited with a suggestive share in any enterprise in which he had a hand. This pencil played over public life, over the sovereign, the ministers, the deputies, the peers, the judiciary, the men and the measures, the reputations and scandals of the moment, with a strange, ugly, extravagant, but none the less sane and manly vigor. Daumier's sign is strength above all, and in turning over his pages to-day there is no intensity of force that the careful observer will not concede to him. It is perhaps another matter to assent to the proposition, put forth by his greatest admirers among his countrymen, that he is the first of all caricaturists. To the writer of this imperfect sketch he remains considerably less interesting than Gavarni; and/or a particular reason, which it is difficult to express otherwise than by saying that he is too simple. Simplicity was not Gavarni's fault, and indeed to a large degree it was Daumier's merit. The single grossly ridiculous or almost hauntingly characteristic thing which his figures represent is largely the reason why they still represent life and an unlucky reality years after the names attached to them have parted with a vivifying power. Such vagueness has overtaken them, for the most part, and to such a thin reverberation have they shrunk, the persons and the affairs which were then so intensely sketchable. Daumier handled them with a want of ceremony which would have been brutal were it not for the element of science in his work, making them immense and unmistakable in their drollery, or at least in their grotesqueness; for the term drollery suggests gayety, and Daumier is anything but gay. *Un rude peintre de moeurs*, M. Champfleury calls him; and the phrase expresses his extreme breadth of treatment.

Of the victims of his "rudeness" M. Thiers is almost the only one whom the present generation may recognize without a good deal of reminding, and indeed his hand is relatively light in delineating this personage of few inches and many episodes. M. Thiers must have been dear to the caricaturist, for he belonged to the type that was easy to "do;" it being well known that these gentlemen appreciate public characters in direct proportion to their saliency of feature. When faces are reducible to a few telling strokes their wearers are overwhelmed with the honors of publicity; with which, on the other hand, nothing is more likely to interfere than the possession of a countenance neatly classical. Daumier had only to give M. Thiers the face of a clever owl, and the trick was played. Of course skill was needed to individualize the symbol, but that is what caricaturists propose to themselves. Of how well he succeeded the admirable plate of the lively little minister in a "new dress"—tricked out in the uniform of a general of the First Republic—is a sufficient illustration. The bird of night is not an acute bird, but how the artist has presented the image of a selected specimen! And with what a life-giving pencil the whole figure is put on its feet, what intelligent drawing, what a rich, free stroke! The allusions conveyed in it are to such forgotten things that it is strange to think the personage was, only the other year, still contemporaneous; that he might have been met, on a fine day, taking a few firm steps in a quiet part of the Champs Élysées, with his footman carrying a second overcoat and looking doubly tall behind him. In whatever attitude Daumier depicts him, planted as a tiny boxing-master at the feet of the virtuous colossus in a blouse (whose legs are apart, like those-of the Rhodian), in whom the artist represents the People, to watch the match that is about to come off between Ratapoil and M. Berryer, or even in the act of lifting the "parricidal" club of a new repressive law to deal a blow at the Press, an effulgent, diligent, sedentary muse (this picture, by the way, is a perfect specimen of the simple and telling in political caricature)—however, as I say, he takes M. Thiers, there is always a rough indulgence in his crayon, as if he were grateful to him for lending himself so well. He invented Ratapoil as he appropriated Robert Macaire, and as a caricaturist he never fails to put into circulation, when he can, a character to whom he may attribute as many as possible of the affectations or the vices of the day. Robert Macaire, an imaginative, a romantic rascal, was the hero of a highly successful melodrama written for Frederick Lemaitre; but Daumier made him the type of the swindler at large in an age of feverish speculation—the projector of showy companies, the advertiser of worthless shares. There is a whole series of drawings descriptive of his exploits, a hundred masterly plates which, according to M. Champfleury, consecrated Daumier's reputation. The subject, the legend, was in most cases, still according to M. Champfleury, suggested by Philipon. Sometimes it was very witty; as for instance when Bertrand, the muddled acolyte or scraping second fiddle of the hero, objects, in relation to a brilliant scheme which he has just developed, with the part Bertrand is to play, that there are constables in the country, and he promptly replies, "Constables? So much the better—they'll take the shares!" Ratapoil was an evocation of the same general character, but with a difference of *nuance*—the ragged political bully, or hand-to-mouth demagogue, with the smashed tall hat, cocked to one side, the absence of linen, the club half-way up his sleeve, the swagger and pose of being gallant for the people. Ratapoil abounds in the promiscuous drawings that I have looked over, and is always very strong and living, with a considerable element of the sinister, so often in Daumier an accompaniment of the comic. There is an admirable page—it brings the idea down to 1851—in which a sordid but astute peasant, twirling his thumbs on his stomach and looking askance, allows this political adviser to urge upon him in a whisper that there is not a minute to lose—to lose for action, of course—if he wishes to keep his wife, his house, his field, his heifer and his calf. The canny scepticism in the ugly, half-averted face of the typical rustic who considerably suspects his counsellor is indicated by a few masterly strokes.

This is what the student of Daumier recognizes as his science, or, if the word has a better grace, his art. It is what has kept life in his work so long after so many of the occasions of it have been swept into darkness. Indeed, there is no such commentary on renown as the "back numbers" of a comic journal. They show us that at certain moments certain people were eminent, only to make us unsuccessfully try to remember what they were eminent *for*. And the comparative obscurity (comparative, I mean, to the talent of the caricaturist) overtakes even the most justly honored names. M. Berryer was a splendid speaker and a public servant of real distinction and the highest utility; yet the fact that to-day his name is on few men's lips seems to be emphasized by this other fact that we continue to pore over Daumier, in whose plates we happen to come across him. It reminds one afresh how Art is an embalmer, a magician, whom we can never speak too fair. People duly impressed with this truth are sometimes laughed at for their superstitious tone, which is pronounced, according to the fancy of the critic, mawkish, maudlin or hysterical. But it is really difficult to see how any reiteration of the importance of art can overstate the plain facts. It prolongs, it preserves, it consecrates, it raises from the dead. It conciliates, charms, bribes posterity; and it murmurs to mortals, as the old French poet sang to his mistress, "You will be fair only so far as I have said so." When it whispers even to the great, "You depend upon me, and I can do more for you, in the long-run, than any one else," it is scarcely too proud. It puts method and power and the strange, real, mingled air of things into Daumier's black sketchiness, so full of the technical *gras*, the "fat" which French critics commend and which we have no word to express. It puts power above all, and the effect which he best achieves, that of a certain simplification of the attitude or the gesture to an almost symbolic generality. His persons represent only one thing, but they insist tremendously on that, and their expression of it abides with us, unaccompanied with timid detail. It may really be said that they represent only one class—the old and ugly; so that there is proof enough of a special faculty in his having played such a concert, lugubrious though it be, on a single chord. It has been made a reproach to him, says M. Grand-Carteret, that "his work is lacking in two capital elements—*la jeunesse et la femme*;" and the commentator resents his being made to suffer for the deficiency—"as if an artist could be at the same time deep, comic, graceful and pretty; as if all those who have a real value had not created for themselves a form to which they remain confined and a type which they reproduce in all its variations, as soon as they have touched the æsthetic ideal that has been their dream. Assuredly humanity, as this great painter saw it, could not be beautiful; one asks one's self what maiden in her teens, a pretty face, would have done in the midst of these good, plain folk, stunted and elderly, with faces like wrinkled apples. A simple accessory most of the time, woman is for him merely a termagant or a blue-stocking who has turned the corner."

When the eternal feminine, for Daumier appears in neither of these forms he sees it in Madame Chaboulard or Madame Fribochon, the old snuff-taking, gossiping portress, in a nightcap and shuffling *savates*, relating or drinking in the wonderful and the intimate. One of his masterpieces represents three of these dames, lighted by a guttering candle, holding their heads together to discuss the fearful earthquake at Bordeaux, the consequence of the government's allowing the surface of the globe to be unduly dug out in California. The representation of confidential imbecility could not go further. When a man leaves out so much of life as Daumier—youth and beauty and the charm of woman and the loveliness of childhood and the manners of those social groups of whom it may most be said that they *have* manners— when he exhibits a deficiency on this scale it might seem that the question was not to be so easily disposed of as in the very non-apologetic words I have just quoted. All the same (and I confess it is singular), we may feel what Daumier omitted and yet not be in the least shocked by the claim of predominance made for him. It is impossible to spend a couple of hours over him without assenting to this claim, even though there may be a weariness in such a panorama of ugliness and an inevitable reaction from it. This anomaly, and the challenge to explain it which appears to proceed from him, render him, to my sense, remarkably interesting. The artist whose idiosyncrasies, whose limitations, if you will, make us question and wonder, in the light of his fame, has an element of fascination not attaching to conciliatory talents. If M. Eugene Montrosier may say of him without scandalizing us that such and such of his drawings belong to the very highest art, it is interesting (and Daumier profits by the interest) to put one's finger on the reason we are not scandalized.

I think this reason is that, on the whole he is so peculiarly serious. This may seem an odd ground of praise for a jocose draughtsman, and of course what I mean is that his comic force is serious—a very different thin from the absence of comedy. This essential sign of the caricaturist may surely be anything it will so long as it is there. Daumier's figures are almost always either foolish, fatuous politicians or frightened, mystified bourgeois; yet they help him to give us a strong sense of the nature of man. They are some times so serious that they are almost tragic the look of the particular pretension, combined with inanity, is carried almost to madness. There is a magnificent drawing of the series of "Le Public du Salon," old classicists looking up, horrified and scandalized, at the new romantic work of 1830, in which the faces have an appalling gloom of mystification and platitude. We feel that Daumier reproduces admirably the particular life that he sees, because it is the very medium in which he moves. He has no wide horizon; the absolute bourgeois hems him in, and he is a bourgeois himself, without poetic ironies, to whom a big cracked mirror has been given. His thick, strong, manly touch stands, in every way, for so much knowledge. He used to make little images, in clay and in wax (many of them still exist), of the persons he was in the habit of representing, so that they might constantly seem to be "sitting" for him. The caricaturist of that day had not the help of the ubiquitous photograph. Daumier painted actively, as well, in his habitation, all dedicated to work, on the narrow island of St. Louis, where the Seine divides and where the monuments of old Paris stand thick, and the types that were to his purpose pressed close upon him. He had not far to go to encounter the worthy man, in the series of "Les Papas," who is reading the evening paper at the café with so amiable and placid a credulity, while his unnatural little boy, opposite to him, finds sufficient entertainment in the much-satirized *Constitutionnel*. The bland absorption of the papa, the face of the man who believes everything he sees in the newspaper, is as near as Daumier often comes to positive gentleness of humor. Of the same family is the poor gentleman, in "Actualités," seen, in profile, under a doorway where he has taken refuge from a torrent of rain, who looks down at his neat legs with a sort of speculative contrition and says. "To think of my having just ordered two pairs of white trousers." The *tout petit bourgeois* palpitates in both these sketches.

I must repeat that it is absurd to pick half a dozen at hazard, out of five thousand; yet a few selections are the only way to call attention to his strong drawing. This has a virtuosity of its own, for all its hit-or-miss appearance. Whatever he touches—the nude, in the swimming-baths on the Seine, the intimations of landscape, when his *petits rentiers* go into the suburbs for a Sunday—acquires relief and character, Docteur Véron, a celebrity of the reign of Louis-Philippe, a Mæcenas of the hour, a director of the opera, author of the *Mémoires d'un Bourgeois de Paris*—this temporary "illustration," who appears to have been almost indecently ugly, would not be vivid to us to-day had not Daumier, who was often effective at his expense, happened to have represented him, in some crisis of his career, as a sort of naked inconsolable Vitellius. He renders the human body with a cynical sense of its possible flabbiness and an intimate acquaintance with its structure. "Une Promenade Conjugale," in the series of "Tout ce qu'on voudra," portrays a hillside, on a summer afternoon, on which a man has thrown himself on his back to rest, with his arms locked under his head. His fat, full-bosomed, middle-aged wife, under her parasol, with a bunch of field-flowers in her hand, looks down at him patiently and seems to say, "Come, my dear, get up." There is surely no great point in this; the only point is life, the glimpse of the little snatch of poetry in prose. It is a matter of a few broad strokes of the crayon; yet the pleasant laziness of the man, the idleness of the day, the fragment of homely, familiar dialogue, the stretch of the field with a couple of trees merely suggested, have a communicative truth.

I perhaps exaggerate all this, and in insisting upon the merit of Daumier may appear to make light of the finer accomplishment of several more modern talents, in England and France, who have greater ingenuity and subtlety and have carried qualities of execution so, much further. In looking at this complicated younger work, which has profited so by experience and comparison, it is inevitable that we should perceive it to be infinitely more cunning. On the other hand Daumier, moving in his contracted circle, has an impressive depth. It comes back to his strange seriousness. He is a draughtsman by race, and if he has not extracted the same brilliancy from training, or perhaps even from effort and experiment, as some of his successors, does not his richer satiric and sympathetic feeling more than make up the difference?

However this question may be answered, some of his drawings belong to the class of the unforgetable. It may be a perversity of prejudice, but even the little cut of the "Connoisseurs," the group of gentlemen collected round a picture and criticising it in various attitudes of sapience and sufficiency, appears to me to have the strength that abides. The criminal in the dock, the flat-headed murderer, bending over to speak to his advocate, who turns a whiskered, professional, anxious head to caution and remind him. tells a large, terrible story and awakes a recurrent shudder. We see the gray court-room, we feel the personal suspense and the immensity of justice. The "Saltimbanques," reproduced in *L'Art* for 1878, is a page of tragedy, the finest of a cruel series. M. Eugène Montrosier says of it that "The drawing is masterly, incomparably firm, the composition superb, the general impression quite of the first order." It exhibits a pair of lean, hungry mountebanks, a clown and a harlequin beating the drum and trying a comic attitude to attract the crowd, at a fair, to a poor booth in front of which a painted canvas, offering to view a simpering fat woman, is suspended. But the crowd doesn't come, and the battered tumblers, with their furrowed cheeks, go through their pranks in the void. The whole thing is symbolic and full of grim-ness, imagination and pity. It is the sense that we shall find in him, mixed with his homelier extravagances, an element prolific in indications of this order that draws us back to Daumier.

AFTER THE PLAY

The play was not over when the curtain fell, four months ago; it was continued in a supplementary act or epilogue which took place immediately afterwards. "Come home to tea," Florentia said to certain friends who had stopped to speak to her in the lobby of the little theatre in Soho—they had been present at a day performance by the company of the Theatre Libre, transferred for a week from Paris; and three of these—Auberon and Dorriforth, accompanying Amicia—turned up so expeditiously that the change of scene had the effect of being neatly executed. The short afterpiece—it was in truth very slight—began with Amicia's entrance and her declaration that she would never again go to an afternoon performance: it was such a horrid relapse into the real to find it staring at you through the ugly daylight on coming out of the blessed fictive world.

Dorriforth. Ah, you touch there on one of the minor sorrows of life. That's an illustration of the general change that comes to pass in us as we grow older, if we have ever loved the stage: the fading of the glamour and the mystery that surround it.

Auberon. Do you call it a minor sorrow? It's one of the greatest. And nothing can mitigate it.

Amicia. Wouldn't it be mitigated a little if the stage were a trifle better? You must remember how that has changed.

Auberon. Never, never: it's the same old stage. The change is in ourselves.

Florentia. Well, I never would have given an evening to what we have just seen. If one could have put it in between luncheon and tea, well enough. But one's evenings are too precious.

Dorriforth. Note that—it's very important.

Florentia. I mean too precious for that sort of thing.

Auberon. Then you didn't sit spellbound by the little history of the Due d'Enghien?

Florentia. I sat yawning. Heavens, what a piece!

Amicia. Upon my word I liked it. The last act made me cry.

Dorriforth. Wasn't it a curious, interesting specimen of some of the things that are worth trying: an attempt to sail closer to the real?

Auberon. How much closer? The fiftieth part of a point—it isn't calculable.

Florentia. It was just like any other play—I saw no difference. It had neither a plot, nor a subject, nor dialogue, nor situations, nor scenery, nor costumes, nor acting.

Amicia. Then it was hardly, as you say, just like any other play.

Auberon. Florentia should have said like any other *bad* one. The only way it differed seemed to be that it was bad in theory as well as in fact.

Amicia. It's a *morceau de vie*, as the French say.

Auberon. Oh, don't begin on the French!

Amicia. It's a French experiment—*que voulez-vous?*

Auberon. English experiments will do.

Dorriforth. No doubt they would—if there *were* any. But I don't see them.

Amicia. Fortunately: think what some of them might be! Though Florentia saw nothing I saw many things in this poor little shabby "Due d'Enghien," coming over to our roaring London, where the dots have to be so big on the i's, with its barely audible note of originality. It appealed to me, touched me, offered me a poignant suggestion of the way things happen in life.

Auberon. In life they happen clumsily, stupidly, meanly. One goes to the theatre just for the refreshment of seeing them happen in another way—in symmetrical, satisfactory form, with unmistakable effect and just at the right moment.

Dorriforth. It shows how the same cause may produce the most diverse consequences. In this truth lies the only hope of art.

Auberon. Oh, art, art—don't talk about art!

Amicia. Mercy, we must talk about something!

Dorriforth. Auberon hates generalizations. Nevertheless I make bold to say that we go to the theatre in the same spirit in which we read a novel, some of us to find one thing and some to find another; and according as we look for the particular thing we find it.

Auberon. That's a profound remark.

Florentia. We go to find amusement: that, surely, is what we all go for.

Amicia. There's such a diversity in our idea of amusement.

Auberon. Don't you impute to people more ideas than they have?

Dorriforth. Ah, one must do that or one couldn't talk about them. We go to be interested; to be absorbed, beguiled and to lose ourselves, to give ourselves up, in short, to a charm.

Florentia. And the charm is the strange, the extraordinary.

Amicia. Ah, speak for yourself! The charm is the recognition of what we know, what we feel.

Dorriforth. See already how you differ.

"SO!"

What we surrender ourselves to is the touch of nature, the sense of life.

Amicia. The first thing is to believe.

Florentia. The first thing, on the contrary, is to *dis*believe.

Auberon. Lord, listen to them!

Dorriforth. The first thing is to folio—to care.

Florentia. I read a novel, I go to the theatre, to forget.

Amicia. To forget what?

Florentia. To forget life; to thro myself into something more beautiful more exciting: into fable and romance.

Dorriforth. The attraction of fable and romance is that it's about *us*, about you and me—or people whose power to suffer and to enjoy is the same as ours. In other words, we *live* their experience, for the time, and that's hardly escaping from life.

Florentia. I'm not at all particular as to what you call it. Call it an escape from the common, the prosaic, the immediate.

Dorriforth. You couldn't put it better. That's the life that art, with Auberon's permission, gives us; that's the distinction it confers. This is why the greatest commonness is when our guide turns out a vulgar fellow—the angel, as we had supposed him, who has taken us by the hand. Then what becomes of our escape?

Florentia. It's precisely then that I complain of him. He leads us into foul and dreary places—into flat and foolish deserts.

Dorriforth. He leads us into his own mind, his own vision of things: that's the only place into which the poet *can* lead us. It's there that he finds "As You Like It," it is there that he finds "Comus," or "The Way of the World," or the Christmas pantomime. It is when he betrays us, after he has got us in and locked the door, when he can't keep from us that we are in a bare little hole and that there are no pictures on the walls, it is then that the immediate and the foolish overwhelm us.

Amicia. That's what I liked in the piece we have been looking at. There was an artistic intention, and the little room wasn't bare: there was sociable company in it. The actors were very humble aspirants, they were common—

Auberon. Ah, when the French give their mind to that—!

Amicia. Nevertheless they struck me as recruits to an interesting cause, which as yet (the house was so empty) could confer neither money nor glory. They had the air, poor things, of working for love.

Auberon. For love of what?

Amicia. Of the whole little enterprise—the idea of the Théâtre Libre.

Florentia. Gracious, what you see in things! Don't you suppose they were paid?

Amicia. I know nothing about it. I liked their shabbiness—they had only what was indispensable in the way of dress and scenery. That often pleases me: the imagination, in certain cases, is more finely persuaded by the little than by the much.

Dorriforth. I see what Amicia means.

Florentia. I'll warrant you do, and a great deal more besides.

Dorriforth. When the appointments are meagre and sketchy the responsibility that rests upon the actors becomes a still more serious thing, and the spectator's observation of the way they rise to it a pleasure more intense. The face and the voice are more to the purpose than acres of painted canvas, and a touching intonation, a vivid gesture or two, than an army of supernumeraries.

Auberon. Why not have everything—the face, the voice, the touching intonations, the vivid gestures, the acres of painted canvas, *and* the army of supernumeraries? Why not use bravely and intelligently every resource of which the stage disposes? What else was Richard Wagner's great theory, in producing his operas at Bayreuth?

Dorriforth. Why not, indeed? That would be the ideal. To have the picture complete at the same time the figures do their part in producing the particular illusion required—what a perfection and what a joy! I know no answer to that save the aggressive, objectionable fact. Simply look at the stage of to-day and observe that these two branches of the matter never do happen to go together. There is evidently a corrosive principle in the large command of machinery and decorations—a germ of perversion and corruption. It gets the upperhand—it becomes the master. It is so much less easy to get good actors than good scenery and to represent a situation by the delicacy of personal art than by "building it in" and having everything real. Surely there is no reality worth a farthing, on the stage, but what the actor gives, and only when he has learned his business up to the hilt need he concern himself with his material accessories. He hasn't a decent respect for his art unless he be ready to render his part as if the whole illusion depended on that alone and the accessories didn't exist. The acting is everything or it's nothing. It ceases to be everything as soon as something else becomes very important. This is the case, to-day, on the London stage: something else is very important. The public have been taught to consider it so: the clever machinery has ended by operating as a bribe and a blind. Their sense of the rest of the matter has gone to the dogs, as you may perceive when you hear a couple of occupants of the stalls talking, in a tone that excites your curiosity, about a performance that's "splendid."

Amicia. Do you ever hear the occupants of the stalls talking? Never, in the *entr'actes*, have I detected, on their lips, a criticism or a comment.

Dorriforth. Oh, they say "splendid"—distinctly! But a question or two reveals that their reference is vague: they don't themselves know whether they mean the art of the actor or that of the stage-carpenter.

Auberon. Isn't that confusion a high result of taste? Isn't it what's called a feeling for the *ensemble?* The artistic effect, as a whole, is so welded together that you can't pick out the parts.

Dorriforth. Precisely; that's what it is in the best cases, and some examples are wonderfully clever.

Florentia. Then what fault do you find? Dorriforth. Simply this—that the whole is a pictorial whole, not a dramatic one. There is something indeed that you can't pick out, for the very good reason that—in any serious sense of the word—it isn't there.

Florentia. The public has taste, then, if it recognizes and delights in a fine picture.

Dorriforth. I never said it hadn't, so far as that goes. The public likes to be amused, and small blame to it. It isn't very particular about the means, but it has rather a preference for amusements that I believes to be "improving," other things being equal. I don't think it's either very intelligent or at all opinionated, the dear old public it takes humbly enough what is given it and it doesn't cry for the moon. It has an idea that fine scenery is an appeal to its nobler part, and that it shows a nice critical sense in preferring it to poor. That's a real intellectual flight, for the public.

Auberon. Very well, its preference is right, and why isn't that a perfectly legitimate state of things?

Dorriforth. Why isn't it? It distinctly *is!* Good scenery and poor acting are better than poor scenery with the same sauce. Only it becomes then another matter: we are no longer talking about the drama.

Auberon. Very likely that's the future of the drama, in London—an immense elaboration of the picture.

Dorriforth. My dear fellow, you take the words out of my mouth. An immense elaboration of the picture and an immense sacrifice of everything else: it would take very little more to persuade me that that will be the only formula for our children. It's all right, when once we have buried our dead. I have no doubt that the scenic part of the art, remarkable as some of its achievements already appear to us, is only in its infancy, and that we are destined to see wonders done that we now but faintly conceive. The probable extension of the mechanical arts is infinite. "Built in," forsooth! We shall see castles and cities and mountains and rivers built in. Everything points that way; especially the constitution of the contemporary multitude. It is huge and good-natured and common. It likes big, unmistakable, knock-down effects; it likes to get its money back in palpable, computable change. It's in a tremendous hurry, squeezed together, with a sort of generalized gape, and the last thing it expects of you is that you will spin things fine. You can't portray a character, alas, or even, vividly, any sort of human figure, unless, in some degree, you do that. Therefore the theatre, inevitably accommodating itself, will be at last a landscape without figures. I mean, of course, without figures that count. There will be little illustrations of costume stuck about—dressed manikins; but they'll have nothing to say: they won't even go through the form of speech.

Amicia. What a hideous prospect!

Dorriforth. Not necessarily, for we shall have grown used to it: we shall, as I say, have buried our dead. To-day it's cruel, because our old ideals are only dying, they are *in extremis*, they are virtually defunct, but they are above-ground—we trip and stumble on them. We shall eventually lay them tidily away. This is a bad moment, because it's a moment of transition, and we still *miss* the old superstition, the bravery of execution, the eloquence of the lips, the interpretation of character. We miss these things, of course, in proportion as the ostensible occasion for them is great; we miss them particularly, for instance, when the curtain rises on Shakespeare. Then we are conscious of a certain divine dissatisfaction, of a yearning for that which isn't. But we shall have got over this discomfort on the day when we have accepted the ostensible occasion as merely and frankly ostensible, and the real one as having nothing to do with it.

Florentia. I don't follow you. As I'm one of the squeezed, gaping public, I must be dense and vulgar. You do, by-the-way, immense injustice to that body. They do care for character—care much for it. Aren't they perpetually talking about the actor's conception of it?

Dorriforth. Dear lady, what better proof can there be of their ineptitude, and that painted canvas and real water are the only things they understand? The vanity of wasting time over that!

Auberon. Over what?

Dorriforth. The actor's conception of a part. It's the refuge of observers who are no observers and critics who are no critics. With what on earth have we to do save his execution?

Florentia. I don't in the least agree with you.

Amicia. Are you very sure, my poor Dorriforth?

266

Auberon. Give him rope and he'll hang himself.

Dorriforth. It doesn't need any great license to ask who in the world holds in his bosom the sacred secret of the right conception. All the actor can do is to give us his. We must take that one for granted, we make him a present of it. He must impose his conception upon us—

Auberon (interrupting). I thought you said we accepted it.

Dorriforth. Impose it upon our *attention*. clever Auberon. It is because we accept his idea that he must repay us by making it vivid, by showing us how valuable it is. We give him a watch: he must show us what time it keeps. He winds it up, that is he executes the conception, and his execution is what we criticise, if we be so moved. Can anything be more absurd than to hear people discussing the conception of a part of which the execution doesn't exist—the idea of a character which never arrives at form? Think what it is, that form, as an accomplished actor may give it to us, and admit that we have enough to do to hold him to this particular honor.

Auberon. Do you mean to say you don't think some conceptions are better than some others?

Dorriforth. Most assuredly, some are better: the proof of the pudding is in the eating. The best are those which yield the most points, which have the largest face; those, in other words, that are the most demonstrable, or, in other words still, the most actable. The most intelligent performer is he who recognizes most surely this "actable" and distinguishes in it the more from the less. But we are so far from being in possession of a subjective pattern to which we have a right to hold him that he is entitled directly to contradict any such absolute by presenting us with different versions of the same text, each completely colored, completely consistent with itself. Every actor in whom the artistic life is strong must often feel the challenge to do that. I should never think, for instance, of contesting an actress's right to represent Lady Macbeth as a charming, insinuating woman, if she really sees the figure that way. I may be surprised at such a vision; but so far from being scandalized, I am positively thankful for the extension of knowledge, of pleasure, that she is able to open to me.

Auberon. A reading, as they say, either commends itself to one's sense of truth or it doesn't. In the one case—

Dorriforth. In the one case I recognize—even—or especially—when the presumption may have been against the particular attempt, a consummate illustration of what art can do. In the other I moralize indulgently upon human rashness.

Florentia. You have an assurance *à taute épreuve*; but you are deplorably superficial. There is a whole group of plays and a whole category of acting to which your generalizations quite fail to apply. Help me, Auberon.

Auberon. You're easily exhausted. I suppose she means that it's far from true everywhere that the scenery is everything. It may be true—I don't say it is!—of two or three good-natured playhouses in London. It isn't true—how can it be?—of the provincial theatres or of the others in the capital. Put it even that they would be all scenery if they could; they can't, poor things—so they have to provide acting.

Dorriforth. They have to, fortunately; but what do we hear of it?

Florentia. How do you mean, what do we hear of it?

Dorriforth. In what trumpet of fame does it reach us? They do what they can, the performers Auberon alludes to, and they are brave souls. But I am speaking of the conspicuous cases, of the exhibitions that draw.

Florentia. There is good acting that draws; one could give you names and places.

Dorriforth. I have already guessed those you mean. But when it isn't too much a matter of the paraphernalia it is too little a matter of the play. A play nowadays is a rare bird. I should like to see ¦ one. **Florentia.** There are lots of them, all the while—the newspapers talk about them. People talk about them at dinners.

Dorriforth. What do they say about them?

Florentia. The newspapers?

268

Dorriforth. No, I don't care for *them*. The people at dinners.

Florentia. Oh. they don't say anything in particular.

Dorriforth. Doesn't that seem to show the effort isn't very suggestive?

Amicia. The conversation at dinners certainly isn't.

Dorriforth. I mean our contemporary drama. To begin with, you can't find it there's no text.

Florentia. No text?

Auberon. So much the better!

Dorriforth. So much the better if there is to be no criticism. There is only a dirt prompter's book. One can't put one's hand upon it; one doesn't know what one is discussing. There is no "authority"—nothing is ever published.

Amicia. The pieces wouldn't bear that.

Dorriforth. It would be a small ordeal to resist—if there were anything in them. Look at the novels!

Amicia. The text is the French *brochure*. The "adaptation" is unprintable.

Dorriforth. That's where it's so wrong, It ought at least to be as good as the original.

Auberon. Aren't there some "rights" to protect—some risk of the play being stolen if it's published?

Dorriforth. There may be—I don't know. Doesn't that only prove how little important we regard the drama as being, and how little seriously we take it, if we won't even trouble ourselves to bring about decent civil conditions for its existence? What have we to do with the French *brochure?* how does that help us to represent our own life, our manners, our customs, our ideas, our English types, our English world? Such a field for comedy, for tragedy, for portraiture, for satire, as they all make-such subjects as they would yield! Think of London alone—what a matchless hunting-ground for the satirist— the most magnificent that ever was. If the occasion always produced the man London would have produced an Aristophanes. But somehow it doesn't.

Florentia. Oh, types and ideas, Aristophanes and satire—!

Dorriforth. I'm too ambitious, you mean? I shall presently show you that I'm not ambitious at all. Everything makes against that—I am only reading the signs.

Auberon. The plays are arranged to be as English as possible: they are altered, they are fitted.

Dorriforth. Fitted? Indeed they are, and to the capacity of infants. They are in too many cases made vulgar, puerile, barbarous. They are neither fish nor flesh, and with all the point that's left out and all the naïveté that's put in, they cease to place before us any coherent appeal or any recognizable society.

Auberon. They often make good plays to act, all the same.

Dorriforth. They may; but they don't make good plays to see or to hear. The theatre consists of two things, *que diable*—of the stage and the drama, and I don't see how you can have it unless you have both, or how you can have either unless you have the other. They are the two blades of a pair of scissors.

Auberon. You are very unfair to native talent. There are lots of *strictly original* plays—

Amicia. Yes, they put that expression on the posters.

Auberon. I don't know what they put on the posters; but the plays are written and acted—produced with great success.

Dorriforth. Produced—partly. A play isn't fully produced until it is in a form in which you can refer to it. We have to talk in the air. I can refer to my Congreve, but I can't to my Pinero. {*}

---

      * *Since the above was written several of Mr. Pinero's plays*

           have been published.

Florentia. The authors are not bound to publish them if they don't wish.

Dorriforth. Certainly not, nor are they in that case bound to insist on one's not being a little vague about them. They are perfectly free to withhold them; they may have very good reasons for it, and I can imagine some that would be excellent and worthy of all respect. But their withholding them is one of the signs.

Auberon. What signs?

Dorriforth. Those I just spoke of—those we are trying to read together. The signs that ambition and desire are folly, that the sun of the drama has set, that the matter isn't worth talking about, that it has ceased to be an interest for serious folk, and that everything—everything, I mean, that's anything—is over. The sooner we recognize it the sooner to sleep, the sooner we get clear of misleading illusions and are purged of the bad blood that disappointment makes. It's a pity, because the theatre—after every allowance is made—*might* have been a fine thing. At all events it was a pleasant—it was really almost a noble—dream. *Requiescat!*

Florentia. I see nothing to confirm your absurd theory. I delight in the play; more people than ever delight in it with me; more people than ever go to it, and there are ten theatres in London where there were two of old.

Dorriforth. Which is what was to demonstrated. Whence do they derive their nutriment?

Auberon. Why, from the enormous public.

Dorriforth. My dear fellow, I'm not talking of the box-office. What wealth of dramatic, of histrionic production have we to meet that enormous demand? There will be twenty theatres ten years hence where there are ten to-day, and there will be, no doubt, ten times as many people "delighting in them," like Florentla. But it won't alter the fact that our dream will have been dreamed. Florentia said a word when we came in which alone speaks volumes.

Florentia. What was my word?

271

Auberon. You are sovereignly unjust to native talent among the actors—I leave the dramatists alone. There are many who do excellent, independent work; strive for perfection, completeness—in short, the things we want.

Dorriforth. I am not in the least unjust to them—I only pity them: they have so little to put *sous la dent*. It must seem to them at times that no one will work for them, that they are likely to starve for parts—forsaken of gods and men.

Florentia. If they work, then, in solitude and sadness, they have the more honor, and one should recognize more explicitly their great merit.

Dorriforth. Admirably said. Their laudable effort is precisely the one little loop-hole that I see of escape from the general doom. Certainly we must try to enlarge it—that small aperture into the blue. We must fix our eyes on it and make much of it, exaggerate it, do anything with it that may contribute to restore a working faith. Precious that must be to the sincere spirits on the stage who are conscious of all the other things—formidable things—that rise against them.

Amicia. What other things do you mean?

Dorriforth. Why, for one thing, the grossness and brutality of London, with its scramble, its pressure, its hustle of engagements, of preoccupations, its long distances, its late hours, its nightly dinners, its innumerable demands on the attention, its general congregation of influences fatal to the isolation, to the punctuality, to the security, of the dear old playhouse spell. When Florentia said in her charming way—

Florentia. Here's my dreadful speech at last.

Dorriforth. When you said that you went to the Théâtre Libre in the afternoon because you couldn't spare an evening, I recognized the death-knell of the drama. *Time*, the very breath of its nostrils, is lacking. Wagner was clever to go to leisurely Bayreuth among the hills—the Bayreuth of spacious days, a paradise of "development."

272

Talk to a London audience of "development!" The long runs would, if necessary, put the whole question into a nutshell. Figure to yourself, for then the question is answered, how an intelligent actor must loathe them, and what a cruel negation he must find in them of the artistic life, the life of which the very essence is variety of practice, freshness of experiment, and to feel that one must do many things in turn to do any one of them completely.

Auberon. I don't in the least understand your *acharnement*, in view of the vagueness of your contention.

Dorriforth. My *acharnement* is your little joke, and my contention is a little lesson in philosophy.

Florentia. I prefer a lesson in taste. I had one the other night at the "Merry Wives."

Dorriforth. If you come to that, so did I!

Amicia. So she does spare an evening sometimes.

Florentia. It was all extremely quiet and comfortable, and I don't in the least recognize Dorriforth's lurid picture of the dreadful conditions. There was no scenery—at least not too much; there was just enough, and it was very pretty, and it was in its place.

Dorriforth. And what else was there?

Florentia. There was very good acting.

Amicia. I also went, and I thought it all, for a sportive, wanton thing, quite painfully ugly.

Auberon. Uglier than that ridiculous black room, with the invisible people groping about in it, of your precious "Duc d'Enghien?"

Dorriforth. The black room is doubtless not the last word of art, but it struck me as a successful application of a happy idea. The contrivance was perfectly simple—a closer night effect than is usually attempted, with a few guttering candles, which threw high shadows over the bare walls, on the table of the court-martial. Out of the gloom came the voices and tones of the distinguishable figures, and it is perhaps a fancy of mine that it made them—given the situation, of course—more impressive and dramatic.

Auberon. You rail against scenery, but what could belong more to the order of things extraneous to what you perhaps a little priggishly call the delicacy of personal art than the arrangement you are speaking of?

Dorriforth. I was talking of the abuse of scenery. I never said anything so idiotic as that the effect isn't helped by an appeal to the eye and an adumbration of the whereabouts.

Auberon. But where do you draw the line and fix the limit? What is the exact dose?

Dorriforth. It's a question of taste and tact.

Florentia. And did you find taste and tact in that coal-hole of the Théâtre Libre?

Dorriforth. Coal-hole is again your joke. I found a strong impression in it—an impression of the hurried, extemporized cross-examination, by night, of an impatient and mystified prisoner, whose dreadful fate had been determined in advance, who was to be shot, high-handedly, in the dismal dawn. The arrangement didn't worry and distract me: it was simplifying, intensifying. It gave, what a judicious *mise-en-scène* should always do, the essence of the matter, and left the embroidery to the actors.

Florentia. At the "Merry Wives," where you could see your hand before your face, I could make out the embroidery.

Dorriforth. Could you, under Falstaff's pasteboard cheeks and the sad disfigurement of his mates? There was no excess of scenery, Auberon says. Why, Falstaff's very person was nothing *but* scenery. A false face, a false figure, false hands, false legs—scarcely a square inch on which the irrepressible humor of the rogue could break into illustrative touches. And he is so human, so expressive, of so rich a physiognomy. One would rather Mr. Beerbohm Tree should have played the part in his own clever, elegant slimness—-that would at least have represented life. A Falstaff all "make-up" is an opaque substance.

This seems to me an example of what the rest still more suggested, that in dealing with a production like the "Merry Wives" really the main quality to put forward is discretion. You must resolve such a production, as a thing represented, into a tone that the imagination can take an aesthetic pleasure in. Its grossness must be transposed, as it were, to a fictive scale, a scale of fainter tints and generalized signs. A filthy, eruptive, realistic Bardolph and Pistol overlay the romantic with the literal. Relegate them and blur them, to the eye; let their blotches be constructive and their raggedness relative.

Amicia. Ah, it was *so* ugly!

Dorriforth. What a pity then, after all, there wasn't more painted canvas to divert you! Ah, decidedly, the theatre of the future must be that.

Florentia. Please remember your theory that our life's a scramble, and suffer me to go and dress for dinner.

1889.

About Author

Henry James OM (15 April 1843 – 28 February 1916) was an American-British author regarded as a key transitional figure between literary realism and literary modernism, and is considered by many to be among the greatest novelists in the English language. He was the son of Henry James Sr. and the brother of renowned philosopher and psychologist William James and diarist Alice James.

He is best known for a number of novels dealing with the social and marital interplay between émigré Americans, English people, and continental Europeans. Examples of such novels include The Portrait of a Lady, The Ambassadors, and The Wings of the Dove. His later works were increasingly experimental. In describing the internal states of mind and social dynamics of his characters, James often made use of a style in which ambiguous or contradictory motives and impressions were overlaid or juxtaposed in the discussion of a character's psyche. For their unique ambiguity, as well as for other aspects of their composition, his late works have been compared to impressionist painting.

His novella The Turn of the Screw has garnered a reputation as the most analysed and ambiguous ghost story in the English language and remains his most widely adapted work in other media. He also wrote a number of other highly regarded ghost stories and is considered one of the greatest masters of the field.

James published articles and books of criticism, travel, biography, autobiography, and plays. Born in the United States, James largely relocated to Europe as a young man and eventually settled in England, becoming a British subject in 1915, one year before his death. James was nominated for the Nobel Prize in Literature in 1911, 1912 and 1916.

Life

Early years, 1843–1883

James was born at 2 Washington Place in New York City on 15 April 1843. His parents were Mary Walsh and Henry James Sr. His father was intelligent and steadfastly congenial. He was a lecturer and philosopher who had inherited independent means from his father, an Albany banker and investor. Mary came from a wealthy family long settled in New York City. Her sister Katherine lived with her adult family for an extended period of time. Henry Jr. had three brothers, William, who was one year his senior, and younger brothers Wilkinson (Wilkie) and Robertson. His younger sister was Alice. Both of his parents were of Irish and Scottish descent.

The family first lived in Albany, at 70 N. Pearl St., and then moved to Fourteenth Street in New York City when James was still a young boy. His education was calculated by his father to expose him to many influences, primarily scientific and philosophical; it was described by Percy Lubbock, the editor of his selected letters, as "extraordinarily haphazard and promiscuous." James did not share the usual education in Latin and Greek classics. Between 1855 and 1860, the James' household traveled to London, Paris, Geneva, Boulogne-sur-Mer and Newport, Rhode Island, according to the father's current interests and publishing ventures, retreating to the United States when funds were low. Henry studied primarily with tutors and briefly attended schools while the family traveled in Europe. Their longest stays were in France, where Henry began to feel at home and became fluent in French. He was afflicted with a stutter, which seems to have manifested itself only when he spoke English; in French, he did not stutter.

In 1860 the family returned to Newport. There Henry became a friend of the painter John La Farge, who introduced him to French literature, and in particular, to Balzac. James later called Balzac his "greatest master," and said that he had learned more about the craft of fiction from him than from anyone else.

In the autumn of 1861 Henry received an injury, probably to his back, while fighting a fire. This injury, which resurfaced at times throughout his life, made him unfit for military service in the American Civil War.

In 1864 the James family moved to Boston, Massachusetts to be near William, who had enrolled first in the Lawrence Scientific School at Harvard and then in the medical school. In 1862 Henry attended Harvard Law School, but realised that he was not interested in studying law. He pursued his interest in literature and associated with authors and critics William Dean Howells and Charles Eliot Norton in Boston and Cambridge, formed lifelong friendships with Oliver Wendell Holmes Jr., the future Supreme Court Justice, and with James and Annie Fields, his first professional mentors.

His first published work was a review of a stage performance, "Miss Maggie Mitchell in Fanchon the Cricket," published in 1863. About a year later, A Tragedy of Error, his first short story, was published anonymously. James's first payment was for an appreciation of Sir Walter Scott's novels, written for the North American Review. He wrote fiction and non-fiction pieces for The Nation and Atlantic Monthly, where Fields was editor. In 1871 he published his first novel, Watch and Ward, in serial form in the Atlantic Monthly. The novel was later published in book form in 1878.

During a 14-month trip through Europe in 1869–70 he met Ruskin, Dickens, Matthew Arnold, William Morris, and George Eliot. Rome impressed him profoundly. "Here I am then in the Eternal City," he wrote to his brother William. "At last—for the first time—I live!" He attempted to support himself as a freelance writer in Rome, then secured a position as Paris correspondent for the New York Tribune, through the influence of its editor John Hay. When these efforts failed he returned to New York City. During 1874 and 1875 he published Transatlantic Sketches, A Passionate Pilgrim, and Roderick Hudson. During this early period in his career he was influenced by Nathaniel Hawthorne.

In 1869 he settled in London. There he established relationships with Macmillan and other publishers, who paid for serial installments that they would later publish in book form. The audience for these serialized novels was largely made up of middle-class women, and James struggled to fashion serious literary work within the strictures imposed by editors' and publishers' notions of what was suitable for young women to read. He lived in rented rooms but was able to join gentlemen's clubs that had libraries and where he could entertain male friends. He was introduced to English society by Henry Adams and Charles Milnes Gaskell, the latter introducing him to the Travellers' and the Reform Clubs.

In the fall of 1875 he moved to the Latin Quarter of Paris. Aside from two trips to America, he spent the next three decades—the rest of his life—in Europe. In Paris he met Zola, Alphonse Daudet, Maupassant, Turgenev, and others. He stayed in Paris only a year before moving to London.

In England he met the leading figures of politics and culture. He continued to be a prolific writer, producing The American (1877), The Europeans (1878), a revision of Watch and Ward (1878), French Poets and Novelists (1878), Hawthorne (1879), and several shorter works of fiction. In 1878 Daisy Miller established his fame on both sides of the Atlantic. It drew notice perhaps mostly because it depicted a woman whose behavior is outside the social norms of Europe. He also began his first masterpiece, The Portrait of a Lady, which would appear in 1881.

In 1877 he first visited Wenlock Abbey in Shropshire, home of his friend Charles Milnes Gaskell whom he had met through Henry Adams. He was much inspired by the darkly romantic Abbey and the surrounding countryside, which features in his essay Abbeys and Castles. In particular the gloomy monastic fishponds behind the Abbey are said to have inspired the lake in The Turn of the Screw.

While living in London, James continued to follow the careers of the "French realists", Émile Zola in particular. Their stylistic methods influenced his own work in the years to come. Hawthorne's influence on him faded during this period, replaced by George Eliot and Ivan Turgenev. 1879–1882 saw the publication of The Europeans, Washington Square, Confidence, and The Portrait of a Lady. He visited America in 1882–1883, then returned to London.

The period from 1881 to 1883 was marked by several losses. His mother died in 1881, followed by his father a few months later, and then by his brother Wilkie. Emerson, an old family friend, died in 1882. His friend Turgenev died in 1883.

Middle years, 1884–1897

In 1884 James made another visit to Paris. There he met again with Zola, Daudet, and Goncourt. He had been following the careers of the French "realist" or "naturalist" writers, and was increasingly influenced by them. In 1886, he published The Bostonians and The Princess Casamassima, both influenced by the French writers he'd studied assiduously. Critical reaction and sales were poor. He wrote to Howells that the books had hurt his career rather than helped because they had "reduced the desire, and demand, for my productions to zero". During this time he became friends with Robert Louis Stevenson, John Singer Sargent, Edmund Gosse, George du Maurier, Paul Bourget, and Constance Fenimore Woolson. His third novel from the 1880s was The Tragic Muse. Although he was following the precepts of Zola in his novels of the '80s, their tone and attitude are closer to the fiction of Alphonse Daudet. The lack of critical and financial success for his novels during this period led him to try writing for the theatre. (His dramatic works and his experiences with theatre are discussed below.)

In the last quarter of 1889, he started translating "for pure and copious lucre" Port Tarascon, the third volume of Alphonse Daudet adventures of Tartarin de Tarascon. Serialized in Harper's Monthly Magazine from June 1890, this translation praised as "clever" by The Spectator was published in January 1891 by Sampson Low, Marston, Searle & Rivington.

After the stage failure of Guy Domville in 1895, James was near despair and thoughts of death plagued him. The years spent on dramatic works were not entirely a loss. As he moved into the last phase of his career he found ways to adapt dramatic techniques into the novel form.

In the late 1880s and throughout the 1890s James made several trips through Europe. He spent a long stay in Italy in 1887. In that year the short novel The Aspern Papers and The Reverberator were published.

Late years, 1898–1916

In 1897–1898 he moved to Rye, Sussex, and wrote The Turn of the Screw. 1899–1900 saw the publication of The Awkward Age and The Sacred

Fount. During 1902–1904 he wrote The Ambassadors, The Wings of the Dove, and The Golden Bowl.

In 1904 he revisited America and lectured on Balzac. In 1906–1910 he published The American Scene and edited the "New York Edition", a 24-volume collection of his works. In 1910 his brother William died; Henry had just joined William from an unsuccessful search for relief in Europe on what then turned out to be his (Henry's) last visit to the United States (from summer 1910 to July 1911), and was near him, according to a letter he wrote, when he died.

In 1913 he wrote his autobiographies, A Small Boy and Others, and Notes of a Son and Brother. After the outbreak of the First World War in 1914 he did war work. In 1915 he became a British subject and was awarded the Order of Merit the following year. He died on 28 February 1916, in Chelsea, London. As he requested, his ashes were buried in Cambridge Cemetery in Massachusetts.

Biographers

James regularly rejected suggestions that he should marry, and after settling in London proclaimed himself "a bachelor". F. W. Dupee, in several volumes on the James family, originated the theory that he had been in love with his cousin Mary ("Minnie") Temple, but that a neurotic fear of sex kept him from admitting such affections: "James's invalidism ... was itself the symptom of some fear of or scruple against sexual love on his part." Dupee used an episode from James's memoir A Small Boy and Others, recounting a dream of a Napoleonic image in the Louvre, to exemplify James's romanticism about Europe, a Napoleonic fantasy into which he fled.

Dupee had not had access to the James family papers and worked principally from James's published memoir of his older brother, William, and the limited collection of letters edited by Percy Lubbock, heavily weighted toward James's last years. His account therefore moved directly from James's childhood, when he trailed after his older brother, to elderly invalidism. As more material became available to scholars, including the diaries of contemporaries and hundreds of affectionate and sometimes erotic letters written by James to younger men, the picture of neurotic celibacy gave way to a portrait of a closeted homosexual.

Between 1953 and 1972, Leon Edel authored a major five-volume biography of James, which accessed unpublished letters and documents after Edel gained the permission of James's family. Edel's portrayal of James included the suggestion he was celibate. It was a view first propounded by critic Saul Rosenzweig in 1943. In 1996 Sheldon M. Novick published Henry James: The Young Master, followed by Henry James: The Mature Master (2007). The first book "caused something of an uproar in Jamesian circles" as it challenged the previous received notion of celibacy, a once-familiar paradigm in biographies of homosexuals when direct evidence was non-existent. Novick also criticised Edel for following the discounted Freudian interpretation of homosexuality "as a kind of failure." The difference of opinion erupted in a series of exchanges between Edel and Novick which were published by the online magazine Slate, with the latter arguing that even the suggestion of celibacy went against James's own injunction "live!"—not "fantasize!"

A letter James wrote in old age to Hugh Walpole has been cited as an explicit statement of this. Walpole confessed to him of indulging in "high jinks", and James wrote a reply endorsing it: "We must know, as much as possible, in our beautiful art, yours & mine, what we are talking about — & the only way to know it is to have lived & loved & cursed & floundered & enjoyed & suffered — I don't think I regret a single 'excess' of my responsive youth".

The interpretation of James as living a less austere emotional life has been subsequently explored by other scholars. The often intense politics of Jamesian scholarship has also been the subject of studies. Author Colm Tóibín has said that Eve Kosofsky Sedgwick's Epistemology of the Closet made a landmark difference to Jamesian scholarship by arguing that he be read as a homosexual writer whose desire to keep his sexuality a secret shaped his layered style and dramatic artistry. According to Tóibín such a reading "removed James from the realm of dead white males who wrote about posh people. He became our contemporary."

James's letters to expatriate American sculptor Hendrik Christian Andersen have attracted particular attention. James met the 27-year-old Andersen in Rome in 1899, when James was 56, and wrote letters to Andersen that are intensely emotional: "I hold you, dearest boy, in my innermost love, & count on your feeling me—in every throb of your soul". In a letter of 6 May 1904, to his brother William, James referred to himself as "always your hopelessly celibate even though sexagenarian Henry". How accurate that description might have been is the subject of contention among James's biographers, but the letters to Andersen were occasionally quasi-erotic: "I put, my dear boy, my arm around you, & feel the pulsation, thereby, as it were, of our excellent future & your admirable endowment." To his homosexual friend Howard Sturgis, James could write: "I repeat, almost to indiscretion, that I could live with you. Meanwhile I can only try to live without you."

His numerous letters to the many young gay men among his close male friends are more forthcoming. In a letter to Howard Sturgis, following a long visit, James refers jocularly to their "happy little congress of two" and in letters to Hugh Walpole he pursues convoluted jokes and puns about their relationship, referring to himself as an elephant who "paws you oh so benevolently" and winds about Walpole his "well meaning old trunk". His letters to Walter Berry printed by the Black Sun Press have long been celebrated for their lightly veiled eroticism.

He corresponded in almost equally extravagant language with his many female friends, writing, for example, to fellow novelist Lucy Clifford: "Dearest Lucy! What shall I say? when I love you so very, very much, and see you nine times for once that I see Others! Therefore I think that—if you want it made clear to the meanest intelligence—I love you more than I love Others." To his New York friend Mary Cadwalader Jones: "Dearest Mary Cadwalader. I yearn over you, but I yearn in vain; & your long silence really breaks my heart, mystifies, depresses, almost alarms me, to the point even of making me wonder if poor unconscious & doting old Célimare [Jones's pet name for James] has 'done' anything, in some dark somnambulism of the spirit, which has ... given you a bad moment, or a wrong impression, or a 'colourable pretext' ... However these things may be, he loves you as tenderly as ever;

nothing, to the end of time, will ever detach him from you, & he remembers those Eleventh St. matutinal intimes hours, those telephonic matinées, as the most romantic of his life ..." His long friendship with American novelist Constance Fenimore Woolson, in whose house he lived for a number of weeks in Italy in 1887, and his shock and grief over her suicide in 1894, are discussed in detail in Edel's biography and play a central role in a study by Lyndall Gordon. (Edel conjectured that Woolson was in love with James and killed herself in part because of his coldness, but Woolson's biographers have objected to Edel's account.)

Works

Style and themes

James is one of the major figures of trans-Atlantic literature. His works frequently juxtapose characters from the Old World (Europe), embodying a feudal civilisation that is beautiful, often corrupt, and alluring, and from the New World (United States), where people are often brash, open, and assertive and embody the virtues—freedom and a more highly evolved moral character—of the new American society. James explores this clash of personalities and cultures, in stories of personal relationships in which power is exercised well or badly. His protagonists were often young American women facing oppression or abuse, and as his secretary Theodora Bosanquet remarked in her monograph Henry James at Work:

> When he walked out of the refuge of his study and into the world and looked around him, he saw a place of torment, where creatures of prey perpetually thrust their claws into the quivering flesh of doomed, defenseless children of light ... His novels are a repeated exposure of this wickedness, a reiterated and passionate plea for the fullest freedom of development, unimperiled by reckless and barbarous stupidity.

Critics have jokingly described three phases in the development of James's prose: "James I, James II, and The Old Pretender." He wrote short stories and plays. Finally, in his third and last period he returned to the long, serialised novel. Beginning in the second period, but most noticeably in the third, he increasingly abandoned direct statement in favour of frequent

285

double negatives, and complex descriptive imagery. Single paragraphs began to run for page after page, in which an initial noun would be succeeded by pronouns surrounded by clouds of adjectives and prepositional clauses, far from their original referents, and verbs would be deferred and then preceded by a series of adverbs. The overall effect could be a vivid evocation of a scene as perceived by a sensitive observer. It has been debated whether this change of style was engendered by James's shifting from writing to dictating to a typist, a change made during the composition of What Maisie Knew.

In its intense focus on the consciousness of his major characters, James's later work foreshadows extensive developments in 20th century fiction. Indeed, he might have influenced stream-of-consciousness writers such as Virginia Woolf, who not only read some of his novels but also wrote essays about them. Both contemporary and modern readers have found the late style difficult and unnecessary; his friend Edith Wharton, who admired him greatly, said that there were passages in his work that were all but incomprehensible. James was harshly portrayed by H. G. Wells as a hippopotamus laboriously attempting to pick up a pea that had got into a corner of its cage. The "late James" style was ably parodied by Max Beerbohm in "The Mote in the Middle Distance".

More important for his work overall may have been his position as an expatriate, and in other ways an outsider, living in Europe. While he came from middle-class and provincial beginnings (seen from the perspective of European polite society) he worked very hard to gain access to all levels of society, and the settings of his fiction range from working class to aristocratic, and often describe the efforts of middle-class Americans to make their way in European capitals. He confessed he got some of his best story ideas from gossip at the dinner table or at country house weekends. He worked for a living, however, and lacked the experiences of select schools, university, and army service, the common bonds of masculine society. He was furthermore a man whose tastes and interests were, according to the prevailing standards of Victorian era Anglo-American culture, rather feminine, and who was shadowed by the cloud of prejudice that then and later accompanied suspicions of his homosexuality. Edmund Wilson famously compared James's objectivity to Shakespeare's:

One would be in a position to appreciate James better if one compared him with the dramatists of the seventeenth century—Racine and Molière, whom he resembles in form as well as in point of view, and even Shakespeare, when allowances are made for the most extreme differences in subject and form. These poets are not, like Dickens and Hardy, writers of melodrama—either humorous or pessimistic, nor secretaries of society like Balzac, nor prophets like Tolstoy: they are occupied simply with the presentation of conflicts of moral character, which they do not concern themselves about softening or averting. They do not indict society for these situations: they regard them as universal and inevitable. They do not even blame God for allowing them: they accept them as the conditions of life.

It is also possible to see many of James's stories as psychological thought-experiments. In his preface to the New York edition of The American he describes the development of the story in his mind as exactly such: the "situation" of an American, "some robust but insidiously beguiled and betrayed, some cruelly wronged, compatriot..." with the focus of the story being on the response of this wronged man. The Portrait of a Lady may be an experiment to see what happens when an idealistic young woman suddenly becomes very rich. In many of his tales, characters seem to exemplify alternative futures and possibilities, as most markedly in "The Jolly Corner", in which the protagonist and a ghost-doppelganger live alternative American and European lives; and in others, like The Ambassadors, an older James seems fondly to regard his own younger self facing a crucial moment.

Major novels

The first period of James's fiction, usually considered to have culminated in The Portrait of a Lady, concentrated on the contrast between Europe and America. The style of these novels is generally straightforward and, though personally characteristic, well within the norms of 19th-century fiction. Roderick Hudson (1875) is a Künstlerroman that traces the development of the title character, an extremely talented sculptor. Although the book shows some signs of immaturity—this was James's first serious attempt at a full-length novel—it has attracted favourable comment due to the vivid realisation of the three major characters: Roderick Hudson, superbly gifted but unstable and unreliable; Rowland Mallet, Roderick's limited but much more mature friend and patron; and Christina Light, one of James's most enchanting and maddening femmes fatales. The pair of Hudson and Mallet has been seen as representing the two sides of James's own nature: the wildly imaginative artist and the brooding conscientious mentor.

In The Portrait of a Lady (1881) James concluded the first phase of his career with a novel that remains his most popular piece of long fiction. The story is of a spirited young American woman, Isabel Archer, who "affronts her destiny" and finds it overwhelming. She inherits a large amount of money and subsequently becomes the victim of Machiavellian scheming by two American expatriates. The narrative is set mainly in Europe, especially in England and Italy. Generally regarded as the masterpiece of his early phase, The Portrait of a Lady is described as a psychological novel, exploring the minds of his characters, and almost a work of social science, exploring the differences between Europeans and Americans, the old and the new worlds.

The second period of James's career, which extends from the publication of The Portrait of a Lady through the end of the nineteenth century, features less popular novels including The Princess Casamassima, published serially in The Atlantic Monthly in 1885–1886, and The Bostonians, published serially in The Century Magazine during the same period. This period also featured James's celebrated Gothic novella, The Turn of the Screw.

The third period of James's career reached its most significant achievement in three novels published just around the start of the 20th century: The Wings of the Dove (1902), The Ambassadors (1903), and The Golden Bowl (1904). Critic F. O. Matthiessen called this "trilogy" James's major phase, and these novels have certainly received intense critical study. It was the second-written of the books, The Wings of the Dove (1902) that was the first published because it attracted no serialization. This novel tells the story of Milly Theale, an American heiress stricken with a serious disease, and her impact on the people around her. Some of these people befriend Milly with honourable motives, while others are more self-interested. James stated in his autobiographical books that Milly was based on Minny Temple, his beloved cousin who died at an early age of tuberculosis. He said that he attempted in the novel to wrap her memory in the "beauty and dignity of art".

Shorter narratives

James was particularly interested in what he called the "beautiful and blest nouvelle", or the longer form of short narrative. Still, he produced a number of very short stories in which he achieved notable compression of sometimes complex subjects. The following narratives are representative of James's achievement in the shorter forms of fiction.

- "A Tragedy of Error" (1864), short story
- "The Story of a Year" (1865), short story
- A Passionate Pilgrim (1871), novella
- Madame de Mauves (1874), novella
- Daisy Miller (1878), novella
- The Aspern Papers (1888), novella
- The Lesson of the Master (1888), novella
- The Pupil (1891), short story
- "The Figure in the Carpet" (1896), short story
- The Beast in the Jungle (1903), novella
- An International Episode (1878)
- Picture and Text
- Four Meetings (1885)
- A London Life, and Other Tales (1889)
- The Spoils of Poynton (1896)

- Embarrassments (1896)

- The Two Magics: The Turn of the Screw, Covering End (1898)

- A Little Tour of France (1900)

- The Sacred Fount (1901)

- Views and Reviews (1908)

- The Wings of the Dove, Volume I (1902)

- The Wings of the Dove, Volume II (1909)

- The Finer Grain (1910)

- The Outcry (1911)

- Lady Barbarina: The Siege of London, An International Episode and Other Tales (1922)

- The Birthplace (1922)

Plays

At several points in his career James wrote plays, beginning with one-act plays written for periodicals in 1869 and 1871 and a dramatisation of his popular novella Daisy Miller in 1882. From 1890 to 1892, having received a bequest that freed him from magazine publication, he made a strenuous effort to succeed on the London stage, writing a half-dozen plays of which only one, a dramatisation of his novel The American, was produced. This play was performed for several years by a touring repertory company and had a respectable run in London, but did not earn very much money for James. His other plays written at this time were not produced.

In 1893, however, he responded to a request from actor-manager George Alexander for a serious play for the opening of his renovated St. James's Theatre, and wrote a long drama, Guy Domville, which Alexander produced. There was a noisy uproar on the opening night, 5 January 1895, with hissing from the gallery when James took his bow after the final curtain, and the author was upset. The play received moderately good reviews and had a modest run of four weeks before being taken off to make way for Oscar Wilde's The Importance of Being Earnest, which Alexander thought would have better prospects for the coming season.

After the stresses and disappointment of these efforts James insisted that he would write no more for the theatre, but within weeks had agreed to write a curtain-raiser for Ellen Terry. This became the one-act "Summersoft", which he later rewrote into a short story, "Covering End", and then expanded into a full-length play, The High Bid, which had a brief run in London in 1907, when James made another concerted effort to write for the stage. He wrote three new plays, two of which were in production when the death of Edward VII on 6 May 1910 plunged London into mourning and theatres closed. Discouraged by failing health and the stresses of theatrical work, James did not renew his efforts in the theatre, but recycled his plays as successful novels. The Outcry was a best-seller in the United States when it was published in 1911. During the years 1890–1893 when he was most engaged with the theatre, James wrote a good deal of theatrical criticism and assisted Elizabeth Robins and others in translating and producing Henrik Ibsen for the first time in London.

Leon Edel argued in his psychoanalytic biography that James was traumatised by the opening night uproar that greeted Guy Domville, and that it plunged him into a prolonged depression. The successful later novels, in Edel's view, were the result of a kind of self-analysis, expressed in fiction, which partly freed him from his fears. Other biographers and scholars have not accepted this account, however; the more common view being that of F.O. Matthiessen, who wrote: "Instead of being crushed by the collapse of his hopes [for the theatre]... he felt a resurgence of new energy."

Non-fiction

Beyond his fiction, James was one of the more important literary critics in the history of the novel. In his classic essay The Art of Fiction (1884), he argued against rigid prescriptions on the novelist's choice of subject and method of treatment. He maintained that the widest possible freedom in content and approach would help ensure narrative fiction's continued vitality.

James wrote many valuable critical articles on other novelists; typical is his book-length study of Nathaniel Hawthorne, which has been the subject of critical debate. Richard Brodhead has suggested that the study was emblematic of James's struggle with Hawthorne's influence, and constituted an effort to place the elder writer "at a disadvantage." Gordon Fraser, meanwhile, has suggested that the study was part of a more commercial effort by James to introduce himself to British readers as Hawthorne's natural successor.

When James assembled the New York Edition of his fiction in his final years, he wrote a series of prefaces that subjected his own work to searching, occasionally harsh criticism.

At 22 James wrote The Noble School of Fiction for The Nation's first issue in 1865. He would write, in all, over 200 essays and book, art, and theatre reviews for the magazine.

For most of his life James harboured ambitions for success as a playwright. He converted his novel The American into a play that enjoyed modest returns in the early 1890s. In all he wrote about a dozen plays, most of which went unproduced. His costume drama Guy Domville failed disastrously on its opening night in 1895. James then largely abandoned his efforts to conquer the stage and returned to his fiction. In his Notebooks he maintained that his theatrical experiment benefited his novels and tales by helping him dramatise his characters' thoughts and emotions. James produced a small but valuable amount of theatrical criticism, including perceptive appreciations of Henrik Ibsen.

With his wide-ranging artistic interests, James occasionally wrote on the visual arts. Perhaps his most valuable contribution was his favourable assessment of fellow expatriate John Singer Sargent, a painter whose critical status has improved markedly in recent decades. James also wrote sometimes charming, sometimes brooding articles about various places he visited and lived in. His most famous books of travel writing include Italian Hours (an example of the charming approach) and The American Scene (most definitely on the brooding side).

James was one of the great letter-writers of any era. More than ten thousand of his personal letters are extant, and over three thousand have been published in a large number of collections. A complete edition of James's letters began publication in 2006, edited by Pierre Walker and Greg Zacharias. As of 2014, eight volumes have been published, covering the period from 1855 to 1880. James's correspondents included celebrated contemporaries like Robert Louis Stevenson, Edith Wharton and Joseph Conrad, along with many others in his wide circle of friends and acquaintances. The letters range from the "mere twaddle of graciousness" to serious discussions of artistic, social and personal issues.

Very late in life James began a series of autobiographical works: A Small Boy and Others, Notes of a Son and Brother, and the unfinished The Middle Years. These books portray the development of a classic observer who was passionately interested in artistic creation but was somewhat reticent about participating fully in the life around him.

Reception

Criticism, biographies and fictional treatments

James's work has remained steadily popular with the limited audience of educated readers to whom he spoke during his lifetime, and has remained firmly in the canon, but, after his death, some American critics, such as Van Wyck Brooks, expressed hostility towards James for his long expatriation and eventual naturalisation as a British subject. Other critics such as E. M. Forster complained about what they saw as James's squeamishness in the treatment of sex and other possibly controversial material, or dismissed his late style as difficult and obscure, relying heavily on extremely long sentences and excessively latinate language. Similarly Oscar Wilde criticised him for writing "fiction as if it were a painful duty". Vernon Parrington, composing a canon of American literature, condemned James for having cut himself off from America. Jorge Luis Borges wrote about him, "Despite the scruples and delicate complexities of James, his work suffers from a major defect: the absence of life." And Virginia Woolf, writing to Lytton Strachey, asked, "Please tell me what you find in Henry James. ... we have his works here, and

I read, and I can't find anything but faintly tinged rose water, urbane and sleek, but vulgar and pale as Walter Lamb. Is there really any sense in it?" The novelist W. Somerset Maugham wrote, "He did not know the English as an Englishman instinctively knows them and so his English characters never to my mind quite ring true," and argued "The great novelists, even in seclusion, have lived life passionately. Henry James was content to observe it from a window." Maugham nevertheless wrote, "The fact remains that those last novels of his, notwithstanding their unreality, make all other novels, except the very best, unreadable." Colm Tóibín observed that James "never really wrote about the English very well. His English characters don't work for me."

Despite these criticisms, James is now valued for his psychological and moral realism, his masterful creation of character, his low-key but playful humour, and his assured command of the language. In his 1983 book, The Novels of Henry James, Edward Wagenknecht offers an assessment that echoes Theodora Bosanquet's:

> "To be completely great," Henry James wrote in an early review, "a work of art must lift up the heart," and his own novels do this to an outstanding degree ... More than sixty years after his death, the great novelist who sometimes professed to have no opinions stands foursquare in the great Christian humanistic and democratic tradition. The men and women who, at the height of World War II, raided the secondhand shops for his out-of-print books knew what they were about. For no writer ever raised a braver banner to which all who love freedom might adhere.

William Dean Howells saw James as a representative of a new realist school of literary art which broke with the English romantic tradition epitomised by the works of Charles Dickens and William Makepeace Thackeray. Howells wrote that realism found "its chief exemplar in Mr. James... A novelist he is not, after the old fashion, or after any fashion but his own." F.R. Leavis championed Henry James as a novelist of "established pre-eminence" in The Great Tradition (1948), asserting that The Portrait of a Lady and The Bostonians were "the two most brilliant novels in the language." James is now prized as a master of point of view who moved literary fiction forward by insisting in showing, not telling, his stories to the reader. (Source: Wikipedia)

NOTABLE WORKS

NOVELS

Watch and Ward (1871)

Roderick Hudson (1875)

The American (1877)

The Europeans (1878)

Confidence (1879)

Washington Square (1880)

The Portrait of a Lady (1881)

The Bostonians (1886)

The Princess Casamassima (1886)

The Reverberator (1888)

The Tragic Muse (1890)

The Other House (1896)

The Spoils of Poynton (1897)

What Maisie Knew (1897)

The Awkward Age (1899)

The Sacred Fount (1901)

The Wings of the Dove (1902)

The Ambassadors (1903)

The Golden Bowl (1904)

The Whole Family (collaborative novel with eleven other authors, 1908)

The Outcry (1911)

The Ivory Tower (unfinished, published posthumously 1917)

The Sense of the Past (unfinished, published posthumously 1917)

SHORT STORIES AND NOVELLAS

A Tragedy of Error (1864)

The Story of a Year (1865)

A Landscape Painter (1866)

A Day of Days (1866)

My Friend Bingham (1867)

Poor Richard (1867)

The Story of a Masterpiece (1868)

A Most Extraordinary Case (1868)

A Problem (1868)

De Grey: A Romance (1868)

Osborne's Revenge (1868)

The Romance of Certain Old Clothes (1868)

A Light Man (1869)

Gabrielle de Bergerac (1869)

Travelling Companions (1870)

A Passionate Pilgrim (1871)

At Isella (1871)

Master Eustace (1871)

Guest's Confession (1872)

The Madonna of the Future (1873)

The Sweetheart of M. Briseux (1873)

The Last of the Valerii (1874)

Madame de Mauves (1874)

Adina (1874)

Professor Fargo (1874)

Eugene Pickering (1874)

Benvolio (1875)

Crawford's Consistency (1876)

The Ghostly Rental (1876)

Four Meetings (1877)

Rose-Agathe (1878, as Théodolinde)

Daisy Miller (1878)

Longstaff's Marriage (1878)

An International Episode (1878)

The Pension Beaurepas (1879)

A Diary of a Man of Fifty (1879)

A Bundle of Letters (1879)

The Point of View (1882)

The Siege of London (1883)

Impressions of a Cousin (1883)

Lady Barberina (1884)

Pandora (1884)

The Author of Beltraffio (1884)

Georgina's Reasons (1884)

A New England Winter (1884)

The Path of Duty (1884)

Mrs. Temperly (1887)

Louisa Pallant (1888)

The Aspern Papers (1888)

The Liar (1888)

The Modern Warning (1888, originally published as The Two Countries)

A London Life (1888)

The Patagonia (1888)

The Lesson of the Master (1888)

The Solution (1888)

The Pupil (1891)

Brooksmith (1891)

The Marriages (1891)

The Chaperon (1891)

Sir Edmund Orme (1891)

Nona Vincent (1892)

The Real Thing (1892)

The Private Life (1892)

Lord Beaupré (1892)

The Visits (1892)

Sir Dominick Ferrand (1892)

Greville Fane (1892)

Collaboration (1892)

Owen Wingrave (1892)

The Wheel of Time (1892)

The Middle Years (1893)

The Death of the Lion (1894)

The Coxon Fund (1894)

The Next Time (1895)

Glasses (1896)

The Altar of the Dead (1895)

The Figure in the Carpet (1896)

The Way It Came (1896, also published as The Friends of the Friends)

The Turn of the Screw (1898)

Covering End (1898)

In the Cage (1898)

John Delavoy (1898)

The Given Case (1898)

Europe (1899)

The Great Condition (1899)

The Real Right Thing (1899)

Paste (1899)

The Great Good Place (1900)

Maud-Evelyn (1900)

Miss Gunton of Poughkeepsie (1900)

The Tree of Knowledge (1900)

The Abasement of the Northmores (1900)

The Third Person (1900)

The Special Type (1900)

The Tone of Time (1900)

Broken Wings (1900)

The Two Faces (1900)

Mrs. Medwin (1901)

The Beldonald Holbein (1901)

The Story in It (1902)

Flickerbridge (1902)

The Birthplace (1903)

The Beast in the Jungle (1903)

The Papers (1903)

Fordham Castle (1904)

Julia Bride (1908)

The Jolly Corner (1908)

The Velvet Glove (1909)

Mora Montravers (1909)

Crapy Cornelia (1909)

The Bench of Desolation (1909)

A Round of Visits (1910)

OTHER

Transatlantic Sketches (1875)

French Poets and Novelists (1878)

Hawthorne (1879)

Portraits of Places (1883)

A Little Tour in France (1884)

Partial Portraits (1888)

Essays in London and Elsewhere (1893)

Picture and Text (1893)

Terminations (1893)

Theatricals (1894)

Theatricals: Second Series (1895)

Guy Domville (1895)

The Soft Side (1900)

William Wetmore Story and His Friends (1903)

The Better Sort (1903)

English Hours (1905)

The Question of our Speech; The Lesson of Balzac. Two Lectures (1905)

The American Scene (1907)

Views and Reviews (1908)

Italian Hours (1909)

A Small Boy and Others (1913)

Notes on Novelists (1914)

Notes of a Son and Brother (1914)

Within the Rim (1918)

Travelling Companions (1919)

Notebooks (various, published posthumously)

The Middle Years (unfinished, published posthumously 1917)

A Most Unholy Trade (1925, published posthumously)

The Art of the Novel : Critical Prefaces (1934)